Small Communities
in Religious Life

Small Communities
in Religious Life

Making them Work

Catherine Widdicombe

The Lutterworth Press
Cambridge

First Published in 2001 by

The Lutterworth Press
P.O. Box 60
Cambridge
CB1 2NT
England

e-mail: **Publishing@Lutterworth.com**
website: **www.Lutterworth.com**

ISBN: 0 7188 3012 1

British Library Cataloguing in Publication Data:
A catalogue record is available from the British Library

Cover Design: Mike Shennan Associates

Printed in the United Kingdom by Redwood Press, Trowbridge

To George Lovell
dear colleague and friend
who has added immeasurably
to my life and work
and to that of
the Grail,
the 'beloved community'
as he calls it.

CONTENTS

LIST OF FIGURES

LIST OF TABLES

Foreword and Acknowledgements

I am greatly indebted to members of many communities and congregations who have given me the inestimable privilege of working closely with them, struggling and agonising as well as creating and achieving. There have been times of tedious and painstaking work, but my memories are more of the excitement of challenge and discovery, moving moments of silence as well as moments of tears and of much laughter. Without the trust and openness of these people, the work could not have been done nor this book written. I have been immensely enriched by them and I thank each congregation, community and member from the bottom of my heart.

Before I began to work with religious in this way, I had experience of working with members of communities, both lay and religious, Anglican, Roman Catholic and ecumenical, men and women in the *Community Weeks* which I initiated with Patrick Fitzgerald SMA. Held at the Grail Centre in Pinner, members of Lee Abbey and Scargill rubbed shoulders with monks from Nashdom and nuns in full habits. Those were the days when we needed to spend much of the introductory session deciding what people would call each other! Those weeks, over several years, deepened my awareness of the need we all had to tackle the difficulties of community life and work at forming community: it does not just happen. Doing that together, I became increasingly conscious of the richness of the ecumenical dimension: whatever our community, we faced similar human problems as we strove to develop communion with those with whom we lived. I am grateful to those who led the weeks with Patrick and myself: Patricia White CSA, Michael Mitchell then of the Franciscans, and Jackie Rolo of the Grail community, and to all who participated in this early ecumenical community venture.

I came to those weeks with my on-going experience of living as a member of the Grail, one of the rare secular institutes which emphasises community life. For fifty years this community has nurtured, supported, challenged and inspired me. I have found it, at times, both demanding and unreasonable, as well as overwhelmingly generous and understanding. It has taught me, above all, that living in community is not an easy option, but it *is* a rewarding one. As a member, both living in community and for fourteen years living alone, I have learnt a great deal about love, compassion and forgiveness. Belonging to the extended Grail community, I have been stimulated and enabled to pursue my inner journey and have come increasingly to see life as a process of falling in love with God, who is so deeply in love with each of us – warts and all. I thank God for bringing me to this community and I thank the Grail for accepting me and for all it has done to allow and encourage me to take up opportunities to learn, and, through consultancy, courses, projects and writing, to share what I have learnt with others.

There are two people to whom I owe more than I can ever say. First, T. R. Batten, from whom I learnt about promoting community development through the non-directive approach. He has not only been my teacher and consultant but a close and greatly valued friend. Meeting Reg Batten was a significant turning point in my life for which I will always be deeply grateful. Second, George Lovell, my close colleague and soul-friend for over thirty years. His critical eye, his patience, and his painstaking and hidden hand on so much of what I have done, including drafts of this book, have added invaluable dimensions and insights to my life and work. His support gave me courage when the going was rough and I was in danger of giving up. For all this and his loyal friendship I can never thank him enough.

Several other people have given generously of their time and effort. I thank Margaret O'Connor DHS and Jean Daniel RLR whose encouragement and suggestions as they read early drafts have been so beneficial to me and to the text. I am grateful also to those who, at various times, have patiently typed and re-typed my manuscript: Diana Kirk, May Farina, Cynthia Mee, and above all, Sandra Baker and her husband Chris. Sandra and Chris were not only long-suffering in correcting version after version; their critical feedback, which I took into account, meant more work for them. The diagrams, also altered many times, are the skilled work of Judy Turner. I am immensely grateful to her as she made time in her busy life.

Lastly, my thanks go to Maureen Connor OSA, my colleague in some of the work and with whom I hatched the idea for this book. Her initial help gave me courage to begin.

Small Communities in Religious Life

INTRODUCTION

THE TREND TO COMMUNITY LIVING

Over the last fifty and more years there has been an increasing movement throughout the world towards living in community, a conscious awareness of the values of what some call 'this more humane way of living.[1] This is to be seen in the large number of 'intentional' communities which are based on religious, ecological, and educational ideologies and concerned with projects to meet particular needs. Many communities are small, fairly informal, and not widely known, but for those who live near them they are oases of peace and good sense in the turmoil of life. Their variety is enormous: ashrams in the centre of big cities; rural sustainable communities; religious men and women living on council estates; communities for those with special mental health or physical needs; families living separately but organised communally and sharing facilities; and retreat, training and conference centres run by people for whom community is a core value; and many others.[2]

This book has grown primarily out of working with many different kinds of religious communities. I also draw on my experience of the Grail Community[3] of which I am a long-standing member. For several years I was closely connected with the Lindore Road Community in south London.[4] I currently belong to the Global Eco-Village Network[5] and the National Association of Christian Communities and Networks,[6] both of which are in touch with large numbers of communities in this country and overseas. All this convinces me that much that I have learnt and which I want to share through this book is applicable to all who live in community.

Wherever human beings strive to form community, the experience will inevitably include challenge and struggle. Commitment to community living with its close involvement with other people is not an easy option. Being an Anglican or Roman Catholic religious and endeavouring to live the evangelical gospel counsels does not automatically rid people of the less desirable human features. Indeed religious who live in small communities often describe themselves as a microcosm of humanity with all its hopes and fears, gifts and foibles, strengths and weaknesses. It is, in part, struggling with those that makes community living immensely enriching.

SMALL COMMUNITIES OF RELIGIOUS

Small communities of religious living alongside and easily accessible to ordinary people are now a recognised and established feature of parish landscapes. They emerge from a revolution in religious life going back to Vatican Two and spurred on by the reduction in vocations. In both Catholic and Anglican traditions small communities are increasing, large ones decreasing. This transition, unimaginable at one time, has far-reaching consequences for religious, for the church, and for local neighbourhoods. Understandably the shrinkage or demise of large convents and their traditional apostolic work is painful and confusing to those who have devoted a major part of their life's energy and effort to them. For some time there was a propensity to equate smallness with failure. This is changing with the advent of small communities and religious life is once more exciting and galvanising. Religious are seeing the Spirit stirring new 'fire in these ashes' as new opportunities for ministry open up and religious collaborate with non-religious to their mutual enrichment, live closer to those who are poor and marginalised, and engage with people who have urgent human and spiritual needs. Notwithstanding and not surprisingly, this process has its difficulties. There is no well-trodden path to follow and an underlying and constant problem is that, while Vatican Two pointed to visionary and fundamental changes in religious life, inadequate attention was given to the ways and means of making them. Recently, I heard a cry from the heart, "Why is the setting up and living in small communities so much more difficult than we had imagined?"

For thirty years I have been privileged to work with religious as they faced these challenges and the problems encountered. This book has grown directly from that experience. I have been closely involved with all concerned, from those in positions of overall responsibility, to those at the grass roots; with single communities, and with congregational gatherings: both informal assemblies and with decision-making chapters; and I have worked with individuals on consultations and training courses. It was exciting to engage with them as they started radically re-thinking their situation as never before, and they are continuing to do so.

Small communities have mushroomed and become established. Much has been achieved and gained from these years of experience. I am convinced that now is an opportune moment to gather together the many valuable lessons which have been learnt from deeply satisfying and apostolically fruitful ministries, struggles against unexpected and sometimes overwhelming odds, and from the malpractice resulting from oscillating between new and outmoded habits of thinking and working. As I engaged with people on this material, I identified the basic issues and questions involved in forming, developing, living in, re-forming, healing, and repairing small communities, and in closing them when their life cycle is spent. The process is endless because communities are living, ever-changing organisms. Having provided various kinds of help through innumerable workshops and courses, I wanted to make continuing help more readily available, especially for those who do not always have people able to help them think things through, nor immediate access to a consultant or facilitator. That is how the idea for this book was born. *Gradually I became convinced that a handbook of this kind, giving ready access to key processes, could be of use. It is therefore a self-help manual to be used in working at tasks, rather than a book to be read or a blue print for action. My intention is to enable members of communities to be their own facilitators and become more reflective practitioners in relation to difficulties they face and the changes they seek to make in their everyday life and ministry in what is an on-going period of transition.*

UNDERLYING THEOLOGY AND SPIRITUALITY

This book is about becoming, being and living in small communities, particularly as vowed religious. The approaches and processes are firmly grounded in the evolving theological and spiritual insights of Vatican Two. This entails taking seriously such dynamic concepts as co-responsibility, subsidiarity and *koinonia* as they apply to living the evangelical counsels of poverty, chastity and obedience. It also involves determining the interactive processes necessary if religious are both to serve and learn from their contemporary ecumenical, spiritual, and secular context. It is therefore a book of the practice theory necessary to enable people to help their own and other communities to work out the practical and theological implications of Vatican Two in the hurly-burly of life.

Experience has proven that the practice theory embodied in this book is effective with people of widely differing spiritualities and with a variety of charisms. It is acceptable and beneficial to them and promotes human development and spiritual growth.

The book is about what is involved in making a small community an effective instrument of mission. Mission is the *raison d'etre* of apostolic religious community and needs to be in the forefront of the thinking, prayer and reflection of community members. The quality of a community's life together affects the quality of the mission and ministry of its members. Ministry and community overlap, interweave and are complexly inter-related. Both need to be kept in mind even when the immediate focus is on one or other.

This is a practical workbook. It takes spiritual aspirations seriously by paying careful attention to the mundane and seemingly trivial matters which go into creating, maintaining and developing community. Communities thrive through attention to such things and often fail through neglect of them, rather than through a lack of vision.

I try to avoid the use of religious terminology because I find that ordinary language often helps people to see old truths in a fresh light: it is so easy to become immune to religious jargon.

WHO THIS BOOK IS FOR

This book is for all who deal directly or indirectly with small communities, although my primary reference is to apostolic religious. It is for those with overall responsibility for forming and supporting them; potential and existing members of small communities; those living alone; those who remain in large communities; and both new and experienced members of a congregation. The approach advocated throughout this book is about maximising the creative participation of everyone involved and implicated in making and maintaining small communities. Clearly, some sections are more applicable to some people, occasions, and phases of community life than others. Where appropriate, I indicate to whom a section is likely to be primarily relevant.

I write out of extensive experience with, and research into, women's congregations, but I have done enough work with male religious and non-religious to feel confident that the basic principles and approaches are relevant and applicable to communities of men, and to all kinds of religious and secular communities of both women and men.

My work with communities has taken place in the United Kingdom and Ireland, but these have included members from various parts of the English-speaking world. I know, from this experience, that the approaches and processes embodied in this book can be of use wherever people are living in or working with small intentional communities.

Whilst this book is not written primarily for external facilitators and consultants, they may find it useful. Furthermore, the way in which it is structured makes it a form of distance learning for those who wish to acquire consultancy or facilitation skills to help those in small communities.

THE SHAPE OF THE BOOK

The shape of the book is designed to make its use as easy as possible for people who are involved in or with small communities. It consists of the following parts:

Part One: Small communities in religious life. This part is an introduction to the internal and external context of the movement from large to small communities. It identifies the nature of the changes being experienced, why they are occurring, and how they can best be facilitated. It describes characteristics and models of local religious community, and its context in the congregation and in society.

Part Two: Opening and closing small communities. Part Two presents a sequence for thinking constructively about the factors that need to be taken into account at the starting up of a community and in closing a house:

– exploring the initial idea; deciding its membership, location and timing; informing the congregation and others outside; preparing to move in; and its early days;

– closing a house so that withdrawal is experienced as life-giving and leading to development rather than a negative event; decision making; informing others; and preparing to depart.

Part Three: Religious life in small communities. Part Three presents those things that make up the life of a small community:

– living as a community: its purpose; how members organise themselves; the tackling of inevitable difficulties; community meetings; and leadership;

– determining mission and ministry; exploring the needs of an area; starting new work; designing work programmes; working collaboratively; and mutual support;

– reviewing and evaluating community life and ministry; and reporting or sharing what they have learnt with the leadership and congregation;

– exercising co-responsibility between communities and the congregation.

This however, makes the life cycle and decisions associated with each phase look more neat and tidy than it can ever be in reality. Life is messy. Progress is often made through cyclical rather than linear processes. A systematic presentation of these phases helps one to work more constructively: it is not to suggest that things can be worked through rigidly in a given order or in isolation from the rest. In real life there will be repetition and overlap, periods when the way seems clear and ideas tumble over themselves, and times of stagnation, deep uncertainty, and struggle. Working out these things is a matter of the heart and the head; the order, rate, and depth varies with different people.

Part Four: Transition between communities. This part considers the move of individuals from one community to another. Such a transition starts when they begin to consider the possibility of moving from where they are and ends after they have been in the new situation a year or more. It considers this critical path and offers suggestions to help people reflect on and learn from the past; to withdraw from a ministry; and to settle into a new situation. It also deals with changes in the membership of a community, and relationships with members who are living elsewhere for a period. A new member, or a member moving out or dying, changes the shape and dynamics of a community. Taking cognisance of this can be important.

Part Five: Towards equipping small communities. This part is about those things which all communities have to do in order to become increasingly effective in mission and ministry and be the sort of community which is life-enhancing to live in: tackling problems, making decisions, evaluating their life and work, and having community meetings. It also includes exercises and discussion outlines on a variety of topics such as community life, charism, faith sharing, poverty, and mission, and some longer-term exercises.

USING THIS BOOK

As this book is meant to stimulate thought, promote creative ideas, and be used for reference, there is an extended list of contents, many cross references, and a full index. My hope is that it will spark off other questions of particular relevance to those who use it. Ventures often stumble and fail, not because people are incapable of achieving success, but because they do not ask, and then work through, the essential questions. However, even asking the essential questions does not automatically or always guarantee success; working things out carefully and systematically will not necessarily ensure the smooth running of any human venture. But it invariably helps. My intention is to help those concerned with small communities to do some things more effectively, to prevent some excursions down cul-de-sacs, to reduce some of the pain experienced because things do not turn out as expected, and to see ways of working through the consequences of unexpected difficulties or mistakes. The book will be of greatest help to those who enter into a dialogue with it, questioning it from their own experience, as well as allowing it to question and challenge them and their ways of doing things.

A NOTE ABOUT TERMINOLOGY

Definitions of some of the terms used throughout this book are as follows:

Congregation: I use the word congregation synonymously with religious order: Groups variously use one description or the other. Some congregations are divided into provinces and regions, others are not. For the sake of simplicity I usually use the word 'province' to refer to the national or regional grouping of religious, and 'congregation' to refer to the international grouping.

Community: refers to a local community of religious or lay people rather than to the congregation or national grouping as a whole.

Leadership team: refers to those who have been elected or appointed to positions of authority at national, provincial, or international level. I often use the word 'team' rather than council, because this is a more accurate description of the common and preferred way of exercising these functions.

Priesthood: I refer to those ordained as priests. They may be parochial or non-parochial. Also, following common usage, when I talk about lay people I refer to those who are secular, rather than religious.

Personal pronouns: As the English language does not have unisex pronouns I have alternated the use of 'he' and 'she' as appropriate.

REFERENCES AND NOTES

1   Metcalfe, Bill: 'The Wisdom of the Elders: Communal Conflict and Conflict Resolution' in *Creating Harmony: Conflict resolution* edited by Hildur Jackson (Gaia Trust, Denmark, in association with Permanent Publications, UK 1999).
2   ibid. That most world religions include a community dimension, and most communities a spiritual one occurred to me forcibly after reading this book which has contributions from some twenty-seven people closely associated with or living in eco-villages or sustainable communities, the vast majority of which have no religious affiliation.
3   The Grail, a Roman Catholic foundation although it welcomes people of all faiths community, has been in the U.K. since 1933. It has a core residential membership of women who have made a long-term commitment to a simple life-style, to helping individuals to grow, and to caring for the earth on a small scale. Men and women who share this ethos and the work that flows from it, become part of this community for longer or shorter periods of time. There is also a large non-residential network of members throughout the British Isles. The community is based at Waxwell Farm House, 125 Waxwell lane, Pinner, Middlesex HA5 3ER.
4   The Lindore Road community existed for several years in Clapham in the 1970s to 1980s. It had a small residential group and a larger number of associates who met weekly for a eucharistic or liturgical celebration and discussion. It attracted many who called themselves 'fringe Christians'.
5   The Global Eco-Village Network (GEN) consists of communities and settlements that focus on ecological issues and sustainable living. GEN was inaugurated in Istanbul in 1996 and is now on the Internet (http://www.gaia.org). It has national groupings in many countries.
6   NACCAN is a network of Christians interested in or living in a wide variety of communities throughout the United Kingdom. It has a quarterly mailing and an annual assembly. Its headquarters is NACCAN Community House, Eton Road, Newport, NP19 0BL.

PART ONE

Small Communities in Religious Life

I. Transition in Religious Life: Its Nature and Facilitation

1. A PERIOD OF TRANSITION

Religious life is changing dramatically. Religious are caught up in an exciting, challenging and somewhat frightening period of change in the church stimulated by Vatican Two. Challenged to read the signs of the times, the church gave up seeing itself as a bastion of stability in a chaotic world, and set out on a painful struggle to interact with and respond to all that was happening in society, a society which itself was also in a period of revolutionary change. Gerald Arbuckle writes, "Surely one of the Council's major achievements was to destabilise, in order to renew a religious culture that had grown old and tired and could hardly comprehend, let alone cope, with the demands of a rapidly changing world."[1]

The newly emphasised theological understanding that the church exists in and for the world was accompanied by another: that all the people of God, not just ordained priests and religious, are called to holiness and apostolic activity. Lay people responded by going as missionaries overseas, working full-time in parishes or dioceses, and giving themselves to all manner of good causes, becoming engaged in many activities which, to a large extent, had previously been the province of religious. At the same time religious congregations were encouraged to stand in the shoes of their prophetic founders who, acutely aware of and disturbed by some crying need or injustice and fired by a particular charism, had with a few companions embarked on a new path. Returning to their roots in this way, led contemporary members to catch the fire and apply it to the very different needs of today's world. A variety of initiatives were undertaken. Many left large schools and hospitals for smaller pastoral projects and opted to live and work for and alongside poor and marginalised people in any number of different ways. In addition, the dramatic drop in vocations in the last thirty to forty years has meant that many large religious institutions were no longer viable and have had to be closed or handed over to lay management. All this has resulted in a change from large to small communities and from the involvement of the majority of members in a corporate apostolate to people undertaking a wide variety of apostolic activities.

These new insights and activities led to several long-established traditions in religious life being called into question, a questioning that still continues: what does living in community, in communion, as opposed to living alongside one another, really mean? A friend wrote to me recently, "It seemed at the time, that it was a feeling of deep frustration at living an inappropriate, unreal, institutional life-style that drove us to push for smaller communities in the early days after Vatican Two. The thrusts and insights of the Council made it possible to do something about what was wrong. What a liberation that was! The positive vision of church signalled a possible path to tread". Diamuid O'Murchu talks of the creation of small communities as being "more conducive to deeper dialogue, greater sharing of life and vision and the possibility of exploring in greater depth the search for community in today's world".[2] But this is not without its stresses and pain. The opening up and questioning of religious life that has led to the creation of smaller communities causes suffering as well as satisfaction, and the consequent growth of individuals, communities and congregations is dearly bought.

Over thirty years after the Vatican Council, religious life, in many respects, still retains some of its former rigidity and this despite the overt and expressed desire to change, and some fairly violent rocking of the boat. Is this because, at some unconscious level, congregational disunity is felt to be too high a price to pay for a more radical living out of the gospel, or because members slow down the rate of change to a pace they can or want to cope with, or which is within the boundaries they realistically are able to face together? Yet, despite any slowing down of the overall process of change, most congregations feel themselves to be, and in fact are, engaged in the process.

In renewing themselves they are being asked to differentiate between the essence and core values of religious life and their particular congregation, and the ways these have been lived and expressed, the methods used and the various accretions which, until Vatican Two, were for so many characteristic of, if not central to, religious life in their perception and experience. The fact that religious life had changed significantly down the ages has largely been lost sight of. "Living things maintain their integrity and identity not by eliminating change, but by continuous dynamic interaction with their environment. It is equilibrium, not change, that is fatal!"[3] Identifying what a congregation needs to conserve and what needs to be changed to make that conservation possible, is a vital part of living as an apostolic religious in a time of transition.[4] This can be uncomfortable as only times of deep questioning can be. It is often made more disturbing by those who find change burdensome, who are deeply distressed and even angered by the changes. Too often they believe that religious life itself is being undermined and destroyed and therefore feel justified in resisting all change. For others resistance is caught up with an overwhelming and misplaced need for security.

In this situation it can take continuous courage to hold to the vision that the current re-shaping of religious life is gradually strengthening it to become a vital force contributing to a more human and spiritual quality of life in church and society. So, while some may feel depressed and see religious life in decline, others are exhilarated and energised as imaginative ideas bear fruit and new ways forward are forged and found to work.

Participation in this process entails hard work: a commitment to thinking, questioning, exploring, trying things out, and taking considered – and at times considerable – risks.

2. THE NATURE OF THE CHANGES EXPERIENCED

The change from large communities to small is intimately connected with more far-reaching changes in religious life. In the past, although the life and work of congregations varied, there was some uniformity and permanence within each one. This has now largely gone. The nature of the changes being experienced is a movement:

From	To
living in a large institutional community regulated by a monastic horarium marking times of prayers, meals, work and recreation	a more informal, human life style in an ordinary house with a few other members with a flexible timetable adapted to ministry and mission
living to a greater extent in a closed institution distanced from ordinary people	becoming immersed in the life and relationships of the neighbourhood and parish
living and working with the same people, often in the same building, on a common work (e.g. teaching or caring for the sick)	members becoming engaged in diverse ministries
working primarily in a ministry directed and controlled by the congregation	working with external organisations, religious or secular, at times in highly professional or specialised jobs
hierarchical, authoritarian, directive relationships in life and work	those characterised by collaboration, collegiality and subsidiary
being directed to apostolic tasks within a given apostolate	participation in a discernment process to determine a person's unique vocation within the overall calling of the congregation

3. THE CHANGED ROLE OF THE PROVINCIAL TEAM

Sandra Schneiders summarises the pre-Vatican Two pattern of religious leadership, "We understood our congregations as Newtonian machine-like systems composed of virtually identical parts, operating according to established laws of motion codified in Rules and customs books and functioning best when no part acted in original, that is, 'singular' ways. Leaders functioned somewhat like factory managers maintaining strict control (erroneously seen as order) for the sake of spiritual and ministerial efficiency."[5]

From the nature of the changes outlined above it will be obvious that those with overall responsibility for the well-being of a congregation are now faced with a very different scenario. Whereas before they were dealing with a number of large communities and institutions which were to a great extent uniform and standardised, they are now called on to design, re-design, create, organise and administer many diverse units, some large but many small and unique. This is illustrated in Figure 1.1.

Before, they were dealing with members whose life style and work experience were similar to their own; now, they are dealing with people whose life and work experience is very different. Some members become highly trained and specialised in a field of professional expertise well beyond that of those in leadership positions. This can make for difficulties when members working in such areas as theology and psychotherapy begin to question the nature of the church and religious life, or the way authority is exercised. A distance can grow up between the attitudes and articulation of beliefs of such members and others who are not in a position to keep up with them due to lack of time, opportunity, ability or desire.

Before, they were dealing with closed institutions; now they are working within ones which are very open. Schneiders writes: "New information of all kinds flooded the system. Sisters studied new disciplines in secular as well as religious universities and interacted with a variety of people they formerly would never have encountered in any meaningful way. The mass media and the uncensored contents of libraries burst through the boundaries of the closed system."[6]

Maintaining the unity and cohesion of the congregation in this changed situation makes very different demands on those in positions of leadership and requires very different attitudes and skills.

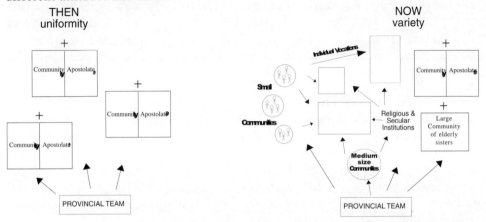

Figure 1.1
The role of the provincial team

The role of the provincial team and how it is exercised is crucial both for the congregation as a whole and for every community. It influences and to a large extent determines the climate in the congregation: whether it is one which is open to and welcomes new local initiatives so they are encouraged and supported, or one in which innovations are merely tolerated, looked at with suspicion or criticised.[7] The part the leadership team plays in a particular community will be influenced by the current congregational setting, the phase of a community's life cycle, and its specific situation.

Clearly, before a community is set up and in its early stages and in the processes which lead to its closure, the team will be heavily involved. During the rest of a community's life span there are likely to be times not only of obvious crisis, but times when a close working relationship between community and team are called for: when key decisions are to be made, an impasse is reached, new members arrive or others depart, superiors are appointed, the community life or work is under review, or there seems to be an unhelpful atmosphere of tension or general malaise.

The management of change both within and between each phase in the life of a community requires thought and skill. A leadership team which is committed to principles of collegiality, collaborative ministry and subsidiarity, and skilled in their use, will act very differently from one which is over-controlling on the one hand or highly permissive on the other. There may also be communities or individuals who have an attitude of dependence and look to the leadership team to do for them what they should be doing for themselves; and others who keep their distance, view any intervention as interference, and leave the leadership team in the dark.

Faced with all this, members of a provincial team may well feel they are walking a tight-rope and that to exercise their role effectively is well nigh impossible. Undoubtedly there will be times when they fail to do so – just as there will be times when communities are seriously wanting. To acknowledge openly and sincerely that both leadership team and community members are fallible, forms a good basis for genuine collaboration.

Professor Gillian Stamp outlines three activities of leadership as "tasking, trusting and tending".[8] A leadership team which missions a small community, trusts it to carry out that mission and yet supports it as appropriate, knowing when and where not to intervene, is very different from one which hands work over, mistrusts, and controls. She also talks of a "triad of trust". In relation to a small community the implications are that a community *trusts* its own judgement, the leadership team *trusts* the community to use its judgement in relation to its purpose, and the community is *entrusted* with the purpose or mission of the congregation.[9]

4. FACILITATING TRANSITION

Whether transition is gradual or sudden, unexpected or intended, welcome or unwelcome, it can be problematic. Transition is not a straightforward simple exercise for an individual, a community group or a complex organisation such as a congregation. It presents an opportunity for both human and spiritual development which, at all levels, can be maximised or wasted. The personal effects of transition are considered in Part Four. The focus in what follows is on the approach most likely to facilitate, throughout a congregation, this movement to small communities in a way that is life-enhancing for all concerned and that is part of the transformation of religious life itself.

Many people in authority intend to work collaboratively but are not doing so, because they lack, not only the necessary skills, but clarity as to what this approach entails in practice. As a result, too often the action taken is authoritarian, directive or manipulative. A provincial can also be *laissez-faire* and with mistaken generosity allow too much freedom to those at grass roots, who in their turn become manipulative, working things out to their own advantage with no thought for the good of the whole: other members and communities simply do not enter into their thinking. Rather than providing overall well-being, these approaches can lead to dissatisfaction and distrust and be destructive of genuine community at local and provincial level. Redeeming such a situation can be a long and painful process.

In working with religious congregations, communities, and individuals engaged at various points in their journey, I have agonised with them over difficult, often seemingly impossible situations, problems and issues. No two have been alike; each had its own unique nuance or twist. There were no ready-made answers. Together we struggled to find a way forward which would fit the situation and the people who lived in it, which would enable them to achieve their purposes, and which they felt was both feasible and held out some promise of success.

As a facilitator, my approach is based on the belief that those engaged in the actual situation are capable – indeed are usually the only people capable – of working out a solution. In order to take a non-directive[10] and reflective approach which characterises my face to face work and which is a central thrust of this book, it is necessary:

– *to enable people to think broadly and deeply about the matter in hand and support them as they do so.* This entails working out ways of getting people to explore clearly, systematically and theologically where they have come from, where they now are, and where they are going. In turn, this means listing various options open to them, considering the pros and cons of each, and helping them make their decision. In the process of doing this, in a multitude of situations, I have worked out many facilitating structures, that is, ways of tackling an issue or problem in steps and stages.

– *to stand in their shoes.* Being alongside people, listening to them and their story takes time and patience, but is the only way to build up as realistic and accurate a picture of the situation as necessary. My basic tool is to ask people questions and, with them, to reflect on their answers. These questions need to be searching but non-threatening, open rather than loaded, and asked objectively rather than judgementally. The central question I ask myself is, "What are the questions I need to ask in order to explore this issue or situation?". I find diagrams help us to think objectively and can summarise, clarify, correct and fill out the emerging picture, while raising issues and questions not apparent before.

– *to form a relationship of mutual trust and openness.* I need to demonstrate that I empathise with and am 'for' those with whom I am working. It requires an attitude of humility rather than arrogance, based on the realisation that at different moments in our lives we all need to turn to someone for help and support. No one is self-sufficient. To enter into the life of another person or community at a point of crisis, pain or decision making is an enormous privilege. Only a relationship of mutual trust and openness makes a firm enough base to risk challenging people when the need arises.

Being non-directive is not an easy option: it is far harder to work out ways of helping people to think and decide for themselves than to do it for them. It can, however, be appropriate and even necessary at times to do some thinking and deciding *for* people. This is so when people are not in a position to think for themselves. Obvious examples are when there is an accident or fire or when people are ill. It may also be necessary when someone is emotionally overwrought or has never been expected to think in this way.[11] Directive and non-directive action are dealt with in more detail on p. 101.

Working with a group or community I not only try to be non-directive myself, but I actively encourage everyone else to be so. I stress the unique insights and experience of each person, the necessity to listen to each other with the heart as well as the head, building on what others are saying or questioning them in order to understand what lies behind it. Such an approach rules out of court such things as pressurising to get a point of view accepted, maintaining fixed positions, lack of interest in other people's ideas, jumping on the first solution put forward, attacking or shooting down an opinion, and non-acceptance of other people's feelings and hunches.

Some congregations, communities and individuals may want to work from first principles as I have done. Others may want a facilitator. Most congregations and communities engaged in promoting and managing change can be helped, at times, by an outsider to alert them to necessary questions or unseen pitfalls, to remind them of their purpose, to draw their attention to the implications of their decisions or actions, and to help them stop in their tracks to check their progress or to face what is blocking them. Few of us have sufficient sophistication and skill in working non-directively, especially in relation to tricky situations and concerns in which we are emotionally involved, not to need such help occasionally.

This is a facilitating book which I hope will give some of the help required. Within it I have gathered together various ways that I have found useful in helping religious work through the issues confronting them in small communities. I put forward methods, facilitating structures, checklists, exercises, steps and stages, ideas and suggestions. Above all, I ask questions to help people to think both together and separately. There is, however, a danger inherent in using this book: that you stick to the rubrics rather than being true to the essential process at the heart of this approach. Exercises and outlines for meetings will usually need modifying to suit your particular situation and community. Working through them could become mechanical, rather than stimulating you to question and develop your own thinking. The intention underlying all that follows is to help you embody the approach which promotes overall development; one that is collaborative, reflective and basically non-directive.

REFERENCES AND NOTES

1. Arbuckle, Gerald: *Strategies for growth in religious life* (St Pauls 1986 ISBN 085439 261 0) p. 21. This is not the place for a thorough analysis of the transition taking place in religious life. In chapter 1 of his book Arbuckle talks about the culture shock experienced by the entire western world, including religious. If they are to be people of their time, loyal members of the

church and true to their Christian calling they will be caught up in the turmoil of church and society rather than cocooned against it.

2. Diamuid O'Murchu MSC in a talk on 'Religious Decline and Revival'. See *Signum*, 18, March 1988, Vol. 16, No. 5, p. 39 .

3. Schneiders, Sandra: 'Congregational Leadership and Spirituality in the Postmodern Era', *Review for Religious*, Jan-Feb 1998, p. 9.

4. I am indebted to Peter Marris for this concept of change and conservation. See *Loss and Change* (Routledge and Kegan Paul, 1974, ISBN 0 7100 8908 2) p. 17.

5. Schneiders, op. cit. (ref. 3 above), p. 9.

6. Ibid. p. 10.

7. I am grateful to Sr. Rosarii O'Connor, SMG for this notion of congregational climate. See her research thesis *'Collaborative Ministry in the Poor Servants of the Mother of God'* for the Avec Diploma in Church and Community Development 1991. John Carroll Futrell SJ STD also mentions it in 'Evaluating Apostolate Communities' in *Human Development*, Volume Seven, Number Two, Summer 1986. He writes "by *climate* is meant the positive or negative sense of being members of a community, determined by shared experiences of the high or low quality of its community life and its achievement of its mission through ministries", p. 14.

8. Stamp, Gillian: A Brunel Institute of Organisation and Social Studies Occasional Paper (BIOSS) The University of West London, *'The Tripod of Work'*, February 1987.

9. Stamp, Gillian: *'Well-Being and Stress at Work'*, BIOSS Occasional Paper, September 1988, p. 2.

10. The non-directive approach was developed as a way of working by T.R. Batten. It is described in *The Non-Directive Approach* by T.R. and M Batten (Avec Publications 1988, ISBN 1 8717 0900 8). See also *Church and Community Development: An Introduction* by George Lovell (Grail Publications and Chester House Publications 1972, Revised 1980); reprinted in 1988 (Avec Publications, ISBN 1 8717 0900 8). Both books are available from Avec Resources, at 125 Waxwell Lane, Pinner, Middlesex, HA5 3ER.

11. T. R. Batten emphasised the need to avoid imposing on dependent groups of inexperienced people responsibilities for decision making in excess of those they are willing or able to bear. See *The Non-Directive Approach*, ibid. pp. 16-17 & 21-22.

II. Community in Apostolic Religious Life

1. COMMUNITY

For many founders and foundresses of apostolic religious, community was a by-product of their desire to do something to meet an immediate, tangible and all too obvious need in their local environment: children needed education or shelter; poor people needed care; sick people needed medical facilities; the dying needed comfort and support. In order to meet these needs, a group of committed people formed a community which enabled them to support each other in the work – physically, psychologically and spiritually. Community was, and still is, an extremely important base for mission and ministry.

The living of apostolic religious community has to be done in the hurly burly of life. Talking about community in non-technical and non-religious terminology is an aid to bringing high religious ideals down to earth and making them newly meaningful in everyday situations. Esther de Waal[1] talks about 'the workshop' in which we live out and forge our Christian lives. Community is such a workshop.

Today, with the breaking down of the nuclear family and the fragmentation of society the need for community is widely recognised. Books and articles have been written about forming community in a neighbourhood, parish or school; about extended non-residential communities; catholic and ecumenical communities; and about community development in urban and rural areas in this country and overseas. Sociologists define community in over ninety different ways.[2] Many religious periodicals have inspiring and challenging articles about the ideals and theology of apostolic communities and 'faith communities of corporate mission'.[3] My task here is a down to earth one: that of stimulating a group of religious to reflect, discuss and come to a common mind on the sort of community they aim to be. What will fit them as a group, be consistent with their purposes for mission and ministry, and be appropriate in their local situation and context?

i. Some characteristics of local religious communities

Religious communities are similar to, but significantly different from, other types of community. The following characteristics, based on work done by George Lovell and myself, clarify the particular strengths and also the difficulties of living in this way.

Members have chosen religious life in a given congregation. As the essential bonding between members is vocational and not personal they will find themselves living with people whom they have not chosen.

Although a new small community may have three or four people who have chosen each other in some way, in the course of time there will be departures and new arrivals, a movement not entirely under the control of the members, although there may well be some degree of consultation. The challenge is to learn to live harmoniously with various people to whom you may not naturally feel attracted as a friend. This commitment means that, as long as you remain a member of your congregation, you cannot, with impunity, walk away from other members with whom you live nor ignore your responsibilities towards them and their well-being. You have thrown in your lot together in the furtherance of the Kingdom for better or worse; at times it feels much better and at times it feels far worse! For most religious this is a major challenge of community life and is ever present.

Members will represent a range of temperaments, outlooks, ages, years in religious life, experience, background, work and theological variations between them (cf. p. 82).

Members participate in many different kinds of exchanges:

- everyday living, meals, celebrations, social activities:
- praying together and discussing or reflecting on religious life and the life of a Christian;
- business meetings in which the practicalities or policy of common life are decided upon;
- discussions about individual or corporate mission and ministry, witness and work;
- discussions, formal and informal, of a personal, pastoral, supportive and challenging nature.

The fact that these exchanges take place with those with whom you live, gives an added dimension: after an emotional meeting or heated discussion, you cannot close the door and leave the situation as you could if it had happened in your separate places of work. You have to go on living cheek by jowl.

The local community is part of a larger whole to which it owes allegiance and obedience, and within which it is co-responsible for the overall well-being and development. The danger is to ignore the rest of the congregation unless help is needed, or letters and directives arrive on the door mat. More about this on p. 127.

Some members are likely to have experienced many years of a more traditional institutional life style. The effects of this may well linger even when overt commitment is given to a more informal way of organising life. More about this on p. 73.

The community members are vulnerable to those with whom and amongst whom they live. The smaller the community the greater interdependence and the personal exposure to vulnerability. Living in a small group makes it more difficult to 'escape' from responsibilities, visitors and crises. The pressures are such that at times escape feels necessary to preserve one's sanity. Even Jesus took his apostles off in this way – although on a least one occasion, that plan was thwarted.[4]

There may well be other characteristics which occur to you. For an outline of a community meeting focused on these characteristics, see p. 207.

ii. Some models of small community living

The models described below illustrate how religious think of their communities. It is for those in a local community to develop their own model to fit themselves and their particular vocation as a small community: it may well change or need reviewing as time passes. A community may reflect one or more of these forms or it may simply be a matter of emphasis.

Parish centred communities. Members are immersed in and work with the local church, sharing in and being part of its on-going life and work. They support, enliven, facilitate and serve. In doing so, they and other parishioners grow together, develop in their Christian lives and promote each other's human and spiritual development. Ministry is mutual, collaborative and reflective.[5]

Mixed communities of growth and wholeness. Members form community in collaboration with others: religious of other congregations and/or lay people who may be of the same denomination or ecumenical, with the aim of exploring new ways of promoting growth and wholeness among themselves and among others in the neighbourhood.

Communities of care and support. Members belong to the same or different congregations and include lay people and those in need of special care and support for one reason or another, physical or emotional, in such a way that all make their maximum contribution to the whole. L'Arche communities are of this kind.

Communities of apostolic support. All or most members are actively engaged in a wide range of work, church-based or secular, including work beyond the local, at diocesan or national level. Such communities may have some members who live at a distance but for whom this is their 'base community' (cf. p. 88).

Communities of prayer. Such a community would be an open centre of prayer in a locality and possibly beyond. In making opportunities for people to deepen their spirituality, a community might provide facilities for people to get away for short periods in a poustinia,[6] provide days or evenings of retreat for individuals or groups, or ways of celebrating the major feasts for families, and so on. Such communities meet the needs and purses of the less well-off and those unable to leave their families or dependants for longer periods.

Small Communities in Religious Life

'Pilgrim' communities. A community moves into a neighbourhood for a short, often specified period, with the aim of building local community and forming lay people to take their part in local church or civic life. When a mutually supportive and active number of lay people can sustain and promote development, the small religious community moves on to a new neighbourhood.

Communities of presence. This model is similar to that of the Little Brothers and Sisters of Charles de Foucauld: to be in an area, praying and working at some manual task with no other explicit form of apostolate. Through very ordinary work and communal prayer, such communities quietly witness to the love of God.

Other models or other ways of modelling community may also be useful when deciding upon the form and purpose of your community[7].

2. SMALL COMMUNITIES IN CONGREGATIONAL LIFE

There is a greater awareness today of the systemic and therefore interdependent nature of all parts of creation. The health and well-being of one part affects the whole in ways which can at times be experienced but more often are unseen and mysterious. Structures set up by human beings necessarily have these same qualities. This is eminently true of religious congregations. St Paul has said it all before, but now that we have a greater understanding of how interdependence is built into the deep structure of our universe and is an essential part of its design, an old truth can become new for us: what it means and its implications for our lives are experienced with a new force.

Congregations are complex entities, often with international, national, and local levels of authority and responsibility, with a variety of decision-making procedures, formal and informal, leading to different types of meetings from general chapters to ad-hoc local gatherings. All parts of a congregation affect and are affected by these procedures.

Small communities have a degree of autonomy but they are not autonomous because they are interdependent parts of the whole congregation. They take their place alongside long-established communities. The experimental and the traditional; the informal and the institutional belong together.

Each and every level of a congregation has its own purpose and value. The most important is the local community, engaged as it is at the coal-face of need in ministry. This is the *raison d'être* of the congregation. Without local communities those at provincial, or general levels would not be needed. Of course they *are* needed. One of the reasons they exist is to facilitate the grass roots work in a wide variety of ways, and those at local level and in specialist areas of work need to keep the congregation's leadership teams *au fait* with the reality of their living and working experience.

The flow is also, and needs to be, between communities. No community is an island. Each community has its unique value, whether it is large or small, traditional or innovative, institutional or with minimum structures. No size or structure necessarily makes for a good community. The criterion for a good community is how closely it lives out and shares Christ's message. This energising flow to and from the central authorities and between communities enables each to function effectively, both in living as religious and in mission and ministry.

In addition, over the years as various members were novices or students together or lived and worked alongside each other in different communities, friendships and informal networks have grown up. In some congregations close bonds are formed as opportunities are made for age groups to meet together. Such networks are largely hidden but nonetheless often carry an immense amount of traffic in the shape of news, ideas, feelings, and attitudes.

Having thrown in their lot together, each individual and community bears some responsibility for the well-being of the whole and may expect to give and receive support and challenge, education and stimulation. Each may at times have to warn against the dangers of the congregation being swept along by unbridled enthusiasms or held back by the over-cautious. Both the enthusiast and the cautious are a part of the rich mix of the congregation. Exploring an innovation put forward by the more radical or a fear expressed by the more cautious often reveals unseen opportunities or pitfalls.

This potentially rich interaction within a congregation can help to bond people together and deepen solidarity between them. It brings about the human and spiritual growth and development of individuals, communities and the congregation as a whole; and ensures the charism lives on and is manifested in new ways appropriate for today.

This is co-responsibility in action. It is worth remembering that the Holy Spirit does not always use the expected channels. The prophetic word may come from the mouth of the youngest or oldest, the team member or the loner, the centre or the periphery.

The overall effectiveness of a congregation depends on the appreciation and healthy practice of all this.

3. THE EXTERNAL CONTEXT OF A CONGREGATION AND ITS COMMUNITIES

Additionally, for a congregation or any part of it to flourish, it must fit well into the wider context, whether one is thinking of the local parish, neighbourhood and the diocese; other Christians and believers of other faiths; or the national or world scene of church or society. A process of mutual interaction makes for healthy functioning and for building up the Kingdom of God.

All parts of the congregation will, in different ways, interact with their context. Those in central leadership are in touch with authorities in the church and in other congregations, internationally, nationally and maybe regionally. Communities and members at every level, to varying degrees, may be in touch with those in the official structures of the church, bishops and priests, as well as others in different congregations. Local communities relate to the local church and neighbourhood. A small group of religious living in a council house has different opportunities and is more accessible to those in its immediate context than those in large institutional communities.

The congregation itself is a pulsating unit of the wider world. Through its extension in many local neighbourhoods in one or more countries and its members in various spheres of work, in associations, organisations, or professional or governmental bodies, there is constant interaction with society.

Just as the interaction within the congregation and between it and other parts of the church may be compared to the life blood flowing in the body, so that between the congregation and society, local and global, may be seen as the air we breathe. Both are necessary for fullness of life. God is to be encountered at work in both.

All this may seem obvious. I call attention to it because the richness of this interaction within and without the congregation can be under-valued. Who has not experienced being so caught up in the needs and demands of their immediate apostolic work, local or congregational, that she has been blind to, forgotten, ignored or resented the opportunities and demands of the wider church or society and thus lost touch with the context in which she and the congregation are set? I am always impressed when visiting a much-loved Cistercian community in South Wales by how much, in prayers and homilies, the monks reveal a knowledge and deep awareness of what is happening in church and world and of their solidarity with it.

4. THE LIFE CYCLE OF A COMMUNITY

The life cycle of any community (cf. Figure 2.1) is not a tidy process. The community composition is likely to change periodically as members join, move out or die. With each change the dynamics are altered and, in a sense, a new community emerges. Although this is true of large as well as small communities, the effects are felt to a greater extent in a small one. In a community of four, for example, a change of one member represents a change in 25% of the community. Despite such periodic alterations, there are three identifiable phases in the overall life cycle of any small community.

Phase I: The formation of a small community: Considering, reflecting, exploring, discerning, decision making, planning and preparing are all involved before a new small community is actually set up.

Phase II: Living and working as a community in mission: This is the major part of a community's life from its early settling-in period to reviewing, reforming and renewing.

Phase III: The closure of a community: This phase includes coming to a decision to close, the closure process, and resettlement of members.

The way each phase is managed, both by those with overall responsibility and those at grass roots, will contribute to or hinder the well-being not only of the community, but of others whose lives it touches. Ways of working effectively in each phase forms the subject matter of this book.

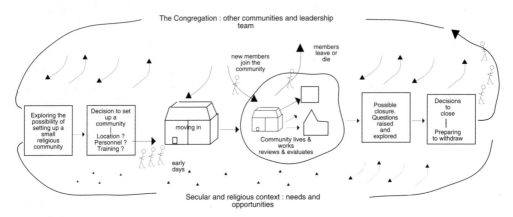

Figure 2.1
Life cycle and context of a small community
(The arrows denote a flow of information, ideas, help and support)

REFERENCES AND NOTES

1. de Waal, Esther: in her commentary for lay people on *The Rule of St Benedict, A Life Giving Way* (Geoffrey Chapman 1995. ISBN 0 2256 6775 4) pp. 38, 40, & 170.
2. Margaret Stacey has found ninety-four definitions of community, so it is not surprising that discussion of what is meant by community continues unabated. O'Murchu warns against definitions and precise description.
3. This phrase is used by John Carroll Futrell (ref. 7) p. 17.
4. Mark 6: 31
5. Lovell, George: *Reflective Practitioners in Church and Community Work,* Avec's 1992 Annual Meeting Lecture (Avec Resources 1994). Also, *Analysis & Design: A Handbook for Practitioners & Consultants in Church & Community Work* (Burns & Oates 1994 ISBN 0 8661 2234 4) p. 251 and p. 196 ff. Lovell talks about the need for reflective communities brought about by key workers 'being effective agents of reflective action for the common good.'
6. This is a term used by Catherine de Hueck Doherty to describe a particular type of Russian hermitage in her book, *Poustinia: Christian Spirituality of the East for Western Man* (Avec Maria Press 1975. ISBN 0 8779 3083 X). It has become a popular form of retreat in the UK, largely through the Grail at Pinner.
7. Browsing through David Clark's *Basic Communities: Towards an Alternative Society* (SPCK 1977. ISBN 0 281 02965 2) might well stimulate you to think along different lines.
   Arbuckle distinguishes three basic models in religious life: the monastic or ascetical; the conventual or relational; and the mission models, in an article "Clarifying Community Models: Essential for Refounding", p. 67 in *Of Clogs and Stocking Feet,* (Ed.) Maureen McCollum (CRC 324 Laurier Avenue East, Ottawa K1N 6P6, Canada, 1992).

PART TWO

Religious Life
and Small Communities

III. Forming Small Communities

Chapter Three is primarily, though not exclusively, addressed to those in leadership positions in the congregation because, however the idea of setting up a small new community came about, the provincial team has the ultimate responsibility.[1] Whoever has been or will be involved inside or outside the congregation, it is the provincial team which is finally answerable for a community's well-being and expected to do something about intransigent problems. The provincial team members, therefore, need to deliberate together on a number of issues concerning the new community even if – and in fact especially if – they intend to involve many other people in the decision making process. If they aim to work collaboratively it is necessary to do their own private thinking and discussion beforehand: the clearer they are about the issues and questions which need to be considered the more likely they are to enable others to think clearly and objectively.

Ideas leading to the setting up of a small community may have evolved in any number of ways. Each community has its own story. Some start life at chapter level when a public decision is made to explore, allow, or encourage the setting up of small communities. In some instances an individual or small group may request to do so because they want, for example, to live alongside disadvantaged people, to try out a more radical life style, or explore new possibilities of being church in the world. Or, it may be that a large house is closing, or members are moving out of an institution such as a school or hospital, the responsibility for which is now being passed over to others. Perhaps a request has come from a diocese or parish to set up a small community for a particular apostolate, or the congregation has decided or been invited to set up a community in another country.

However the initial decision to set up a new community has been taken, a multitude of areas need to be considered and decided about before a community is up and running. It may well be that in some instances the early investigations and discussion lead to a decision *not* to set up a particular community.

The areas that follow are closely and complexly interrelated. Apart from the first (on decision making), they may not all be relevant or in the appropriate order for your situation. There is no standard critical path for setting up a new community, no travel guide to follow. Discussion of these areas will overlap and other areas will occur to you. Map out your own path through the labyrinth in the order that seems best for you and your situation.

1. DECISION MAKING

The principles and practices of decision making I have written about elsewhere are embodied in this book.[2] However, I would like to call attention to two factors that can facilitate the process.

The first is an attitudinal one: an exploratory style goes hand in hand with a collaborative approach. Those engaged in this part of the process ideally provide a searching, open and questioning, rather than categorical or inflexible, role model. All involved need to be genuinely exploring whether or not to set up a particular community and, if it is decided to do so, the most effective way of proceeding with what is a challenging and difficult task. Working in this way avoids 'group think'[3] and is more likely to promote a vibrant and life-giving community team in which all feel responsible, take initiative, struggle together with ideas and tasks, and tackle the problems that are bound to arise. With such attitudes, team-work is built in from the beginning and when the members start to work with others in the locality, collaborative ministry will be a natural extension of their way of working (cf. p. 117).[4]

The second factor is a practical one. It can be helpful to make provisional decisions as you go along, on the understanding that they will be checked out and if necessary altered in the light of further work. This useful device can free up your thinking and enable you to move on to another area.

Decision making in a small community is discussed in Chapter Thirteen. Some of the points made there may well be relevant to the leadership team at this stage.

2. PRELIMINARY EXPLORATIONS

Thought needs to be given to who might participate in some of your early thinking about the membership and location of a new community and the time scale to which you are working.

i. Who to involve and how to do it

The question of who to involve in the early stages of exploring possibilities, making more detailed plans and proposals, and who is responsible for what decisions, is of critical importance if a new community is to get off to a good start. The extent to which it is appropriate to include, closely or otherwise, all who will be affected by the setting up of a new community will vary from situation to situation. In some instances the proposal may be mooted publicly from the start. In other situations, probably the majority, it is more appropriate for only a small number of people to engage in this preliminary stage. This section deals with the question of who to involve in the preliminary explorations and in the actual making of decisions. The further question as to how to inform others, both within and outside the congregation is considered on p. 50, 'Informing the congregation' and on p. 54, 'Going public'.

When three Jesuits were considering setting up a community in Portadown in Northern Ireland, they were in touch with at least seven different categories of people, varying from their own superiors and other Jesuits, to diocesan and local church leaders and people, professional and lay, Catholic and Protestant. Omitting any one group or key person could well have undermined their future ministry.[5]

As the body ultimately responsible, the leadership team will need to consider the following:

· The involvement of the leadership team

The question of how deeply you commit your time and energy as the leadership team to setting up a particular new community will depend on a number of factors such as:

– the overall situation and current programme of the congregation and yourselves as the leadership team: balancing the needs of one community and those of the congregation as a whole is a problem with which you will be only too familiar!

– whether there is anything particularly unusual, new, significant, prophetic, sensitive or problematic which requires your participation;

– whether there are others in the congregation who are experienced, able and available and to whom you would feel confident to delegate the job;

– the particular gifts, skills, abilities and experience you possess, individually or collectively, in relation to this task;

– your own feelings and hunches: these are important and must be taken into account.

There may well be other factors in your situation which will affect your decision about whether or not one or more of you is involved and who else to include in the early stages.

· Involving potential members

The sooner those who are to be members of the new community are part of the thinking process, the more likely it is that the outcome will fit not only the situation but the personnel. In many cases there will be a sliding scale of increasing participation by potential members and decreasing participation by those in the leadership team or those delegated by them. Only too often have I heard of the preliminaries being kept solely in the hands of the leadership team with dire results. I know of one community about which some major decisions were made and action taken with all the good will in the world by the provincial team, and which actually made it impossible for the small community, once it was set up, to operate. An enormous amount of time, energy and heartache resulted and it took several years to re-form that community so that it functioned well, and wounds were healed.

· Involving others outside the congregation

Whether the idea of setting up a community is an initiative of the congregation or a request from a parish or diocese, will influence if, when, and the extent to which others outside the congregation are invited to participate in the decision making process. Once other people are aware of the possibility, undue pressure may be brought to bear on you or expectations may be raised, both by church authorities or secular bodies, making it more difficult to think openly and critically about various options. It may be wise to do a certain amount of private thinking within the confidentiality of the congregation before going public, even to a chosen few.[6]

On the other hand, although the quality of your private thinking affects public dialogue, others outside the congregation may have more information, either hard facts or knowledge of a more intangible kind, which could be crucial to your exploration of the area and its possibilities. Early involvement could therefore be important.[7] Weighing the balance needs to be done through hard thinking, reflection, discernment and prayer. Whatever you decide to do about asking people to participate in the decision making process, it is likely that the generality of people in the local church and neighbourhood will need to be informed at some stage. This is dealt with on p. 50.

· Involving the congregation

Involving and informing the congregation are closely interrelated. The latter is considered on p. 50.

If the decision to set up a community has been made by the chapter, members of the congregation will know about it and therefore have some minimal involvement from the start. Members may be asked not only to support the early explorations by their prayers, but to offer information, ideas or practical help.

· How to involve others

There are different ways in which people, whether inside or outside the congregation, can be involved in the preliminary explorations, decision making and planning. Clarity, both on your part and theirs, is crucial to a satisfying and productive partnership and is more important than the degree of involvement. Whoever you ask to participate, individually or as a group, and whether in one particular aspect or in relation to the whole proposal, you need to make clear what you are asking and expecting of them.

Are you consulting them? Are they being asked, for instance, for information or their ideas on a matter to help you make a decision, or are you asking them to make the decision with or without you? Many consultative processes have led to bad feeling because those consulted thought they were being given authority to make a decision.[8] See Figure 3.1 for a Consultation Flow Chart.

Are you delegating to them? If you are delegating the task to other people, who may or may not include members of the congregation or new community, there are questions

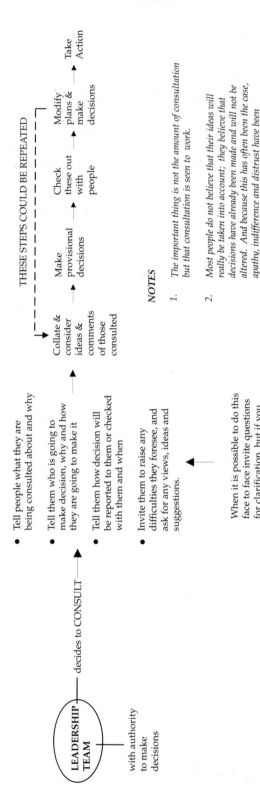

THESE STEPS COULD BE REPEATED

LEADERSHIP TEAM — decides to CONSULT

with authority to make decisions

- Tell people what they are being consulted about and why
- Tell them who is going to make decision, why and how they are going to make it
- Tell them how decision will be reported to them or checked with them and when
- Invite them to raise any difficulties they foresee, and ask for any views, ideas and suggestions.

When it is possible to do this face to face invite questions for clarification, but if you want people's considered opinion, hold them back from giving an immediate response

Collate & consider ideas & comments of those consulted → Make provisional decisions → Check these out with people → Modify plans & make decisions → Take Action

NOTES

1. The important thing is not the amount of consultation but that consultation is seen to work.

2. Most people do not believe that their ideas will really be taken into account; they believe that decisions have already been made and will not be altered. And because this has often been the case, apathy, indifference and distrust have been built up which it takes a long time to break down.

3. Trust will be built up in so far as those in authority are clear, open and honest in explaining what they are doing and why they are doing it; promote the open sharing of ideas and possible difficulties with those concerned; do what they have said they will do.

4. These processes ensure as far as possible that 'right' decisions are made and that decisions are implemented.

**Figure 3.1
Consultation – a Flow Chart**

Small Communities in Religious Life

about how best and when they will keep you informed of developments, when your authority is necessary or could be useful, and the decisions to which you need to be party. Clarifying the area of freedom and the limits beyond which they must not go without further consultation with you, can save misunderstandings and recrimination. Often as people explore, blurred areas will arise, things no one had thought about, or it may be that some hitherto unseen problem or concern occurs to you. It can be important and liberating to have an understanding between both parties, that should such things happen, they will be raised between you and this will not be thought of as over-dependence on the one hand or interference on the other. Table 3.1 lists some factors that should be considered when delegating to others.

Table 3.1:
Checklist for those delegating

What is the task of the group to whom we are delegating?

What are they free to do and not free to do?

What areas do we need to keep within our control?

What difficulties do we foresee?

What sort of time-scale have we in mind?

How and when do we need to be kept informed or receive progress reports?

At what stage do we need to be consulted?

What decisions do we have to make?

Have we reached an understanding about blurred areas and any problems or concerns which may arise later?

---

ii. Membership of a new community

The leadership team is primarily responsible for ensuring that the make-up of any community is such that people are likely to be able to live and work collaboratively and effectively together. This is true when setting up a new community, particularly if it is a pilot project, and even when membership is partially pre-determined by circumstances, such as closure of a house or a request from a small group. The necessity of moving house could provide you with a welcome opportunity for a change-around of members.

Among the factors to consider are such things as criteria for membership, size of community, and how you actually make a choice of people.

· Criteria for membership in relation to the community as a whole

In most selection processes it is useful to draw up criteria before considering individuals. The following may stimulate you to start making your own list when thinking of a particular situation.

Compatibility. Adolph Guggenbuhl Craig says that the struggle involved in forming the sort of household which is supportive, moderately peaceful, stimulating and challenging is a vital ingredient in the process of achieving salvation.[10] Although he is talking of marriage, this is as true, possibly more so, of religious life. As religious rarely find themselves in a community all the members of which they would choose to live with, some degree of incompatibility is usually present. However, if it is too marked, the ensuing tension could stymie rather than promote personal and community well-being and development.

Overall health. Most communities have to contend with some degree of ill-health, whether physical, mental, or psychological: none of us is entirely free from weaknesses and limitations in these fields. How much can a particular community stand without it becoming a major problem? A small community, especially if it will be breaking new ground, is unlikely to be the ideal place for a person suffering from a long-standing health or personality difficulty.[11]

Variety or lack of it. Are you looking for a homogeneous group or a heterogeneous one? This can apply to such things as age, experience, skills, outlooks, nationalities, years in religious life, and so on.[12]

Collaboration and balance. Are these people likely to function as a team? Have they the necessary gifts and graces between them:
  – to cope with the practicalities of living (house, possibly garden, driving, etc.)?
  – to make decisions without dithering for ages or hurrying the process?
  – to manage a crisis?
  – to take a lead when necessary?
  – to encourage the deepening of spirituality among themselves?
  – to see the funny side of things and instil hope during the bleaker times?
  – to take risks and try out new ventures in a responsible way, keeping in touch with the leadership team?

There must be many other questions. Add your own.

Mutual support. What is the potential for giving and receiving support? With this in mind, will it be most helpful to have people who have lived together before or a group of friends or people who do not know each other well?

· Criteria for membership in relation to the individual

The above criteria refer to the community as a whole. You may formulate others concerning the suitability of individuals, for example:

Willingness. What degree of enthusiasm are you looking for? What degree of reluctance will you avoid?

Availability. Some people may be in key positions in their work or be under contract for several more years. Withdrawing such a person suddenly or without proper negotiation and genuine agreement, can cause ill-feeling to all concerned and have a bad effect on that person's ministry.

Other points can be drawn from the general community criteria suggested above.

· Size of community

The number of members may or may not be pre-determined by factors such as the accommodation and the number of people available and willing to join the community. Size is certainly not the criterion by which to judge what makes for a good or poor religious community.[13] If there is any flexibility it could be useful to look at various numbers in relation to such factors as:
- the need for privacy as well as community (cf. p. 80);
- the amount and type of apostolic work which is envisaged by individuals or by the group as a whole;
- sources of income and financial needs;
- viability as a community;
- numbers necessary to ensure the smooth running of the house.

· Making a choice

Clearly, in making a choice of members for a community, a discernment process is a two-way activity involving both those in authority and potential members. Most congregations have their own norms and procedures for this. However, a general group discernment process is given on p. 178 and could be adapted to discerning with a potential community member.

Where the membership is not a given, the leadership team has a choice between selecting and inviting, or asking for volunteers and selecting from those who apply. To resolve this question you could list the pros and cons of these alternative routes. If you decide to ask for volunteers you may be faced with selecting between them. To encourage suitable candidates and minimise disappointing expectations, let people know the criteria you will be using and the number of volunteers required.

iii. Deciding on location

This section is addressed to all those who will be concerned in deciding both on the area in which the new community will live and on their accommodation. This will include the leadership team, and those who explore possibilities, among whom ideally will be several or all members of the new community. This is important because a home-base and how one feels about it, is significant in maintaining the morale of most people.[14] It is a place in which to relax, to be together, and to build up energy and courage to go about one's ministry. Whatever else it is used for, these functions need to be taken into account. It is not indulgent to do so, although if they weigh too heavily in one's choice, it may be!

The model of community will affect the criteria you draw up. It is also likely that suggestions will have been made about the area, or you may have received a request to start up a community from a diocese or parish, and even an offer of accommodation. Whatever your position, you will need to formulate criteria which will help you in your search, be useful to check any proposals or requests received, and by which to assess any property you are considering.

In formulating you own criteria the following questions and ideas may be useful.

The model of religious community you have in mind (cf. p. 34). Ask yourselves:
> Do we already have a model in mind?
> Does it include any of those described?
> Do any of these models or parts of them immediately attract us? If so, why?
> Are there other models we could add to the list?
> Can we formulate our own model, remembering that it can be altered and
>   developed as time goes by?

The area of the country. Ask yourselves:
> How far or near do we want the new community to be to other communities?
> What sort of area are we looking for: inner city, town, suburban, country, etc?
> Are there unmet needs in it which are consistent with our charism?
> What sort of house is acceptable/not acceptable?
> What sort of rail, coach or road links are necessary?

Mission and ministry. A degree of clarity is necessary to explain to others, both within the congregation and in any prospective area, what it is that the community hopes to do. It may only be when it moves into an area and is in contact with people who live and work there, that plans will take a more definite shape. Only so much can be done beforehand. There are, however, questions about the use of the house which may have implications for its location. Will your home be a base from which to go out and work or will it be an integral part of your work? Will it be an 'open house'? We all need some privacy: will you rely on your home base for that or supplement your need for private space by going elsewhere? Mission and ministry is considered in more detail in Chapter Seven on p. 105.

The type of locality. How closely will you identify with those among whom you minister? The number and size of rooms often vary from one locality to another: how much personal space do you need? Is there any possibility of expansion? What about security?

Parish. The choice of parish is not only key if your work is to be parish-based: good relationships with the local parish priests are also important if you are hoping to work with the local people in any way.

There is also the question of finding a local church which meets your spiritual needs. Do you go to your local parish in order to worship with people you live among, or 'shop around' for a satisfying spiritual base, as so many lay people do nowadays?

Practicalities. Depending on whether you will get around by car, by cycle or on foot, questions arise about proximity of public transport, shops, church, etc.

Permanence. How long are you envisaging being in the area? Some groups plan on a five– or ten-year stay, hoping by then to have formed an active laity sufficiently linked together in the equivalent of base communities, to prosper without them. Others plan a long-term apostolate. This answer may affect whether you rent or buy.

Image. This more intangible aspect could affect the influence you will have. How do you wish to be seen by local people, those among whom you work, the parishioners, and others? What are you wanting to communicate by the type of dwelling you have? What image do you want to avoid?

Personal factors. What have you learnt about yourself and your needs and how easy or difficult you have found life in different types of areas, in relation to accommodation, noise levels, amount of built-up area or open space, and security? Considering questions like these may alert you to alight on a danger signal you would do well to take into account.

Information gathering. The time will come when a visit to a prospective area will help you to assess how closely it meets your criteria. Consider where and whom you might visit in order to get information not available on the surface of things: the town hall, public library, church, medical centre, social services, schools, or launderette? Are there any local events you could attend? To begin with, you may want to visit anonymously until you are more sure of your ground (cf. p 232).

iv. Timescale

How long you hope to take in deciding about these factors must be discussed and agreed between the leadership team, the exploratory group and the community members. The timescale will be affected by numerous factors: the time necessary for prospective members to get to know each other well enough to be fairly sure they will be able to make a go of it together; time to orientate themselves as they make the transition from one community and style of life and work to another, and for the communities they are leaving to do likewise (cf. p. 136); time for anyone involved in the locality to orientate themselves to the arrival of a new community; time to make the other more tangible and practical decisions.

At the start of your exploration, ideas about time-scale may be vague. As you go along things will become clearer. At some stage you will need to agree on when your move will be. Timing is important because at one end of the scale are dangers of rushing through the process of exploration and making ill-thought out decisions, and at the other, of drifting, and losing momentum and building up frustration. In order to find the balance which is right for you and your situation it may be useful to:

– *put parameter dates on this first stage.* For example, "We will not move before September this year, but hope to have done so by Easter next year". Use these parameters as guides, do not be enslaved by them.

– *check up on how you are feeling about the progress you are making.* If you are feeling breathless, rushed, pressurised, frustrated or losing interest or hope, discuss and think through the implications.

– *check out informally how other people, who are also involved in some way, are feeling.* For instance, how are members of communities from which people are moving, feeling? What about the feelings of the rest of the congregation (cf. p. 52)? Is anyone in the locality to which the new community will be moving, adversely affected by the length of time the process is taking?

3. INFORMING OTHERS

When and how you inform other people, whether inside or outside the congregation, is of crucial importance. It can make all the difference as to whether the new community gets off to a good start or is hampered by negativity from various quarters. An exercise in developing sensitivity towards all who are likely to be affected by the setting up of a new community and which, ideally, could be done by the provincial team and members of a new community is outlined in Table 3.2. If it is done at an early stage, the insights gained will inform future relationships, not only between all concerned as the new community is being set up, but when it moves in and begins to settle down.

i. Informing the congregation

The systemic nature of a congregation must be borne this in mind when considering when and how to share news of the new community with others in the congregation. The timing and way this is done can have far-reaching effects, for good or ill. As with the birth of a new baby in a family, so the advent of a new community affects and alters the shape of the whole and the relationships between the parts. I believe that the whole process of setting up a new community can be, in varying degrees, a life-giving exercise for the whole congregation. I fear that, at times, it is not thought of in this way and sends negative ripples throughout the system. This is a tragic waste of energy which could be used to support new ventures and to profit from them, even if people are not participating in them actively. "We must recognise new small communities as new shoots, not as broken branches and give them a sense of belonging".[15]

Small Communities in Religious Life

Table 3.2
THE EFFECTS OF OUR COMMUNITY ON OTHERS

One member sketches out the categories of people with whom the community are to a greater or lesser extent in touch, such as those in the figure below.

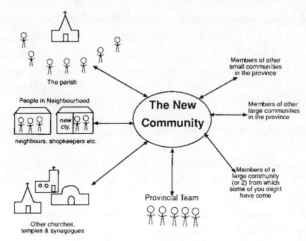

The exercise consists of standing in the shoes of each group and viewing your community from their perspective, either by focusing together on one group in turn and asking the questions below or by dividing up with each person or pair focussing on one group. Whichever you do, it is useful to begin by centring yourselves and taking some time in personal reflection before pooling your thoughts. It is important that provincial team members do not stand in their own shoes for this role play. Hints for leading a guided fantasy on p. 206 may be helpful in introducing and de-briefing.

Question 1: What are (a) your positive feelings and (b) your negative feelings about this new community? How will the setting up of it affect you?

Question 2: What sort of relationship do you want with the community? What sort of relationship do you not want? What are your hopes and your fears?

Question 3: What would you like to say to them about these things?

After each group has been discussed it could be useful to return to stand in your own shoes and pause to reflect on the total impact of the new community before saying what has struck each of you.

· **The perspective of the new community members**

As central actors in this development, those setting up a small community have an enormous amount to do as they re-organise and re-orientate their lives. They are likely to become preoccupied by their move and all that it entails by way of decision making and planning, unexpected responsibilities, questions, opportunities and problems, as they adjust to forming themselves into a viable community. It is therefore understandable, but regrettable,

Small Communities in Religious Life 51

if they give little thought to others for whom it brings change. The attitudes and actions of the new community members at this early stage, will affect their on-going relationships.

· The perspective of those remaining in large communities

The very setting up of new ways of living religious life raises questions about the authenticity and value, not only of the new, but also of the old. Those who carry on in the well-tried way may well become defensive, feel undervalued, confused, hurt or abandoned, or see an implicit criticism of their own life style. They may worry as to who will care for them as they grow older, or how to maintain and use an over-large building. Jealousy and envy may go unrecognised and unchallenged and lead only too easily to a souring of relationships within a congregation.

· The perspective of existing small communities

If other small communities already exist, the creation of a new one entails changed relationships. Members of existing communities may well realise that they have a wealth of experience from which a new community might learn. They may feel aggrieved if this is not asked for, is ignored, or if they see "obvious" mistakes being made. On the other hand they may feel jealous if the past has been learnt from and the new community is given more help and support than they had. They may, of course, feel overjoyed and encouraged that small communities are gradually becoming the accepted norm. Co-responsibility between communities is considered further on p. 132.

· Preparing to tell other communities

Some of the ideas below may help as you prepare to tell the congregation about the new community and its progress.

Articulate your purpose. Clarify what you are trying to achieve. What response are you hoping for? What reactions do you want to avoid?

Stand in the shoes of those who will be affected. This is a valuable technique. Pay particular attention to people who are most likely to feel negative about the new community. A group exercise is set out in Table 3.3.

Consider the questions below.

When to tell them? What is the best time for them to know? How long might they need to get used to the idea? Do you need their help or support and if so, what for and when? Might they be hurt or angry if they hear later rather than earlier? If you need to keep the information confidential, are they likely to respect confidentiality? Does your decision rest on their response? Do you tell people when the decision is a *fait accompli* or part-way through the process?

Where to tell them? What is likely to be the best setting: formal or informal, individually or together, face to face, or by letter or telephone?

Table 3.3
PREPARING TO TELL THE CONGREGATION

One member needs to guide the others through the process.[16] See hints on leading a guided fantasy on p. 206.

1. Sit in a relaxed way, close your eyes and take a few deep breaths to still yourself.

2. Quietly imagine yourself as one of those in the congregation who may well be unhappy at the news of the setting up of this small community. (If this is done in a group without mentioning names you could suggest that individuals stand in the shoes of different types of people affected in a variety of ways, for instance, an elderly person who is always negative to change, someone who believes in institutional communities with traditional practices, someone who would dearly like to be going to the new community but will not be doing so, someone from the community of one or more of the new members, a volunteer who was not selected as a member, and so on.)

3. As this type of person, reflect for a minute or more on all you have achieved in your life as a religious, the struggles and successes, ups and downs, your feelings then and now as you reflect on your experience.

4. Then consider the setting up of this new community. How will it affect you? What do you feel about it? What are your fears about it? Do you feel sad, angry or let down? Why do you feel like this? Have you any hopes for it? What sort of relationships would you like to see developed between you? (Other similar questions may occur to you as you think about your specific situation and your own members.)

5. Gradually return to the present and become yourselves again. Share what you thought and felt. What strikes you? What have you learnt? What are the implications for the way you communicate news of the new community to the rest of the congregation?

Who might tell them? Who they hear from can be a factor in whether people respond positively or negatively. Who is the best person to communicate the information, for example, the general, provincial or a councillor, the local superior, another member of the community, or a member of the new community?

How to tell them? Most people are reasonable if things are explained to them carefully and openly. A brief announcement or explanation will be enough for some but those who more deeply affected may need more information as to the whys and wherefores.

How to deal with negative feedback? It may be wise to think about this before it happens so that you are ready for criticism or adverse comments and can deal with them in a helpful way rather than exacerbating the situation. What is the likeliest negative feedback? How far is it justified? Stand in the shoes of the person concerned: what would help you to see other sides of the question and be open to other points of view? Read off the implications for your response. The most helpful response may be to remain open and calm and really listen to what is being said and explore with those concerned why they feel as they do. The phrasing of your response is important, for example:

"We gave a lot of thought to this question and took what seemed the wisest course."
"We may have been wrong about that, but could see no other way at the time."
"People clearly see this very differently; we honestly think that what we decided was for the best."
"We're really sorry you feel like this about it, but we can't see any alternative."

ii. Going public:

This part is addressed primarily to the leadership team but also to those who will form the new community. Whoever transmits the information or however it is done, it is primarily the members of the new community who will have to live with the results.

At some stage the setting up of a new community will become public knowledge. How and when this happens needs consideration so that the response of people outside the congregation is most likely to be positive. I have often heard of anger and hurt experienced by people who are implicated but feel their interests and situations have not been taken into account. This may be objectively true, but if it is not, feelings are likely to have been aroused through the way in which the news was communicated.

The advent of a new community may be viewed in different ways by the various people in the locality.

· The perspective of the parish

Ordained and lay members of a parish may not have experienced a small group of religious living alongside them as part of the parish community; they may only know large communities with their own chapel and chaplain. If they have known a small community, they may well expect the new one to follow the same pattern. The shape of the parish will change and all sorts of fears, hopes and questions could arise when the idea of a new community becomes known. Why have these religious come? How will it affect the parish, current arrangements, established groups? Will they help us or take over from us?

· The perspective of the neighbourhood

Although some local people may have met, been taught or nursed by religious, many may have had nothing to do with organised religion, let alone religious, before. Others may have known of large communities living at a certain distance in a large institutional type of house, possibly surrounded by extensive grounds or high walls. There may well be a variety of misunderstandings and even suspicion around. Are they here to proselytise? Are they do-gooders? Will they patronise our local shops or be fleecing us for 'a good cause'? Will they keep themselves to themselves? Why are they coming to live in our street? The personal reflection suggested on p. 51 may be helpful at this stage.

Small Communities in Religious Life

Having considered the potential responses and reactions, ask yourselves questions like:

What are we trying to achieve through going public?

What information shall we give before we move in? How and why the idea emerged, how the decision was made and why, relevant hopes, fears and feelings, who the members will be, and so on. Too little information could sound secretive, too much could overwhelm.

Who should give the information? One of the local people, the leadership team, a member of the new community, or a church or civil dignitary from the diocese or area?

What is the best way to go public? Face to face, formally or on the grapevine, by letter or an article in a local newspaper or bulletin, by phone? These are not necessarily mutually exclusive.

Who shall we inform? Are there some people who are in positions of leadership who need to know first? Is there any individual or group who might be offended if not told personally, or who is told after other people?

4. OTHER ASPECTS

Other aspects of community life and mission may well be considered at this early stage. How deeply they are discussed before members actually start their community life together in their new setting will vary from place to place. Factors to do with such things as lifestyle, prayer together, leadership, and mission are dealt with in subsequent chapters.

5. MOVING IN

i. Preparing to move in

How you enter a situation determines, in large measure, the response you will receive from those already there. It is wise, therefore, to spend a little time thinking ahead and preparing yourself internally as well as externally. In fact, the internal preparation is the more important of the two: it is good to do and say certain things and to avoid others, but it is your inner attitudes which communicate on a deeper and less conscious level.

THEN   NOW

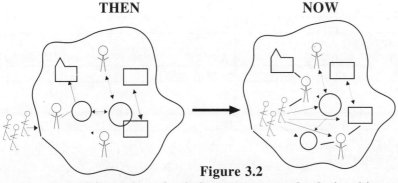

Figure 3.2
Disruption of existing patterns and relationship

· **Envisaging the situation**

When we leave somewhere in which we have been living and working, it is relatively easy to realise that that situation, whatever happens to it for better or worse, will not be the same without us. Looking forward, you could equally well say that the situation, whether community, parish, locality, school or office, once you are there, will not be the same as it is now. When a new community moves into the area it cannot just slot into the situation, it necessarily disrupts existing patterns and relationships. The parish and neighbourhood are affected and their shape is changed. Because your arrival will change the shape (Figure 3.2) adjustment will be needed on the part of all concerned. For you, moving into a house or flat is relatively straightforward, but for your neighbours, as the Jesuits moving into Portadown discovered, it could be a dramatic event.[17] Your entry is an important moment and its effect on all you hope to achieve should not be underestimated. Other people have hopes and fears about you. Some in the parish and neighbourhood may not be expecting you, others may be looking forward to your coming, and yet others may not want you. You could help yourself to become more sensitive by standing in the shoes of those with whom you will be living and working. The exercise on p. 51could, if you have not already done it, be done alone or, preferably, the new community could do it together, slightly adapted.

· **Your early objectives**

Together those moving in and those already in the situation are creating something new. Realising the potentially disruptive effect of your advent can help you go there with an attitude of humility, tiptoeing as it were, and wanting to look, to listen and to learn. Realising that your arrival heralds the birth of a new situation with different possibilities and opportunities can be exciting. In the light of this, reflecting alone and together and articulating as a community what your immediate objectives will be during the first few days and weeks, will help you to move in more purposefully. You may want to do this informally. Another way is to use a grid like that in Table 3.4.

Table 3.4: Objectives for the initial few months			
Our/My objectives in relation to	the first few days	the first few weeks	the first few months
myself	to . . .	to . . .	to . . .
my/our religious community	to . . . to . . .	to . . . to . . .	to . . . to . . .
the parish	to . . .	to . . .	to . . .
our neighbours	to . . . to . . .	to . . . to . . .	to . . . to . . .
the . . .	to . . .	to . . .	to . . .

Decide which groups to include in the first vertical column, e.g. the province; the people with whom you will work; colleagues; people such as social workers, doctors, teachers, clergy, other churches. Tailor the lists to your situation, and to be manageable, short and simple. Having worked on your grid, go through each objective, deciding how to achieve it. For example, if your objective during the first few days in relation to yourself is 'to survive', ask yourself "what will help me/us to do so?". Or, if you are hoping to form friendly relationships with your neighbours, think what would help them to take to you and what might put them off (the way you dress, talk, behave, etc). These may seem trivial, but "for want of a nail, the horse was lost. . .".

· Getting to know each other

In my experience the most effective way for people who have never lived together to get to know each other is through joint thinking, discussing, deciding, making and carrying out plans. However, if you want to supplement this, the exercises or activities given in

Chapter Sixteen may be helpful. You might go away on holiday, for quiet days, or for a course together and in this way you gradually build up some shared history, and experience each other in a more relaxed or at least a non-work setting.

· Practicalities check list

Having had a fortnight in which to furnish a penthouse flat in a foreign country, before four of us moved in and were ready to provide secretarial services for a lengthy international meeting, I know the value of listing all that will be needed in order to be able to live and work. In the general disruption of moving house it is all too easy, and can be disastrous to morale, to find that there is no tea available or that no one has thought of contacting the electricity suppliers. It is useful to sit down together sometime beforehand, and brainstorm what will have to be done or provided so you are able to eat, sleep, cook, feel secure, and generally sort yourselves out. Then decide who will be responsible for what, before and during the first few days. Posting up your practicalities check list in a prominent place is a reminder which can save a lot of hassle.

· Congregation, family and friends

It may be difficult in the turmoil of moving to think of other people, but there are those who are interested in your move and may be waiting to hear how you are getting on. A change of address card, accompanied by some indication of how things are, may be all that is necessary to keep them happy.

ii. Moving in and early days

Thomas Merton has said "The place where I am is the place where I belong". 'Place' in this quotation may refer to a geographical location, but to me it means far more than that. There is the outer 'place' in terms of situation: where you are living and working, who you are living and working with, and what you are working at. There is also the 'place' where you are on your inner journey: your motivating beliefs, feelings, attitudes, your hopes, fears and struggles. Some aspects of Part Four *Transition between communities* may help individual members to think about their personal move.

Some places in which we find ourselves, both externally and internally, seem to require more of us than others. Setting up a new community house in a new location is one such place. There are so many decisions to be made on every front on a daily or weekly basis and, being in a new situation, uncertainties replace a familiar routine. There are the sudden eruptions of the unexpected, the excitement of new discoveries, and the forming of new relationships. All this demands a lot of emotional energy. This will be especially true when the plumbing goes awry, the neighbours are over-friendly or hostile, or the differences between you become more obvious and make life uncomfortable and challenging.

This 'place' is unavoidable, it has to be lived and worked through. Moving house is high on the list of major traumas in life, and for some people the experience will be more demanding and draining than for others. Be patient with yourself and with each other: take time to rest or relax together; avoid rushing to get everything shipshape.

Every situation will vary as to how much planning and decision making is best done before moving in and what it is wiser or more practical to leave until you are *in situ*. There is no ideal formula or blueprint about the timing: it is up to each community to make its own schedule. Doing so can avoid misunderstandings and frustration. However, there are decisions which need to be made earlier rather than later if you want to start off on the right foot. If left too late, you may unthinkingly have formed habits which are dysfunctional and hard to break.

When on the move it may not be possible to talk through these issues to everyone's satisfaction: you may need to make provisional arrangements and build up an agenda for later discussion. So early decisions are best not seen as carved in stone. This is a trial period, and as has already been said, seeing your decisions as provisional during the initial settling-in phase avoids inflexibility later on: "We decided to do it this way, and you are wanting to change. . .", or "We've always done it this way". 'Living provisionally' is a phrase coined by Brother Roger Schutz of Taizé. It is particularly apt during your settling in period. Discussing the practicalities of living together touches deeper issues about which people often have strong feelings. Decisions will be made in the light of your varied experience of life, but you will have little or no experience of actually living together as *this* group, here in *this* new place, at *this* moment in your lives. These here and now elements are significant factors. You may think you know each other because you have lived together in the past, but it is likely that you have each grown and changed during the intervening period. You may think you know each other because you are 'only' moving house, but a changed environment may well alter your behaviour and that of others.[18]

REFERENCES AND NOTES

1. According to Canon Law the provincial or general is the ultimate authority. I refer to 'provincial team' or 'leadership team' because increasingly authority is exercised and decisions are formulated in a collaborative way by the provincial or general and the councillors.
2. Widdicombe, Catherine: *Meetings That Work, A Practical Guide to Team Work,* (St Paul's, 1994; 2nd edition The Lutterworth Press, 2000,). The process of decision making and various practical suggestions are dealt with on pp. 161-168.
3. Group Think is a phrase coined by Irving Jarvis to describe errors of decision-making based on group conformity and misplaced loyalty to a leader or institution. The thinking of the group becomes 'frozen' and members resist outside pressure to re-examine their views. New information is ignored or used in such a way as to reinforce, rather than challenge their stance. See *Group Think* by Irving Jarvis and Leo Mann (Collier MacMillan 1977)
4   Collaborative ministry is now officially recognised by the Catholic Church in the UK. See *The Sign We Give* (Matthew James Publishing 1995 ISBN 1 898366 14 4). This is the report from the Working Party on Collaborative Ministry which was set up by the Bishops' Conference of

England and Wales, 1995. (It is available from The Secretariat, 39 Ecclestone Square, London SW1V 1BX.)

5. *Analysis and Design,* op. cit. (ref 5, p. 38). Lovell gives a full and instructive account of the setting up of a Jesuit community, pp. 93-106.

6. Ibid. pp 193-196. See also *Human and Religious Factors in Church and Community Work* by George Lovell (A Grail Publication 1982) p.43. Lovell stresses the need to do some private thinking in order to be in a position to make the best use of the time and energy of other people in discussion and decision making. Such private thinking is *not* done in order to manipulate the outcome but to promote genuine participation and collaboration.

7. Op. cit. (ref 5, above). Lovell describes how priests and curates of the Armagh diocese were enabled to make a free decision about the possibility of a Jesuit community in Portadown, Northern Ireland, pp 96-97.

8. Ibid. p. 256.

9. This diagram and notes are adapted from one by George Lovell.

10. Guggenbuhl Craig, Alolph: *Marriage, Dead or Alive?* (Spring Publications, Geneva, 1977). Although he makes out a case for couples to struggle through the relationship difficulties, this is not to deny that in some instances divorce or separation are an unavoidable way out of a situation.

11. Sperry, Len: 'Neurotic Personalities in Religious Settings', *Human Development*, Volume Twelve, Number Three, 1991.

12. I often find the trite use of Myers-Briggs Typology unhelpful when people use it to describe themselves as though fixed in a position. However, thinking about the personnel for a new community may well be an occasion when it would be useful in selecting a mix of people likely to be able to carry out various community building and work functions. *The Manual for Myers-Briggs Type Indicator* by Isabel Briggs-Myers (Consulting Psychological Press, 1962).

13. 'Trends in Spirituality' in *Review for Religious*, March/April 1988. Frederick McLeod writes, "What is more critical, in my opinion, for a community's well-being today is not its size . . . but the community structures that are established to challenge and guide its members to live with each other securely, smoothly and religiously." p. 241.

14. The importance of place on our psychological well-being is being realised increasingly. Alteration of behaviour due to environmental factors is a well-attested fact and is being researched by Claire Cooper Marcus, Professor of Architecture and Landscape Architecture, University of California. She is author of *Easter Hill Village: Some Social Implications of Design.*

15. This was said at the General Chapter of the Mercy Union (UK) in April 1993.

16. Anthony de Mello talks about 'the untapped source of power and life in a fantasy' in *Sadhana, A Way to God* (Image Books, Doubleday, 1984) p. 65. Several such exercises are suggested throughout this book.

17. Op. cit. (ref 5 above). "They worked out how best to move into such a house. They thought about it from their own perspective and they tried to stand in the shoes of their new neighbours and to speculate on the possible effects upon them of three Jesuits moving in next door. Through looking at it this way they really saw and felt that their entry was a dramatic event which could have positive and negative effects. Three Jesuit priests moving in to a closely knit homogeneous community of deprived people was indeed a serious discontinuity!", p. 100.

18. Cooper Marcus, op. cit. (ref 14 above).

IV. Closure of a Small Community

Addressed to all with the responsibility, whether in decision or implementation, for closing a small community. It is important to involve as far as possible those with whom the community has collaborated. The clearer members are about the issues and quetions, the more likely they are to enable others to think objectively.

Closing a religious house, whatever its size, is inherently problematic.[1] Good reasons can usually be put forward for keeping any house open: worthwhile work is being done by the community or individuals; its closure removes the symbolic religious presence from that neighbourhood and also the support and hospitality given by the community. There are also the practical difficulties of closing some work down or handing it over to others without people feeling let down. Added to which are the emotional ties of present and possibly past community members, and maybe of the congregation which has invested heavily in the venture. The life and work of those who have to move will be disrupted: they may not see clearly where and how the next stage of their life and ministry will work out; they may be full of fears as to whether they will be able to cope with the change, whether they will find some equally worthwhile ministry or even another job. People will have put down their roots with varying degrees of tenacity and some will be constitutionally more open to change than others. I myself have been caught up in some of this trauma. I remember as a facilitator looking up from my breakfast to find an elderly sister behind me wielding a bread knife over my head as she asked me to do my best for their community in the forthcoming chapter! I was torn between amusement at what a wonderful illustration it would make and a feeling of deep sympathy at the very real distress she felt at the possibility of closure after years of faithful service in the area.

1. WHO TO INVOLVE IN DECISION MAKING

This question has been considered in relation to setting up a new community on p. 31. The same categories of people need to be involved in considering closure.

· The leadership team

The leadership team are ultimately responsible for making the decision – unless it is done in chapter. If they stand in the shoes of those who will be affected by the closure it will help them to consult and act sensitively. They also need to avoid being pressurised by others, and to keep their objectivity and be free to make the best possible decision. Decision making is discussed on p. 163 and in Chapter Thirteen on p. 171.

· Members of the community

The closure of a house is of major concern to those living in it. They are conversant with the situation and in a position to give information which is pertinent not only to deciding whether to close the house, but how and when and who else might be involved at what stage, and about possible futures for themselves.

· Others outside the congregation

Local people in the neighbourhood and parish, work colleagues and clients, other religious, parish priests and bishop may all be affected by the closure. Early consultations in which they can express their feelings and possibly raise objections allow you to be open about your situation, explain the predicament you are in, and your reasons for considering closure, and ask for their help, support and prayers in a difficult time of decision making. Too often decisions about the closure of a house or apostolic work have been made behind closed doors, and the news when it has been made known – or leaked – has caused a furore and much ill-feeling.

If the congregation and community are really working collaboratively, it will be natural to open the discussion to those outside and together seek to discern what God is asking, both of the religious and of others in the area at this time.

I often feel that religious seldom realise what their presence and activities mean to those who live near or work with them, and how deeply they are valued. Breaking the news about the possibility of closure and consulting those who will be affected needs great skill and sensitivity. Given that, the congregation and community can often be surprised by joy at people's understanding, sympathy and generosity.

· The province or congregation

That the closure of a house is of concern to the whole province or congregation is a natural corollary of co-responsibility. If the community is of long-standing, there are likely to be members elsewhere who have strong ties with it or may have been involved in setting it up or supporting it. What they have to say by way of views and feelings adds to the information available and helps those concerned to know that they have been heard. The backing of support and prayer is much needed both during the decision making and the actual closure. Some of the ideas about involving and informing others in the congregation when setting up a small community may well be relevant at this stage of possible closure (cf. p. 50).

· Chapter delegates

When a province or congregation needs to retrench, the subject of closures may feature on the chapter agenda and research be done during the time of preparation. Such research may be to do with:

- criteria for closing houses or keeping them open;

- a review and evaluation by each community for presentation at the chapter. A way of doing this is suggested on pp. 183-6 and 194-5;

- a sociological survey of economic and social needs based on ranking areas of the country on a sliding scale of those which are more or less deprived or affluent;

– feasibility studies of houses in area groupings which include information about their physical resources, current work, personnel and possible developments were they to remain open.

Except in a few clear-cut cases, it is often wiser for chapter delegates to make recommendations rather than actual decisions about possible closures. They are unlikely to have sufficient information, or may be unable to get their minds round all the facts pertaining to an individual house and its situation in relation to all the other houses. Furthermore, several participants may well be emotionally involved and unable to decide to close their own house or be reluctant to vote to close a house with whose members they have close ties. Added to which some people may be unwilling or unable to shoulder responsibility for decisions which bite. Pressure of time and other important issues often prevent the reflective discernment and hard thinking which is needed.

On the other hand, a chapter may make recommendations and give instructions about the need for thorough consultation and other conditions which need to be met before a decision is reached and before a house is actually closed.

2. DECISION MAKING

Some of the suggestions concerning decision making in Chapter Thirteen on p.171may be useful. In making decisions about closing a house there are several areas you could consider.

· Timing

Undue haste and working to deadlines can raise anxiety levels and cause you to omit vital factors, make ill-considered decisions, or ride roughshod over people's feelings. Much time and effort can be expended later in trying to overcome the harm done by too much haste. On the other hand working to flexible deadlines can prevent the process dragging on interminably.

· Theological reflection

Where appropriate it is important to suggest that those who will be involved in making the decision, engage in some form of theological reflection as a basis for the discernment process. Reflecting on the sacrificial cost of closure, on death and resurrection, may motivate them to be open and generous. One community formulated challenging questions for themselves to reflect on: Are we called to a building, a place, or a particular work? Are we extending God's kingdom? Where is our security – in a house, a ministry, or in God? What do we fear most?

· Choosing between houses

When a choice has to be made to close one of a number of houses there are some communal exercises which could be done with those concerned:

– Consider the pros and cons of continuing, developing, and closing each house. Focusing on one house and helping everyone, including its own members, to formulate both pros and cons will make for greater objectivity.

– Get individual members to imagine an alternative future for themselves if or when their house closes or their work folds up: a future they find acceptable or exciting.

– Get each community to work out the conditions under which it could face closure with equanimity.

· **Criteria for closure**

Each congregation needs to work out its own criteria. The list below, drawn from frequently used criteria, may serve as a check list or stimulant for further thought.

No valid or ongoing apostolate. Consider such factors as: duplication of services; the work could be done equally well or better by lay people; its scope is seriously limited by those in authority in the secular sphere or local church; the community is no longer wanted; the work itself is no longer needed or is proving ineffective; the work while good in itself, is no longer one of the congregation's priority areas.

Shortage of personnel. Members may no longer be able to continue what they were doing, be needed elsewhere, have lost heart or feel a call to an alternative way of life or other work; or congregational retrenchment is necessary.

Unsuitable location. The style of life may not be in conformity with the message; the house may be in an area made unsuitable because it has become 'gentrified' or too rough and unsafe; the work does not warrant the property which may be too large, or pretentious, or its upkeep is too much of a drain on resources or personnel.

The emphasis is on provision rather than development. The service being provided relies on community members: others are not being trained to do it or take responsibility for it, thus making for dependency. Also, the charism is not being transmitted so that it flowers and develops in lay people.

The work and life of the community is out of tune with current thinking in the church.

No valid or overwhelming reasons can be given for keeping it open. It is possible that, despite a house meeting many of the above criteria for closure, it is kept open for a particular reason: it is involved in a pilot project; the foundation is only for a limited period of time; or it serves some practical purpose.

Lack of financial viability. While some houses may well not be required to be financially viable in themselves and have to rely on central funds, it may be that such funds are simply not available, need to be used elsewhere, or reserved for future development or contingencies. A community, however much its work is needed, might become too much of a drain on financial resources.

· **Consultation**

Consultation and a flow chart of consultative procedures have already been considered on p. 43-4.

3. INFORMING OTHERS OF CLOSURE

Those you have consulted during the decision making will, to some extent, be prepared for the news that the community house is to close. They may, however, still find this difficult to accept. It could help people to do so if you explain your own feelings and the agonising decisions you have had to make. Lay people particularly, know all too well about reaching decisions of this kind and are more likely to be supportive when taken into your confidence in this way. Too often decisions are publicised with no indication of the human cost to those who had to make them, and people are left feeling, at some level of their being, that they were made easily by those who will not bear the brunt of the effects.

4. PREPARING TO DEPART

What is written in relation to individuals at times of transition in Part Four will be relevant to the community as a whole.

A community might well be helped at this stage by having someone who will accompany it, listen to people's feelings, and support members during the time of withdrawal.

A final celebration planned in collaboration with those with whom the community has been working could stress the closure of one phase in the life of the parish, neighbourhood, and community, and the opening of another.

NOTE

1. I am drawing largely on work I have been involved in with the Mercy Union and the Mercy Institute, both in the UK.

Part Three

Religious Life in Small Communities

V. LIVING AS A SMALL COMMUNITY

This section is addressed primarily to the members of small communities, but clearly those who have overall responsibility for them and others who may be involved with them through facilitation work would also find parts of it relevant.

1. AIMS, PURPOSES AND MISSION STATEMENTS

Articulating the mission of your community will give you direction and drive, become an invaluable and practical touchstone to guide your decisions and activities, and help you when you come to review and evaluate. Such a statement is therefore not something which is merely framed and hung in a prominent place, or just used as a book mark. Ideally it is in constant use: remembered, referred to, and used in explanation of your *raison d'etre*. Without such a statement, a community is in danger of drifting, stagnating, or dissipating its energies as it is blown first in one direction and then in another. You may think in terms of aims, purposes or mission statements; whatever terminology you prefer, they all answer the basic question: *what are we here for?* Getting an agreed answer to that question, one which is clear, sufficiently specific, and relevant to your situation, and which as a group you find deeply motivating, is of fundamental importance to your community and can be of genuine benefit to those among whom you live and work. Such a statement is a public expression of what you are hoping to bring about in and through your life and work. Your congregation may well have a mission statement. I suggest you formulate one for your own community. Clearly there needs to be consistency between them, but your community statement could be more specific for your particular situation.

If your statement is to be one which will serve you well, it is unlikely to be arrived at without some heart searching and hard thinking. Even when you have one which is eminently satisfactory, as time goes on, you may well find it needs amending to express some new insight or perspective. It needs to be a living statement.

i. Exploring your beliefs[1]

Thinking about beliefs can facilitate the articulation of purpose or mission. People who are purposeful and committed have deep inner beliefs which motivate them. Their exterior activity is bound up with their very being. Erich Fromm talks of alienated and non-alienated activity.[2] Alienated actions are those which are done mechanically and are divorced from oneself. Non-alienated activity is that which springs from the depth of one's being and is therefore creative. Clearly, the effective setting up of a new community requires such non-alienated activity in those directly involved in the process. Spending time reflecting on and discussing motivating beliefs, is a helpful, and at times essential step to formulating purpose (cf. Table 5.1).[3]

Table 5.1: Beliefs in life, work and ministry

In order to use your beliefs in your work/ministry, you need to understand and believe in:

How they affect all you do	Their value in our personal development	Their value in the corporate development of a group or community
In alienated activity beliefs // actions are separate and distinct from each other *In non-alienated activity* beliefs ⟷ actions support, challenge, question, stimulate each other. Acting in a non-alienated way is powerful for good (or evil). This is true of groups as well as individuals.	Being aware of what you believe: – promotes your theological growth, equips you to engage creatively in theological dialogue, and helps you to embody your beliefs in action because you: – understand what you do or do not believe and your commitment to a particular belief. – make your beliefs more readily available for use in decision making, and reviewing what you are doing and why. – can be true to your inner self, you become authentic in your work and ministry.	Being aware of and in touch with what you believe as a group: – helps you to see where others are coming from, their theological/belief motivation and commitment. – engenders mutual understanding and trust, and builds a common experience and history. – enables people of different beliefs to work together with integrity for the common good. – promotes communal theological development.

Table 5.1: Beliefs in life, work and ministry (cont'd)

Beliefs underlie action

In general: they motivate you in your vocation and ministry and give an on-going thrust to all you do and how you do it.

In particular situations: applying your beliefs to your work in hand enables you to assess its value and your commitment to it.

What is required: As honest a statement as possible of any beliefs upon which you are operating in relation to your work and life in general and in relation to a specific aspect at a given time.In thinking about your beliefs it helps to differentiate between:

> *Public theology* – what we say we believe: more rational, better organised, easier to get at.

> *Head theology* – what we believe or think we believe: what we are consciously in touch with.

$$\uparrow$$

> more personal, pervasive, profound, and elusive.

$$\downarrow$$

> *Visceral/gut theology* – what we show we believe through actions, decisions, life-style and commitments: our feeling self.

In using your beliefs there are two modes of action:

– Active mode – applying our beliefs to work, actions, events, decisions, etc.

– Attentive/Reflective mode – listening to what your beliefs are saying to you about your work activities, decisions, etc., and what these are saying to you about your beliefs.

These modes interact and alternate.

Based on the work of GL

By beliefs I am not talking about overall credal formulas but those beliefs which set us alight. George B Wilson talks about "uncovering where our passion lies, what would excite us and move us to commitment."[4] Bruce Rahjen differentiates between *public theology*, what we say we believe, *head theology*, what we believe we believe, and *visceral theology*, what we demonstrate we believe through what we do and how we live; or our public, thinking, and feeling selves.[5] Here we are talking about visceral beliefs, what burns within us. Statements of purpose based on such beliefs are powerful and affect the totality of our beings. Those which are not remain uncreative. This exploration of beliefs needs to be done both individually and corporately. Beliefs are furthered considered on p. 113. Your corporate statement of purpose or mission springs from the deep beliefs you hold in common. This theological reflection is not easy but well worth the effort. It gives a quality to your action, deepens your motivation and commitment, and makes it more likely that your new community is truly Christian and a force for good in building up the Kingdom. It is hard to put your heart into things you do not believe in, and questionable whether you should expend time and energy in trying to do so. Aids to theological reflection are suggested in Chapter 16.

ii. Formulating your purpose or mission statement [6]

Arriving at an agreed statement of purpose or mission is likely to take time, energy, and quite probably a lot of paper before you are satisfied. In view of its value it is worth the effort. Purpose is further considered on p.114. A way of formulating one's purpose is considered on p. 72. The suggestions below may also enable you to decide whether to formulate your aims as a statement of purpose or a mission statement.

· Some basic questions:

Consider your model of local religious community (cf. p. 34); your charism (cf. p. 74); if appropriate, your option for the poor (cf. p. 75); your mission and ministry (cf. p. 105); and reflect on what you hope to achieve in the light of any thinking you have done on your beliefs. As appropriate, ask yourselves questions such as: What are our gut feelings about what is needed?

What are we hoping will happen in our own lives as individuals and as a community?

> What changes for the better do we hope to bring about:
> – in the lives of those with whom we work, whether in parishes, secular or church jobs?
> – in the lives of those among whom we live in parish and neighbourhood?
> – in our province or congregation?

Have we any wider purposes in relation to other groups?

Wilson suggests another set of questions, such as:
> What kind of people are we, really? What has shaped us – or deformed us?
> What patterns are important to us, and what is just unexamined custom?
> What experiences ground our conviction that we have a task in front of us that no one else can do?
> What makes us, and therefore our call and gift, different?
> What do we want so badly that we're willing to say no to other attractive possibilities?
> What dreams are so compelling that we will fight for them?

· What do you want to avoid?

Both Lovell and Wilson emphasise the need to be clear about what you are *not* trying to be or to do, what you want to avoid, the noxiants. This enables you to put limits or boundaries on what you aim to achieve. To spell these out can both help to clarify your purpose and give a cutting edge to your work. As Lovell says: "Purposes and noxiants help to check in a positive and negative manner whatever is emerging from the process. A purpose, for example, might be to promote love and care in a neighbourhood; a noxiant to avoid mistrust. Using these to check ideas for action involves asking, "Will our plans help people to love and care for each other? Can they possibly lead to mistrust?" Each question has its own potential not possessed by the other for checking things out and faulting plans. Together they have a pincer checking effect."[7]

· Terminology

Formulating your replies in ordinary language rather than religious jargon will give them an immediacy and freshness.

· Distinguish between your underlying purpose and short term objectives

Short-term objectives enable you to work towards achieving your purpose. As Lovell points out, " to build a community centre is an objective; to help people differing widely in belief and culture to use the centre and to love and care for each other is a purpose because it is about developing Christian attributes."[8] To have a participative liturgy is an objective; to have a liturgy which draws people into ever deeper communion with each other and their God is a purpose. An objective is something you can see completed; a purpose is something you make progress towards but can never fully achieve. Once you have established your purpose, you are more likely to see various objectives, all of which might contribute towards it.

· A statement of purpose or a mission statement ?

Consider the examples below. Which kind of statement appeals to you?

(a) The members of a good neighbour scheme stated their purpose as:
"1. to help people to live more satisfying lives through the development of a sense of community;
2. to enable Christians, as an expression of their faith, to care and to help others to care, for people in the area;
3. to show that people in the churches care for others and are prepared to help them regardless of their attitudes to the Church;
4. to fulfil one of the Romsey Council of Churches objectives, that is, to give service to the local community."

They then agreed to work to achieve their purposes by:

"1. helping people to care for each other, help each other and help themselves;
2. helping people to obtain the support and care they require without depriving them of dignity, self respect or independence;
3. providing opportunities for members of different churches and people who are not church members to serve their neighbours;
4. working with other organisations and services."[9]

(b) Wilson suggests two possible mission statements of a parish:

"We're a tough bunch of mining folk struggling with the demands of an inclusive gospel in the face of militant racism and an anti-government town. Our mission – for a long time to come – will be to use all the toughness that characterises our heritage while developing vulnerability and sensitivity and neighbourliness to people who harbour deep hostility in their blood." Or, "We are a deeply wounded community. Our mission for the next five years will be to support and help one another and our children to recover trust in one another, in our church, and in the Lord after the painful discovery of paedophilia in a beloved pastor."

· **Be provisional**

Formulating a provisional or 'good enough' statement of purpose or mission may enable you to do further work in clarifying your mission and ministry (cf. p. 105), which in turn will enable you to write your statement with more exactitude. The Jesuits who were setting up a project in Portadown, Northern Ireland, found they had to go through this process several times until they had a sufficiently clear statement which they could use when they had moved in and were at work.[10]

2. LIFESTYLE

Your life-style as religious is influenced by many factors including the vows of poverty, chastity and obedience, the opportunities and demands of mission, aims and purposes as outlined above, and the area, situation and context in which you live. Living in a small community requires thinking about ways of living as religious in a new and different, less institutional way, and making the necessary interior as well as exterior changes.

i. Traditional practices of the congregation

For many congregations, the setting up of small communities is a break with tradition, a move from an institutional, more monastic life-style to one in which you are freer to organise your lives and routines to suit the requirements of your mission and ministry.

Traditional ways and customs are the fruit of learned experience about how groups of religious can live together in harmony and mutual support and challenge, and in a way that both safeguards them and enables them to carry out their corporate mission and ministry. It is too easy to speak disparagingly of inherited monastic customs without realising and ensuring the continued living out of the values at their heart. For instance, since the custom of silence at certain times and places has been largely abandoned, a need for privacy and space in busy lives is felt. Peter Marris talks about the need to make appropriate changes to conserve what is of enduring value.[11] Not to do so can invite a mechanical performance, endangering the life-giving values the traditional practices originally enshrined. On the other hand, there is the danger of moving to a small community with an institutional mind-set which predetermines how traditional values will be lived.

A new community needs to decide what traditional values it wishes to conserve and how it will aim to do so in similar and in different ways, through asking itself:

What was the original purpose, or need, that a particular practice grew up to meet?

Do we still have that need in our new situation?

If so, how can we meet that need in a way which is appropriate for us now?

What change in the outer form will conserve the inner core of value in a meaningful way for us?

ii. Charism

It has often been the rediscovery of a congregation's founding charism that has led to the setting up of small communities. Those who founded religious orders did so in response to an inner urge to do something about some need in society or in the church. Their original charism, or gift of the Spirit, attracted others who banded together to meet that need. Down the years the charism was handed on from one generation to the next, from one culture to another. It was lived by faithful, and possibly not so faithful, members in times of stability and in times of change. Through this process, the charism, at best, changed, deepened and developed in ways appropriate to the place and time. At worst, it was handed on like a sacred parcel or became a form of words with little meaning for day-to-day life and work. Vatican Two challenged congregations to make changes which would put them in touch with their founding charism, in such a way that they could once more be set alight by it in relation to the needs of today (cf. Figure 5.1).

Living in a small community provides an opportunity to explore both your initial charism and ways in which it may have been developed, reformed, redesignated or clarified down the years, and to verify its relevance for your current situation while working out practical ways of using it and being inspired by it. Doing this will help ensure that you are not only faithfully living your charism but that you will be sharing it, enhanced and enlivened, with others – be they the next generation of religious, or lay people who adopt its vision. Ways of exploring your charism are suggested on p. 219-21.

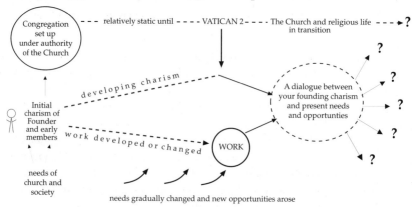

Figure 5.1
The development of charism in religious life

Small Communities in Religious Life

iii. An Option for the Poor

Most, if not all, congregations have followed the church's lead in making a preferential option for the poor. For many it was already part of their charism. There are numerous books and articles about taking an option for the poor and exhorting and encouraging individuals and communities to do so . Worthy as that is, in my experience, it has caused problems in many congregations. A major difficulty has faced those at a chapter who have been inspired and deeply motivated by the concept and have made a corporate commitment to it on behalf of their congregation. How are they to help others who have not undergone what is often called a conversion experience, to commit themselves to it in an effective way? This is a problem often faced by chapter delegates in relation to many of their decisions. Nevertheless, the option for the poor, which is so fundamental a stance, has particular difficulties.

When a chapter does not manage to avoid or mitigate these negative effects, and so ensure that taking this option has an overall positive rather than a negative effect on the congregation, varying degrees and kinds of commitment to it may well be given by different members. To be committed, some real understanding of the concept and its implications is necessary. Yet there is often confusion and conflict, both within an individual and between people, as to how and to what extent this option is to be earthed in both individual and communal practice. In any community, even a small one, there may well be members who think and feel very differently about the option for the poor. In reflecting on the variety of responses below, and there will surely be others, it is worth remembering that we are not responsible for our feelings, and it is profitable to own them. What we do about them is another matter (cf. p. 140).

Apart from deep commitment and motivation, there may be less worthy responses felt in varying degrees:

> Some people give overt and nominal consent out of loyalty, obedience, a desire to preserve unity, suppressing qualms or misgivings. This causes an inner alienation which is destructive rather than creative. For the option for the poor to have an overall positive effect, our hearts as well as our heads need to be engaged. Such people may variously feel guilty and worry about their lack of enthusiasm; do small actions to assuage their conscience; talk big and do nothing; feel helpless and try to forget the option altogether; justify themselves by looking at what they are doing in other fields or what the congregation as a whole has done to adopt the option; or they may try to force themselves to feel motivated and even think that they have succeeded.

> Some people experience, at some level of their being, resentment and anger at having the option for the poor imposed on them by chapter decree. They may express their resentment inappropriately and exacerbate their own and other people's negative feelings.

> Some people simply shrug it off, refuse to become involved or to consider it seriously. Their apathy keeps its demands at bay.

This book is not the place for an analytical exploration of the meaning of religious poverty today or of the preferential option for the poor. Hundreds of books have expounded a wide variety of different understandings and analyses of the global context of poverty and oppression which is the back drop against which religious, like all Christians, have to live their lives. There is no substitute for serious reading, reflection and prayer in order to decide on the implications for you, both individually and as a small community, of your vow of poverty and the preferential option for the poor.

Your decision depends to some extent on resources and opportunities. While face-to-face work with poor people is one way, other worthwhile activity can take place at a distance, e.g. through educative work with the better off, advocacy, or working to change unjust structures.[12] The suggested community meetings on p. 255-9, may enable you to think and feel your way to a group decision about what the option will mean for you.

iv. Mission and ministry

The mission and ministry of a small community is a major factor in determining its life style. So too is the chosen model of community, and its location. A basic question in relation to practical community arrangements is, "Is this likely to help our mission and ministry or to hinder it?".

Such domestic arrangements may be thought of as minor, but the way they are decided enhances or impoverishes community life. Our attitudes to ordinary everyday matters of life have been formed by experience. Attitudes laid down in the formative years of childhood may have been modified or developed through later experience, particularly of religious life, but they are rarely completely changed. Therapists talk of a 'birth script' that we each have, whether or not we are aware of it. This affects the way we face and tackle life events and relationships.[13] Knowledge of different personality types, through participating in Myers Briggs or Enneagram workshops[14] can increase mutual understanding through showing differences in basic attitudes. Our attitudes are a deep part of us. It takes time and patience to change ones we are not happy to own. By talking over domestic matters, however seemingly trivial, you may avoid one of them suddenly hitting you like a rake handle!

The following may help facilitate the smooth talking-out of the practical details of life:

Try to understand attitudes different from your own and where they may have come from, before evaluating them. Talk out the differences in as open and unjudgemental a way as possible. What is normative for one may be exceptional for another.

Tolerate the different speeds with which you and others change: some are cautious and take time, others welcome change almost too quickly.

Try taking on tasks not experienced before: you may find an unexpected talent or are able to develop a new skill. Take the risk, but avoid pushing people into jobs they are never likely to be good at, while trying to ensure that everyone does their share.

Take people's other responsibilities into account.

Be prepared to make temporary arrangements and to have trial periods.

Avoid comparisons, touchiness and standing on your rights. Try to meet the personal needs of individuals: these vary from one to another (cf. p. 79-83).

If people's emotions erupt, allow them to, and then explore their strong feelings (cf. p. 149).

Don't make mountains out of mole hills: keep your purpose in mind.

Marry orderliness with flexibility.

Make your own agenda, such as Table 5.2, of practical arrangements you need to discuss.

Table 5.2
Practical Decisions

Ask yourselves questions about:

· **Meals:** Taken together or not? Where? Formal or cook our own? How will we indicate absence from a meal?

· **Cooking, etc.:** Who cooks when? Will we cook alone or in pairs? What about washing up? Who decides on menus? Standard of food? Employment of a part-time cook?

· **Catering:** Who does it: the cook? in turn? one person over a period? How indicate shopping needs? Work on a budget? Use and care of fridge and deep freeze?

· **Household chores:** List what needs to be done – housework, washing, rubbish, locking up, ordering supplies, etc. Who will do what? For how long? Use of washing machine?

· **Gardening:** List jobs to be done. Do we employ someone? Who will do what?

· **Heating and Hot Water:** Whose responsibility? How much heating do we need?

· **Car or bicycle:** Their use, security and maintenance?

· **Telephone:** Answer phone? Answering cover? Messages? Use?

· **Conservation and re-cycling:** What will be our policy and practice?

· **Visitors and answering the door:** Who answers the door and when? How much of an 'open house' do we want? Will we have any private areas or sacrosanct times? Any differences between family, friends, and 'clients' or people seeking help? How 'at home' do we want overnight visitors to be? Length of stay? Payment?

· **Recreation:** Free days (cf. p. 213)? Use of TV? Relaxing together and separately? Celebrations? Entertaining? Noise? Drink?

· **Pets:** What is our view on having a dog, cat, bird or. . . ?

· **Equipment:** What is necessary for ministry, chores or leisure? Use and maintenance?

· **Papers and Periodicals:** What papers and magazines will be bought communally? How to ensure they are available or circulating?

· **Use of House:** Criteria for deciding use of rooms for what or for whom? Décor and furnishing responsibilities? Use of personal rooms for visitors when absent? Responsibilities for maintenance and repairs?

· **Timetable:** Time of prayer, meals, meetings etc. When and when not to be flexible?

· **Absences:** What can we do about those whose work makes them absent themselves, for instance, every evening and weekend, or through being on night duty?

· **Illness:** First aid supplies? Caring for the sick?

---

v. Finance

Money is often a highly emotive subject in communities where resources are shared. Individuals have their own deeply held perspectives on the meaning, value and use of money. Our very different concepts are the product of our family, social and cultural backgrounds and have been formed by the circumstances of early childhood. You may also have been deeply influenced by your initial training in religious life. Given the variety among people, it is not surprising that attitudes and feelings about money vary enormously. How easy it is to be shocked by others whom we see as spendthrift and lax, or mean and parsimonious!

It should therefore be a salutary exercise to explore how money has acquired its meaning in your life. Sharing what is learned with your community might help everyone to understand and be more tolerant towards others with very different attitudes. Such a community sharing could make a good basis for communal decisions about budgeting and spending as a community, and about contributing to the congregation and to charity. A community meeting on attitudes to money is outlined on p. 230.

The areas and questions below, which are directly to do with finance or financial implications come from and therefore reflect, the concerns and questions of a wide number of diverse congregations. Some may not be relevant to your situation. Take the suggestions below as a stimulant to your thinking and make your own list of issues to consider.

Community and congregation
Community budget: What does it include/exclude? Who decides on the amount?

Community bursar: What is her responsibility and area of authority? When are accounts given and to whom? Availability of petty cash? Security?

Personal budget or allowance
Where does it come from? How is it decided upon and by whom? Does it rise with inflation? What does it include/exclude? Do we each have a bank account?

Charity
How much do we give? To whom or to what do we give it? When?

Courses
Who decides on who goes to what courses? What are the norms: cost, frequency, length, purpose – for personal development, professional need or use to the congregation?

Retreats
Length? Cost? Timing? Travel?

Professional Expenses
Travel? Gifts? Subscriptions? Materials and equipment? Car?

Compassionate Leave
Special needs of one's family or close friends?

Medical
Routine requirements? Therapy? Special dietary needs?

Holidays
How are decisions made and by whom? What are the norms: length, frequency, cost, style, taken with family or friends within or outside congregation? How do we organise timing? Can the house be closed? Travel: what sort of and cost?

3. THE COMMUNITY AND THE INDIVIDUAL

The issues I focus on here arise directly out of my work with religious and my own experience of living in the Grail. The more I reflect and read, the more I realise how complex is the relationship between the individual and the community. The well-being of one does not automatically result in the good of the other, although it may well contribute towards it. Genuinely holy people can be found in mean-spirited communities, and deeply selfish ones in which the majority of members experience authentic *koinoinia*.

For a long period, religious community life was distorted by an over-emphasis on corporate uniformity, hierarchical discipline and unreflecting obedience to authority at the expense of the individual. Vatican Two and the new human and theological understanding of the person, showed just how undesirable this was and stimulated people to try to redress the balance. Not surprisingly, in making the necessary adjustments, the pendulum was inclined to swing too far towards individualism. Judith Merkle says, "the challenge to congregations today is to learn about community from individualism, but also to critique its fallacies"[9]. Community life, if it is to be more than a group of individuals living together for convenience, necessitates some curtailment of individual freedom: self-control, self-discipline and self-sacrifice on the part of individual members are part and parcel of living the gospel precepts cheek by jowl with others very different from oneself.

Careful continuous attention to the various needs of individuals and communities helps to get at sources of dissatisfaction and frustration and to build up communities and congregations that are fulfilling for all members. What follows is a needs check list.

i. Individual needs

Individual human and spiritual needs manifest themselves in different ways in different people at different times, and they are satisfied in a great variety of ways. Those noted below are ones I have found particularly relevant to living in community. They overlap and are not in any particular order.

· The need for freedom to be oneself

I believe that Christian community is intended to nourish self-esteem and allow us to be genuinely ourselves: we are not meant to hide behind a facade that subconsciously we believe to be more acceptable. God loves the real me, not the person I often pretend to be or the *persona* I may have cultivated over the years. Freedom to be oneself is closely connected with self-esteem, which to some extent in its turn is linked to the need for affirmation and support.[15] When self-esteem is damaged people can be inhibited from expressing themselves openly or honestly. In its turn, self-esteem depends on the gospel precept to love oneself, a necessary requisite to showing genuine love of others. One of the less happy legacies of traditional religious practice can be an inner urge to conform, to deny one's individuality constantly in order to fit in and please others. This must not be confused with individualism which is at the opposite end of the continuum and is considered on page 80.

· The need for freedom to pursue one's vocation

With Newman I believe that, "God has created me to do some particular service. He has committed some work to me which he has not committed to another".[16] And this is true of religious. They have personal vocations, as it were, within the overall vocation of the religious congregation to which and through which they are called: a call from God to a vocation within a vocation. Personal and community discernment are necessary to know whether inner urges are truly calls from God. Sometimes there is a common agreement. Occasionally there are differences of opinion about individual and collective callings. Then following one's conscience can mean treading a lone path or one very different from the rest of the community. That can be painful, both for oneself, other members, and those in positions of responsibility in the congregation. However, freedom of conscience must be maintained. It is enshrined in Vatican Two and written into most, if not all, religious constitutions, and is closely bound up with this freedom to pursue one's particular vocation.

· The need for privacy and quiet

However naturally extrovert or gregarious people are, everyone has a deep-seated need for privacy. We may not always recognise this or want it. There may be times when we shy away from our own company, but the need is there. It is one we may become more aware of in different circumstances and at different stages of life. There can be a special quality and depth to time spent on our own, which brings renewal and refreshment. Khan points out that too often 'the intoxication of life' prevents us from becoming aware of the value of this moment and the need "to communicate with one's deepest innermost self, as if one were blowing one's innermost spark into a divine fire".[17] Henri Nouwen emphasises the need for empty space in life, when people do not even commune with themselves. "We are so afraid of open spaces and empty places that we occupy them with our minds . . . how can we ever expect something new to happen to us if our hearts and minds are so full of our own concerns, that we do not listen to the sounds announcing a new reality."[18] Interior preoccupation therefore can ensure the *status quo*. Nouwen goes on to say that true hospitality is allowing others such space and helping them into it.

This need is is not to be equated with private prayer and spiritual reading although it is akin to it and may be fostered by prayer, scripture reading and spiritual exercises. Equally, some people engage with themselves in this way as they listen to music, walk, cycle or drive, or when doing such things as knitting, sewing, gardening, painting, slow reflective reading or journalling.

· **The need for personal companionship, friendship, and *koinonia***

As human beings we have a fundamental need for friends: people with whom to share our thoughts and feelings, in whom to confide, and against whom to test out ideas and decisions. They become soul friends when we feel at ease and relaxed with them, know they are 'for' us and will support us through difficult times. They may come from a different walk of life, be of our own or the opposite sex, belong to other denominations or faiths, and have different interests.

Members of a Christian community need and want *koinonia*, a New testament word indicating a special quality of fellowship and communion, that sense of community which is basic to our Christian heritage and way of life. Ideally, a local religious community will satisfy, to some degree, an individual's need for companionship and friendship. It is unlikely to meet it fully, especially when the community is very small. Some religious will have close family ties and also friends beyond the community, whether in their place of work or elsewhere. This can be enriching, although there is the consequent danger that they may isolate themselves from their community. On the other hand, if people rely solely on the community to meet their need for companionship and friendship, they may well suffer from unmet needs, have unrealistic expectations of the community, or make inappropriate demands of other members.

· **The need for a creative outlet**

While some people are recognised as creative, that does not mean that the rest of us are not. Too many people are apt to say "I am not creative, never have been." To express yourself and to use your gifts, is a creative activity which is deeply satisfying. Fox has said, "The artist in each one of us needs to be let out of the closet."[19] Casals has written "I have always regarded manual labour as creative and look with respect – and, yes, wonder – at people who work with their hands. It seems to me that their creativity is no less than that of a violinist or writer. It is of a different sort, that is all".[20] While it may be easier to recognise how you are creative at work, it can be valuable to explore ways in which you are creative in your leisure. Having a creative hobby of some sort can be an invaluable life-giving resource at any stage of life including retirement and old age.

· The need for relaxation

Relaxation is an obvious need but achieving a good work-leisure balance is not always easy. Quite apart from times of undue pressure when other things have to take first place, relaxation can so easily be squeezed out when we become absorbed or obsessed by our work. Although some people may be able to relax fully in the community, it is highly likely that there will be times when members need to get right away from the community in order to relax thoroughly. Where and how this need is satisfied depends very much on personality, temperament, and one's current state of well-being; whether or not a person's work is closely associated with the community and house; and on compatibility and personal relationships between community members.

· The need to make time for God

Finding a way of meeting this need and enabling others to do so is vital, not only for our own well-being, but for that of the community. As well as the liturgy and times of corporate prayer, we each need times of solitude and silence to tune in to the reality of God within oneself, to experience the presence of God within the people and events of every day.

Each person must make *their* contribution towards promoting their own spiritual development. However, that does not mean that we cannot help each other to meet this need. Spiritual directors, soul friends, and community members, may help enormously by giving suggestions, encouragement, and above all, challenge. (Some exercises for personal reflection in this area are included in *Building a faith community* on p.216.)

· The need for challenge

Living with others in community provides a constant questioning of the way one lives oneself. There is the silent questioning of my unhealthy attitudes and actions that comes from seeing how others live, and the far more uncomfortable challenge given by word of mouth. In my experience, although I do not always appreciate it at the time, being challenged has been one of the great values of community life and has helped me to grow, but not without pain. Religious have an obligation, because of their commitment to each other, to foster the well-being of other members and not to allow them, by default, to seriously renege on their religious commitment. They have to avoid being judgemental. But they may well have to challenge or confront each other. Help and hurt are closely related to how this is done, when and by whom, and on one's own mood and situation. It is not easy to receive criticism. It is even more difficult to give it in a way that is supportive and loving. Ways of both responding to challenge and preparing to challenge another are suggested on pp. 87 and 102.

· The need for affirmation and support

The amount of encouragement and affirmation people need varies enormously and is affected by many personal factors, including the level of their self-esteem.

Opportunities to make contributions towards meeting this need are often neglected because of the propensity of people living in community to take each other for granted and not to affirm and support one another. Too often it can take an accident or a crisis for the very real support of the community to become tangible. Affirming others so that what you say is heard and accepted is an art, and sincerity is essential in order to avoid sounding – and possibly being – patronising.

Much of the support community members give each other is in ensuring that the needs mentioned above are met. It is too easy in busy apostolic lives to allow one's own needs to be neglected.

ii. Community needs

For a group of people to be an authentic religious community, individual and collective needs have to be taken into account. Each community is unique and its needs will vary with membership and circumstances. Working with communities has involved me, and those with whom I have been engaged, in paying attention to one or more of the needs outlined below.

· The need for community, *koinonia*

There is all the difference in the world between a group of people living alongside each other, and living in communion, *koinonia*: they allow their lives to intersect and interact; they give time to building up each other and the community. Doing this can include working together, praying together, socialising and celebrating as well as planning, making decisions, sorting out problems and discussing issues; times of joint activity as well as times of prayer and quiet. Communities that flourish are usually good at celebrating together, although finding activities which are enjoyable and refreshing for everyone can be more problematic. Celebrations can be serious or hilarious – humour and laughter are important elements in life; mentally or physically nourishing; formal or informal. Taking the trouble to mark occasions with something special, festive, or unexpected, adds spice to life.

· The need for a clearly articulated common purpose

A community needs to articulate its shared purpose in relation to community life and mission, even though members may pursue various ministries. This is true for a religious community even though the overall direction is given by the evangelical counsels and the charism of the congregation. Ideas about formulating a statement of mission or purpose are given on p.71. The practice of commissioning people to carry out their ministries demonstrates the corporate commitment of the community to the apostolic work of each member.

· The need for mutual accountability

The vow of religious obedience requires each member to be accountable to legitimate authority within the congregation and all are expected to live and work according to its constitutions and norms. In part, this is discharged through religious having a sense of responsibility to each other, seeing their community as the local manifestation of the congregation to which they have committed themselves. Accountability is encouraged by openness, tolerance, sensitivity, the ability to empathise and growth in mutual understanding.

· The need to be outward looking

A community exists in, and has responsibilities for, the wider world, whether this is thought of as local, regional, national, international, or all four. There will be a reciprocity of giving and receiving as community members seek to understand others, to work with them, and to contribute to the common good. Most communities, if they pause to reflect, will be only too aware of all they are receiving from others. This mutual ministry can be both enriching and stimulating. Without it, a community is in danger of growing overly inward-looking and losing something of its real life.

· The need for corporate prayer and faith-sharing

Corporate prayer and faith-sharing are essential to the spiritual health and unity of a Christian community. It is not the amount, but the quality of time spent in this way which is life-giving. This is considered more fully on p. 92, and reflecting and sharing together on p.91. Other ideas and suggestions will be found in *Building a Faith Community* on p. 216.

iii. Meeting individual and community needs

Experience shows that the quality of personal and community life and vocational effectiveness is closely related to achieving a good balance between meeting the needs both of individual members and their community. Religious continually have to work at this.

If a community meets the exorbitant needs or demands of an individual, not only is the person in danger of becoming increasingly selfish and dominant, but the community life, harmony and the mission itself are likely to suffer. Trying to cope in such a situation can use – possibly misuse – an enormous amount of emotional energy. The community may have to take courage and harden its heart in order not to be held hostage by one or two individuals. On the other hand, if community needs always take precedence, personal growth and development suffer, as one or more people squeeze themselves into conformity and deny their own legitimate needs. Ultimately, not only does the individual suffer, but the community lacks the enriching contribution of mature adults.

Therefore, for a community and those within it to flourish, the fundamental human and spiritual needs (not wants) of both individual and community must be taken into account, without the needs of one habitually being met at the expense of the other, or priority being constantly given to ministry to the exclusion of both. There will always be a tension between these things. It is important that it is a creative rather than a destructive tension.

· **Avoiding destructive tension**

I start by noting those factors that can cause destructive tension because these are easily recognizable: they are tendencies that, at one time or another, most people may well have identified in themselves.

Lack of concern about personal or community needs: There is a danger of allowing the demands of work or care of others to preoccupy people at the expense of their own or community needs. To sacrifice oneself for the good of another, does not call for the sort of neglect of personal needs that makes for one's overall diminishment as a person. Yeats wrote, "Too long a sacrifice can make a stone out of the heart".[21] Undoubtedly there will be times when people are called to set aside their own needs, but there can also be times when, without meeting them, they will not be able to carry on or make their contribution to the community: they themselves become a liability. This is easier to see with tangible needs like sleep or food, but it is also true of the more hidden emotional and spiritual needs. The same is true of a community. A community that constantly allows the demands of ministry to override its need to meet together for prayer, faith sharing, discussion, or celebration will cripple itself.

Over-concern about personal or community needs. This occurs when individuals or community are concerned about meeting their own needs at the expense of those of others. For example, being over-protective of the legitimate need for privacy, can make for an egoistical inward looking individual or community and be detrimental to both.

Stressing personal and community needs at the expense of mission and vocational requirements. Mission is of paramount importance. Cecil McGarry emphasises that the form community life takes is for the sake of serving the mission, "We should not be saying, 'What is the form of our community life? How do we live together?, so much as 'How do we serve?' and in the service, 'What's the best way for us to live?' . . . How we live, where we live, what apostolates we do, how we dress, all these should be in the service of mission."[22]

Lack of awareness and communication. There is a danger that either the individual or the community gives no thought to or is unaware of their needs, or does not express needs and feelings frankly and in a way which helps others to consider them seriously. Personal and collective reflection heightens individual and collective awareness and generates vital communication. Individuals have a right to have their feelings and requests respected and considered in relation to community needs. The community has a right to have its collective needs considered, even when minorities reject majority felt needs.

· **Maintaining healthy tension**

What follows are notes on things which I have found helpful towards the achievement of healthy tension between the various needs of individuals and the community and the requirements of mission.

Standing in other people's shoes and getting others to do the same. This can help to prevent the pastoral care of either individuals or community from always overriding the pastoral care of the other.

Promoting awareness and discussion about individual and community needs. Unless both individual and community are alert to their own needs, there is a danger of allowing other things to take priority. When people function effectively many demands will probably be made on them to which they feel they must respond. This may cause them to neglect their own needs so much that it leads to burnout. It is important to explain the reason for saying 'no' in a way that helps people understand their dilemma.

Mutual openness. One of the dangers in community life is that people's preconceptions of others may, at times, be prejudices and prevent them seeing the real needs of other members. People are more likely to be candid and open in acknowledging unmet needs and in voicing the needs of the community as a whole where there is mutual understanding and trust, a listening with heart as well as head, and where allowances are made for individual differences (p. 89). This requires sensitivity to verbal and non-verbal expressions of need, tolerance, empathy with others, and conscious desire for their well-being.

Flexibility. Although it is inadvisable for either members or the community as a whole to play fast and loose with the customs and arrangements they have decided upon, for example, times of commmunity meetings, prayers, and meals together, it is unwise to treat such things as rules never to be broken. Flexibility is required to make allowances and realise that at times it is necessary for community fixtures to be postponed or abandoned for the individual or common good.

Working to needs in relation to purpose and priorities. When faced with deciding on the respective needs of the community and individuals and the demands of mission, it can be helpful if you have already articulated your purpose (see p.71). This is then available as a touchstone in working out priorities and in coping with the conflicting needs. At times, for the sake of mission, the satisfaction of individual and community needs must be temporarily deferred. There are circumstances, however, when the mission itself is likely to suffer if the needs of the community or an individual, say for time out, are not met. What is important is to work to *all* needs in relation to purpose, circumstances and priorities. Amongst other things this involves identifying the needs of the community that have to be met immediately because, for example, they are an essential expression of corporate identity; and the needs of the individual that require satisfaction at once, rather than curtailment or deferral. Courage is required to voice the minority or unpopular opinion when it is necessary to defend the need of some individual or to stress the overriding need of the community or its mission. For this to happen, minority views must be taken seriously. The way the Uniting Church of Australia does this in its decision-making process is described on p.172. It may be too formal for a small community but the thinking behind the process is universally relevant.

An exercise *Needs, wants, and expectations* picking up these ideas for personal or communal reflection can be found on p.212.

Small Communities in Religious Life

iv. Speaking the truth in love[23]

When living in community it is sometimes necessary, for the good of the community and of the person concerned, to talk to someone forthrightly about some attitude or action which is having a deleterious effect on the community or its mission. I avoid the word 'confront' because it is a hard word often implying hostility, whereas the action I am describing is most effective if done with gentleness and courtesy. But it is still a difficult task, fraught with danger: relationships may deteriorate or break down; or a person may become defensive, aggressive or lose their self-confidence.

In many communities taking a person to task is left to the person exercising leadership and I have therefore discussed it more fully in Chapter Six. However, in so far as all members of a community are co-responsible, there are times when you may feel called to 'speak the truth in love' to another member. Suggested questions and preparation for doing so are considered on p. 102. All of us, however, are called on to respond to a challenge at some stage. Ways of making the most of this are dealt with in Table 5.3.

Table 5.3
Responding to a challenge

I find myself journalling when people challenge me. I work at such questions as:

What happened? What was said?

What underlying message or meta-communication was being given?

How did I respond?

What do I now feel and think about all this? I allow all my negative feelings to pour out on paper, knowing it is solely for my eyes.

Why do they see things this way? I try to put myself in their shoes in order to understand and, if possible, empathise with their situation. What truth is there in what was said?

What can be done to make changes to improve the situation? This is easier when I am convinced of the truth of the challenge and what lies behind it. It is more problematic when I believe it to be unjustified and based on small-mindedness, unacknowledged envy or jealously, transference, or the result of neurosis.

The choices are to ignore it, to react in a way that exacerbates the situation, or to try and respond positively. This can vary from calmly accepting what has been said or introducing a little humour, to trying to rise above the situation and picture it in a way that helps me to see it differently and form a broader perspective. I find myself agonising over this process and it can take several days in which I take very small steps. Clearly prayer is an integral part of the process. My experience is that it is worth the struggle: I learn much about myself and my reactions and how to act more wisely in the future, and relationships usually improve. At times I need the help of a trusted friend or colleague.

---

v. Living singly

I touch on this here because exercising co-responsibility is essential if communion is to be authentic between those living on their own and the congregation as a whole. The province is responsible, either directly or through a local community to which the member may be attached, for ensuring that the needs of those living alone are being met. Those living singly, in their turn, have some responsibility to do their part in meeting the corporate needs of the congregation as a whole. This subject is considered in more detail in Chapter Eleven.

4. THE CHALLENGE OF COMMUNITY LIFE

There are excellent and endless articles, treatises and books setting out the ideals of living in communion with others, rather than merely alongside them. They variously inspire, exhort, encourage and depress. Their very number witnesses to the worthwhileness and the difficulty of the task. There is a world of difference between aspiring to the ideals of community and facing the hard task of making them a reality, whether life is tortuous and tumultuous or routine and mundane. Futrell speaks about living in community 'in spite of everything'.[24] This section is written in the belief that this is indeed possible, that, in spite of a plethora of differences, people can form supportive, loving, and mutually challenging communities which make for individual and communal human and spiritual growth.

Community relationships and what is needed to build, maintain and repair them, are considered below from various perspectives, and with a practical rather than a theoretical emphasis.

i. Salvation is in the struggle

Christ's way has always been deeply challenging to his followers, whatever their calling or chosen way of life, because it sets forth clear ideals for living. If our final destiny relied on us attaining those ideals we would be in a sorry state. Fortunately our salvation is in the struggle after them. Reading *Marriage: Dead or Alive?* by Guggenbuhl Craig was a happy turning point in my own community journey. In it he argues that it is in tackling the day-to-day difficulties of living in harmony, that a married couple, even though seemingly mismatched, find their salvation.[25] In a flash of insight I realised that I was meant to remain in my community, warts and all – and at that time I could see very little else – and that it was in struggling there together that we would all find our salvation. Every community has warts. All members are at various times both burdens and blessings. I believe that the characteristics and atmosphere sensed by outsiders come not only from sharing a common heritage and history, and living the same constitutions, but from the everyday struggle to be faithful and to help others to be faithful. An outline community meeting on this concept will be found in Chapter Sixteen.

Small Communities in Religious Life

ii. Living with differences

As has been noted already on p. 23, communities are composed of people who differ from each other in many ways. Some differences, such as age, colour, nationality, education, background, health, likes and dislikes, and levels of responsibility, may be obvious; others to do with attitudes, ideas, beliefs, abilities, expectations, reactions, hopes, fears and feelings, degrees of commitment, and personality may only reveal themselves gradually or not become apparent. Differences between people provide potentially creative opportunities. There is some truth in saying "If we all think alike, no one thinks at all".[26]

Particularly when people both live and work closely together or are committed to each other on a long-term basis, the differences between them can assume significant proportions and cause major difficulties. These can be exacerbated where one or two people appear to thrive on conflict. A community in which very different people are seen to live together in reasonable harmony, to be 'for' rather than 'against' each other, can be a significant counter-cultural witness in a society where differences so often cause division and war. In a large community, you are likely to be able to avoid overmuch contact with people whose differences from you cause you problems; in a small community such 'escape' is not possible. To achieve at least relative harmony, the following suggestions, as personal food for thought or even communal discussion, may be helpful. There is no panacea.

· **Recognise the differences between you and other members.**

Accept that this is the position: it is nobody's fault. It is a given when living in community.

· **Allow others to be different**

This is clearly easier with external or historical things which neither you nor they can change, but harder with the less tangible aspects of personality. It seems that part of our socialisation into society has taught us to believe in and be loyal to a certain person, school, organisation, or group, to the detriment of others. Allowing people to be different is not natural to our way of thinking, as it seems to be, for instance, to aboriginals. Marlo Morgan discovered how non-judgemental these people were when she saw them re-erecting a fallen cross above a white person's grave in an isolated spot in the outback. She asked them why they had done this.

> "Why not? We do not understand, agree, or accept your ways, but we do not judge. We honour your position. You are where you are supposed to be, given your past choices and your current free will to make decisions. This place serves for you the same as other sacred sites. It is a time to pause, to reflect, to confirm your relationship to Divine Oneness and all life. There's nothing left here, you see, not even any bones! But my nation respects your nation. We bless it, release it, and become better beings for having passed this way."[27]

Reflecting later she asked herself, "Would I now have the understanding to remain centred, be non-judgemental and let others follow their own path with my blessing?"

Small Communities in Religious Life

· **Rejoice and celebrate differences**

Difference enhances your community life, mission and ministry. Reflect on the creativity and spice which such differences add to life, and or the opportunities they open before you as a group. "The way to build unity, is to nurture differences" according to Sean Ruth.[28] An exercise in living with significant differences is to be found in Chapter Sixteen on p. 212.

iii. Conflict in the community

It seems that wherever there are human beings, except perhaps in some primitive tribes,[29] there is potential conflict. The way it is handled causes it to be a creative, growthful experience or one which is destructive. Some possible reactions, which are not all mutually exclusive, are: to ignore it, to avoid it, to suppress it, to seek help, or to tackle it. There are times and situations which make any one of these appropriate. If a community does nothing about a conflict situation over a period of time the conflict will have a negative effect on the individuals concerned and therefore on the community as a whole. Even though tackling it may not cause it to disappear, ways may be found of ameliorating, containing, or living with it. Where there is conflict in a community some of the ideas discussed in Chapter Twelve, *Problems and problem solving* on p. 166 may well be appropriate, In general it is important to:

· **keep calm and relaxed rather than become tense or panic;**

- if possible, avoid tackling the contentious issue or situation until emotions have calmed down;

- think in terms of reaching a 'win-win' rather than a 'win-lose' solution: this may involve moving from discussing the issues or causes of the conflict, to the sort of outcome wished for;

- enlist everyone's goodwill and determination to work towards a satisfactory solution;

- work for mutual understanding: it has been said that until you can argue convincingly for your opponent's position, you are not able to appreciate it sufficiently to discuss it with her fruitfully.

Some practical methods of tackling a contentious issue or situation in a community are outlined in Chapter Sixteen.

5. JOURNEYING TOGETHER IN FAITH

The spiritual well-being of the community is paramount. The life-giving centre, from which everything you are to each other and others flows, and from which your ministry draws its nourishment and motivation, needs constant attention if it is to remain alive and vibrant. Although the focus is on the faith journey of the community, this needs to be seen holistically. Your faith, your beliefs, your Christian love may be central to your life but they also permeate and are expressed in every aspect of it. The two are inextricably intertwined. It is easy to be glib about this. The challenge is to live consciously aware that God is part and parcel of our ordinary humdrum lives, as well as being both deeper than and utterly beyond them.

i. Co-responsibility and spirituality

Co-responsibility between people in a community means realising one has some real responsibility for the spiritual support and well-being of the others, individually and corporately. This is an awesome thought. How can you carry out such responsibility without interfering or sounding holier-than-thou but as one poor person telling another where bread is to be found? The community needs to consider how it will keep itself spiritually alive. The emphasis below is on what you do together, not because it is necessarily more important than what you do separately, but because community is the focus of this book. In any case, your corporate prayer and sharing should support and stimulate you individually – and vice versa.

ii. Praying together

Ideally community prayer is life-giving for all concerned. Unfortunately but understandably, because of our diversity, it is not always so. We may be at very different stages in our personal journey in faith and will have different spiritual needs at different times. A community would do well periodically to ask itself questions such as the following:

What are we doing about praying together? What do we feel and think about it? It can be useful to allow each person to have their say before having any discussion.

What do we each look for from community prayer? What sort of prayer do we each find life-giving?

What do we think about developing a different pattern to meet our various spiritual needs, or at least most of them, most of the time? How can we avoid becoming mechanical or too loosely structured? How much variety would suit us? Do we want the same person to lead prayers or to take turns in some way?

If we try out some new pattern, when shall we review it?

What do we feel and think about our current arrangement about mass? If we have Mass together occasionally in the house, are the arrangements and organisation satisfactory?

What do we feel and think about any room we have set aside as a chapel or prayer room: its furnishings, the way we use it, and the way we share or do not share it with others?

How do we feel about any everyday rituals and blessings – grace at meals, special occasions, feasts and celebrations? What value do we put on such things? How organised or spontaneous are we or do we want to be?

iii. Reflecting and sharing together

This can be enormously supportive. Many people are well used to it, but for others it may still be a new experience and difficult to enter into. Some of the methods suggested in Chapter Fifteen, *Making community meetings work* on p. 197, may be of use when considering faith-sharing meetings. It is important to keep the following in mind.

We each have a unique relationship with God. Therefore we have our own insights and ways of putting things which are potentially helpful to others. We do not have to rely on a few spiritual high flyers within or outside our community.

We each have a responsibility to contribute to the spiritual well-being of others from our own resources, no matter how meagre we see them to be. We do this not only by speaking but also by listening, listening with the heart. The quality of our listening will help others to articulate their thoughts and insights.

We should not feel under pressure to disclose more than we wish to disclose. Esther Gordon talks about reaching "the threshold of intimacy" and the possibility of heightened emotions. When "this threshold is challenged or breached in some way, people feel vulnerable."[30] This can cause people to retreat or become defensive. Neither make for open sharing. In listening to others talking about their deep beliefs, you are treading on holy ground. When we disclose something close to our hearts or which has moved us deeply, we need to feel it is received with respect and attention. This may encourage us to say more. "What might seem unremarkable for one person, could cost another an immense effort".[31] Sharing at this level is a gift given and received.

Confidentiality needs to be respected. This includes knowing that what I say will not be quoted to others or out of context, and it will not be taken advantage of and used against me at some future date.

It may be necessary to proceed slowly. Do not expect to be able to share deeply before you have grown together as a community and learnt to trust each other. But, remember too, that it is through sharing on a deeper level that trust builds up.

The ambience is important. People need to feel relaxed and comfortable and know they will be undisturbed by other people or the telephone.

Some suggestions for exploring how you can best pray together and share at a deeper level are contained in *Building a faith community* on p. 216.

REFERENCES AND NOTES

1. In what follows, I am drawing on work done over the years with George Lovell. He has written quite extensively on beliefs in *Analysis and Design* (see ref 5, p. 38) p. 125 & 239 ff.
2. Fromm, Erich: *To Have or To Be* (Jonathan Cape 1978) pp. 90-91.
3. When working with an ecumenical Good Neighbours Scheme, members could not decide whether

non-Christian helpers should be allowed in a scheme which was about witnessing to Christian love and care. It was when they clarified their common beliefs that they were able to articulate their purposes and this, in turn, enabled them to solve the problem. See *Churches and Communities: An approach to development in the local church* by George Lovell and Catherine Widdicombe (Search Press 1978, reprinted 1986) p. 127 ff.

4. Wilson, George B: 'Of Mission Statements and Missions' in *Human Development* Volume Seventeen, Number Two, Summer 1996, p. 11.
5. Rahtjen, Bruce with Kramer, Bryce and Mitchell, Ken: *A Work Book in Experiential Theology* (A Publication of Association in Experiential Theology Inc., 1977).
6. Once again I draw on work done by and with George Lovell over the years. See also Lovell op. cit. (ref 1 above) pp 122ff.
7. ibid. p 239ff.
8. ibid. p. 123.
9. ibid. p. 124.
10. Lovell, op. cit. (ref 1 above) p. 104.
11. Marris, op. cit. (ref 4 p. 31) p. 17.
12. See George Lovell's latest book *Consultancy, Ministry and Mission: A Handbook for Practitioners and Work Consultants in Christian Organizations.* (Burns & Oates 2000). Chapter Six on 'The Nature and Properties of Work' has a section 'The Work is Comprehensive and Inclusive' in which he discusses working alongside rich and poor.
13. I was introduced to this concept by Shirley Ward and Carmel Byrne of Amethyst, the healing centre in Killiney, Ireland. See also David Chamberlain in *Babies Remember Birth* (Jeremy Tarcher 1988 ISBN 0 3453 6411 2).
14. The theory on which these workshops are based can be found in Isobel Briggs-Myers *Gifts Differing* (Consulting Psychologists Press Inc. 1980 ISBN 0 8910 6001 1) and in *The Enneagram, A journey in self discovery* by Maria Beesing OP, Robert J Nogosek CSC and Patrick O'Leary SJ (Dimension Books 1984 ISBN 0 8719 3214 8). See also ref 12, p. 60.
15. The Dali Lama was at first unable to comprehend what was meant when someone remarked that many modern Americans lack self-esteem. When he did understand, he was greatly disturbed, for this was not a concept within the thinking of Tibetan Buddhists who grow up with a more healthy regard for themselves.
16. Newman, John Henry: *Meditations and Devotions* 400-1. This is quoted in *A Newman Synthesis* (Sheed and Ward 1930 arranged by Enid Przywara S.J.) p. 215.
17. Khan, Hasrat Inayat: *The Sufi Message, Volume 10,* (Barrie and Radcliffe 1964). Quoted in *Caduceus* Issue Number Eleven, 1990) p. 46. Kabat-Zinn, Jon writes simply but forcefully in *Mindfulness Meditation for Everyday Life* (Judy Piatkins Publications 1994 ISBN 0 7499 1422 X).
18. Nouwen, Henri J.M,: *Reaching Out* (Collins Fount Paperback 1980) pp. 68-72.
19. Fox, Matthew: *Original Blessing* (Bear and Co. 1983 ISBN 0 9396 8007 6) p. 185. In Part III 'Befriending Creativity, Befriending our Divinity: the Via Creativa', Fox emphasises the recovery of faith in our own creativity.
20. Casals, Pablo: *Joys and Sorrows,* (New York 1970) pp. 24ff.
21. Yeats, W B: "Easter 1916" in *Holy Fire*: *The Quest for Enlightenment*, edited by Daniel Halpen, (Harper Perennial 1994).
22. McGarry S.J., Cecil: 'Living the Vision in a Age of Change.' A talk recorded at Anchor House, Ireland in 1991 for the Sisters of Charity.
23. Leonard Schwartzburd writes thought-provokingly in "The Risky Confrontation of Friends" in *Human Development,* Volume Nine, Number Two, Summer 1988.
24. "To be together . . . in Spite of Everything" by John Carroll Futrell, S.J. in *Review for Religious* Volume 32 1972/3 p.54.
25. Guggenbuhl Craig, op. cit. (ref 10, p. 60).
26. Seifat, Harvey and Clinebell, Howard: *Personal Growth and Social Change: A Guide for ministers and laymen as change agents* (Westminster Press 1969) p. 176.
27. Morgan, Marlo: *The Mutant Message Down Under* (Thorsons 1994. First published by Harper

Collins, USA. 1991 ISBN 1 8553 8484 1) p. 74.

28. Ruth, Sean: *Key Stages,* an unpublished paper.

29. Op. cit. (ref 27 above). Morgan notes from her walkabout with the Real People Tribe of Aboriginals that conflict and competitiveness were unknown among them: they found it incomprehensible in western people.

30. Gordon, Esther and Soons, Hubert: *Whole Time: A Handbook for Workshops* (Grail Publications, 1996. ISBN 0 9018 2983 8) p. 43.

31. Ibid. p. 41.

VI
Leadership in the Community

Thought must be given as to how leadership will be exercised in a new community. Whatever label is attached – local superior, co-ordinator, shared responsibility, shared leadership – leadership functions have to be carried out so that the community and its mission and ministry flourish. These functions need to be thoroughly discussed and agreed by all the members. To decide about leadership in the community, it is necessary to clarify its role and function. Leadership functions, unlike organisational or administrative functions, may be few but are key to the development and well-being of a community. In this section we consider different forms of community leadership; coming to a common mind on leadership functions; and approaches to leadership.

1. FORMS OF COMMUNITY LEADERSHIP

Various forms of leadership are currently in use and each can be effective. What is important is that people are clear and agreed about the form in use and its suitability.

· Shared leadership

At the present time, despite the formal requirement for Roman Catholic religious that every community must have a designated superior or co-ordinator, it is not unusual for a system of shared leadership to be in operation in small communities.

Shared leadership can be effective when co-responsibility, in all its facets, is understood and members are committed to it in practice and not just theoretically. This involves:

- leadership functions and other responsibilities or community tasks being either divided between people or undertaken by everyone. In the latter case, it requires everyone to feel a measure of responsibility for everything, if things are to run smoothly. This includes anything from dripping taps to liturgy, from pastoral care to communal events put on for the community or others.

- periodic meetings to assess how things are going, both in their separateness and as a whole, and with an eye to both short-term and long-term development.

Futrell argues that people often react against authority because of the way in which it has been exercised in the past, and that a mature community will want to delegate leadership, as opposed to organisational or administrative functions, to one of its members. "The mutual trust level among the members is such that they desire to delegate the authority function as the best way to enable them to realise their communion in the community."[1]

Shared responsibility is often confused with shared leadership. Shared responsibility involves sharing community tasks, but not leadership functions.[2]

· Rotating leadership

There are two factors which make rotating leadership problematic. First, not every member of the community has necessarily the required abilities and skills. Second, there is a danger of the short-term receiving attention and the long-term well-being and development being ignored. In choosing this model, a community needs to decide on ways of avoiding or overcoming these difficulties.

· Designated or elected leadership

Here leadership rests in the hands of one member. Clearly, much depends on the individual selected for this role and the way in which leadership is exercised. Such a leader may be resident or non-resident. A way of deciding on an appropriate form of leadership is given in Table 6.1.

Table 6.1:
Deciding on an appropriate form of leadership

1. Take each form in turn and consider the pros and cons individually in relation to your situation.

2. Pool and discuss them. At this point, rather than making a decision, you may find it beneficial to allow time for reflection and prayer.

3. Make your decision (See Chapter Thirteen *Decisions and Decision Making*).

   Whatever form of leadership you choose, it could be helpful to:

   – work out ways in which you might help each other in the exercise of these functions. Leadership of any kind requires support and action from everyone. What would be helpful?
   – decide what to do if problems, areas of confusion, or questions arise;
   – check out periodically that the chosen form is serving you well and that nothing is being forgotten. Making a date on the community calendar could ensure that this does not get overlooked.

---

2. SOME LEADERSHIP FUNCTIONS

The functions of leadership are categorised in many different ways by people who have written widely on the subject. This amalgam, which is drawn from discussions over the years with local community leaders, does not claim to be complete and the functions are not discrete. It is included by way of a check list for thinking already done or as a stimulant for further thought.

• A focus of unity

This is both a symbolic and practical function. It is a holding together of people and things; an embodying of the values held in common. It requires:

- keeping one's ears to the ground, being alert as appropriate to what is happening within and between people, and to events and trends both in and beyond the community;

- ensuring people are informed and in touch with each other and with what is going on;

- realising that the corporate welfare of the community is a priority, this includes keeping the purposes, vision and mission before the community;

- encouraging, questioning and challenging both individuals and the community as a whole (oneself included) to ongoing conversion. This entails such things as promoting reflection, articulating core values, stimulating self and community appraisal and evaluation. Suggestions for challenging an individual are considered on p. 102.

- providing faith sharing and both prayerful and social celebrations where people tap into the spiritual wellsprings of the congregation and also enjoy each other's company.

· **Pastoral care**

This is a role of human and spiritual oversight in order to ensure that individual and community needs are met. In addition to some of the actions outlined above, it requires:

- being sensitive to individual members: how they may be feeling and what they are contending with in order to support, help or challenge, as appropriate;

- being aware of the general atmosphere in the community. If there is tension, exhaustion, depression, apathy or similar feelings, suggesting possible action, or raising community awareness and deciding together what to do might help;

- safeguarding both the freedom of the individual and that of the community, trying to keep an appropriate balance between meeting the needs of individuals and the community as a whole (cf. p. 84);

- trying to build up good and creative relationships between people. This entails helping people to listen sensitively and compassionately to each other;

- ensuring that one's own personal needs are being met: to become over-tired, over-stretched or overwhelmed does not contribute to the well-being of the community and can prevent or hinder the carrying out of one's leadership functions. We have a pastoral responsibility towards ourselves.

· **Maintenance**

This is about maintaining the smooth running of community life by:

- ensuring that the various organisational, administrative and practical tasks are carried out. This may be done by one person or shared out according to gifts, abilities and so on;

- co-ordinating the various ideas, activities and events;

– facilitating or getting others to facilitate decision making, reviews and evaluations, the tackling of problems, and the solving of conflicts;

– ensuring that mutual accountability and co-responsibility are exercised .

· Development

This is to do with the longer-term growth and well-being of the individual, the community as a whole and its mission. As well as actions already mentioned, it requires:

– keeping up to date with relevant new ideas, trends, issues and developments in the church, religious life and society;

– having an overall view of the community and its mission and checking out and amending it with other members: raising questions about what the community does, why, and whether changes could be made for the better in current activities or whether new ones are called for. This includes anything from lifestyle, corporate prayer, to mission and ministry. The superior is not necessarily the person with vision: raising questions can call others to visionary thinking and prophetic action;

– challenging, stimulating and enabling individuals to work towards their full potential as human and spiritual beings. "All leadership is an ability to draw others beyond the point where they at present find themselves to a stage of greater realisation of their common aspirations."[3]

· Liaison

Leadership is a boundary function between the community and its environment. This requires:

– representing the community to those outside and, when appropriate, to individual members;

– responding to formal approaches to the community, whether from the provincial team, generalate, another community, church or civic authorities, or individuals;

– being aware of the environment in which the community is set, both religious and secular, and raising questions if there is too much, too little, inappropriate or questionable traffic between the community and its environment;

– approaching the appropriate person in the congregation, church or locality when necessary: e.g., for help or advice that cannot be obtained or dealt with within the community over some project, problem or person. It is important to keep the concept of subsidiarity in mind on such occasions: too often a provincial is expected to solve difficulties which the community could perfectly well deal with itself;

– helping the community become aware of the key factors of the religious and secular, local and global context within which it operates. This includes current trends and issues about which the community might need to be informed, and possibly take some action.

Small Communities in Religious Life

3. COMING TO A COMMON MIND ABOUT
LEADERSHIP FUNCTIONS

Leadership will be exercised best when all are agreed about its key functions. With shared/rotating leadership or before selecting an individual, the following may help:

> *Step 1.* Each list what you consider to be the key leadership functions. Possibly put them in order of importance. Jot down any areas about which you are unclear or which you want to question.

> *Step 2.* Share your ideas and compile a composite list on which you agree. Try to categorise the functions rather than have too lengthy a list.

A superior who has already been designated might amend this exercise by either:

> a. Being clear how you see your role and function and be clear what you are *not* clear about. You may want to ask the community to do some preliminary thinking. Share your ideas with the community and discuss them with a view to coming up with an agreed formulation.

or

> b. Having clarified your own mind, act on what you have come up with and at some stage, check out with the community that things are alright. Ask some leading questions to help them consider your leadership functions critically, e.g.

Is there anything I am *not* doing which would be helpful?

Put yourself in my shoes: is there anything else *you* would be doing if you were me?

What has been helpful? What has been unhelpful?

Although ideally the first way may seem best, it is likely that with all the other things you have to talk about as a community, this second way will be more feasible.

4. APPROACHES TO LEADERSHIP

There are two basic approaches to exercising leadership: promoting development and seeking to control. The developmental approach in often referred to as collaborative. This word can be ambiguous: people may collaborate to exercise control or to do harm. In this context it is to work together for the common good and for development.

Collaboration can take various forms: it can be a full partnership between equals; in some situations it may simply involve consultation or keeping people informed about what is happening; it may entail working interdependently; or it may be between people who have different responsibilities. For instance, the collaboration between a bishop and the diocesan clergy is different from that of a priest with parishioners, or that between members of a project group.

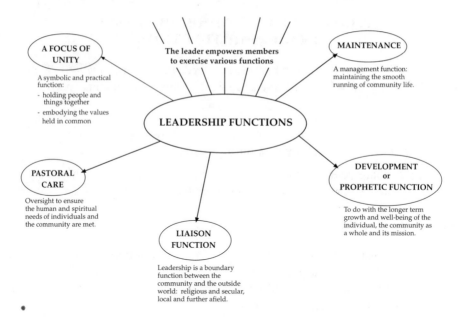

The leader empowers members to exercise various functions

A FOCUS OF UNITY

A symbolic and practical function:
- holding people and things together
- embodying the values held in common

MAINTENANCE

A management function: maintaining the smooth running of community life.

LEADERSHIP FUNCTIONS

PASTORAL CARE

Oversight to ensure the human and spiritual needs of individuals and the community are met.

DEVELOPMENT or PROPHETIC FUNCTION

To do with the longer term growth and well-being of the individual, the community as a whole and its mission.

LIAISON FUNCTION

Leadership is a boundary function between the community and the outside world: religious and secular, local and further afield.

Figure 6.1
Leadership Functions

The collaborative approach to leadership is espoused, at least in theory, in most organisations and communities. This is certainly true of religious congregations. Unfortunately, past experience, hierarchical structures, and habit, too often guide the use of authority into a controlling mode.

To promote collaboration and co-responsibility, the exercise of leadership – whether by a designated superior or in a shared leadership situation – calls for directive action, non-directive action[4] and at times for withdrawal. The controlling approach requires directive action. Figure 6.2 is a summary of directive and non-directive action.

The choice of action is crucial to effective collaborative leadership. No hard and fast rules exist: action must be tailor-made after thinking about the situation, those involved, and what you hope to achieve. The following questions are adapted from Lovell:[5]

What must I do *for* these people?
What must I do alongside them, *with* them?
What must we do *together*?
What must I leave people to do *for themselves* and *with each other* ?

Some guidelines are mentioned on p. 29and on p. 118. However, few people are ad-equately trained in working collaboratively or non-directively, but books are available on the subject, some of which have suggestions for on-going self-training.[6] A checklist for those exercising leadership is given in Table 6.2.

Small Communities in Religious Life

At various times and in different situations you need to work both directively and non-directively. This chart sets out some of the factors affecting the choices open to you between directive and non-directive action.

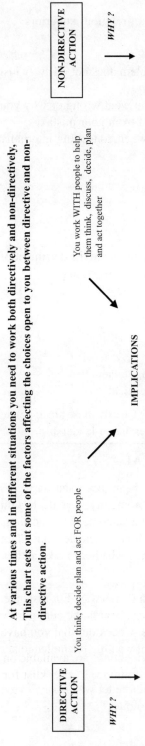
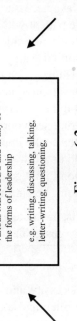

DIRECTIVE ACTION

You think, decide plan and act FOR people

WHY?

Because you believe you are able to decide and act in their best interests; or because people are not in a position to make good decisions for themselves; or because you want to get something done quickly or in your way e.g. in crisis situations; to prevent people harming themselves or others; or to ease the transition from controlling to collaborative ways of working.

HOW?

- by telling people what to do, ordering or enforcing things;
- by providing or making arrangements for people;
- by suggesting, asking, advising or persuading people;
- by inspiring or using loving coercion;
- by bargaining, threatening, manipulating, or by the giving or witholding of information.

The latter are highly questionable ways of proceeding which all too often we fall into.

NON-DIRECTIVE ACTION

WHY?

You work WITH people to help them think, discuss, decide, plan and act together

Because you believe that the people are in a position and have the ability, the information and experience (which you may not have) which will enable them to make good decisions for themselves or share in the making of decisions which affect both you and them; and because you believe that people develop by having increasingly more control over decisions which affect their lives.

HOW?

- by listening to people and asking questions;
- by discussing pros and cons;
- by helping people to assess advantages and disadvantages;
- by providing relevant information as clearly and objectively as possible;
- by ensuring all relevant facts are taken into account
- by making sure all views are considered.

IMPLICATIONS

1. The CHOICE of action is crucial to effective development work with people. You need continually to ask yourself "Is this something I should be doing? Is it something they can and should be doing? Is it something we could best do together?"

2. You need to be clear about your PURPOSE because your choice of action will be determined largely by what you are trying to achieve in the lives of people.

3. The acquisition of directive and non-directive skills are necessary.

You may do these things through various METHODS and in any of the forms of leadership

e.g. writing, discussing, talking, letter-writing, questioning,

Figure 6.2

Approaches to directive and non-directive action

CW based on work of TRB

Table 6.2:
A checklist for those exercising leadership

The following are based on guidelines formulated by a group of religious superiors:
- Value small progressive steps.
- Clarify misunderstandings.
- Tackle major on-going issues rather than bury them: a problem does not go away just because it is ignored.
- Use the case study method (see p. 169) to assess where you went wrong or why you allowed certain unfortunate things to happen, so you learn from your mistakes.
- Consider the use of an outside consultant or confidante, when consulting internally could be problematic.
- Think widely and inclusively and positively.
- Help the good to develop and pay attention to difficult areas.
- Make necessary space and time for yourself.
- Be patient with yourself and others: we all make mistakes.
- Don't take sides.
- Don't use all your energy in dealing with the neurotic or apathetic to the detriment of visionary planning, and ensure you find time for those who really need you.
- Don't allow maintenance to submerge mission.
- Don't do everything yourself.
- Don't see yourself as the solver of all problems.
- Don't take important decisions unilaterally.
- Don't allow yourself to be manipulated.
- Don't play games, polarise, become defensive, or encourage others to.
- Don't be patronising, judgemental, over-anxious or over-critical.

This list in unlikely to be complete. What others would you add? Clearly these are apposite both to designated superiors and to other members in their exercise of leadership.

5. CHALLENGING AN INDIVIDUAL

The necessity and danger of 'speaking the truth in love' has been discussed on p. 87. Since often and ultimately this task falls to the leader of a community, it is dealt with here. Thorough preparation increases the likelihood of a positive outcome. The questions below may help you explore various aspects, on your own or with a colleague, consultant or friend. It may help to work through the points before deciding whether to take action.

· Deciding whether or not to do so
Ask yourself if you have a legitimate reason for facing a person in this way. For instance, your feelings of responsibility towards the person concerned or towards the community raises serious questions for you about their actions or attitudes. Check out that you have the well-being of the person and community at heart and are not wanting to challenge her for an ulterior motive.

Another question is what you hope to achieve. Is there any other better way of achieving the same result? What is likely to happen if you avoid the encounter?

· Deciding who could best do so

To talk forthrightly to a person or group in a way that is both effective and maintains a good relationships it may help to ask: Am I the right person to talk to her? Will our relationship bear the weight of such forthrightness? Could someone else who has a better relationship with her be in on the interview particularly when facing something major?

· Deciding where to do so

The advantages and disadvantages of meeting on the territory of one or other of you, or on neutral ground will vary according to the individual and situation.

· Deciding when to do so

Various questions need to be considered:

Is now the best time? Should I do it while the issue is alive or wait until things have cooled?

Should I make an opportunity or be prepared to take an opportunity when it arises?

If I decide now is *not* the right moment, what am I going to do to ensure I do not 'conveniently forget' because I find it a hard thing to do? Should I review the situation each week or put a date in my diary?

· Preparing yourself to do so

Think of the occasions when another person has challenged you. What helped you to receive what was said and learn from it? What made you feel defensive, angry or closed to what you heard? It can help to jot down your two lists. Now read off the implications in relation to what you want to say to the person concerned.

To stand in their shoes and imagine how they feel and why they act as they do, can be an extremely useful and salutary experience before any encounter.

Both the above exercises may inform your attitude and approach. You are more likely to be effective if you are able to get into a positive frame of mind towards the person.

People are more likely to respond positively to someone who:

– both challenges and affirms them: the challenge is about their attitudes or behaviour, the affirmation is for them as a person of value, and possibly for what they are currently experiencing or struggling with;

– is forthright, clear, honest, specific and non-judgemental: avoiding innuendoes and vague generalities;

– 'fires their own shots': it can be cruel and dysfunctional to imply that other people are disturbed or angry by saying such things as 'people have said to me that you . . .' or 'several people have been upset by you . . .'. This can cause negative feelings towards the community as a whole or towards whoever the person thinks you are referring to and, whether mistaken or not, this can make for a bad relationship;

– is able to identify with the difficulty people face and empathise with them and is thus clearly 'for' them rather than standing in judgement on them.

· Preparing to raise the issue

Here are some important questions you may want to consider.

> Should I give some indication beforehand that I want to talk about this? Could I send a note raising the issue(s) to give the person time to prepare rather than take them by surprise? Which would be least likely to cause defensiveness?

> Am I prepared for the pain I will cause? Am I prepared to work through the pain? Am I prepared to be hurt myself in the encounter? Can I accept that I may have some responsibility in this? For example, perhaps I should have said something earlier.

> How can I best introduce this matter? It may be wise to draft on paper what you want to say and to stick closely to your script. You may want to try it on a trusted colleague to ensure that it comes across as you wish. How will you begin? Your opening gambit is likely to affect the openness or defensiveness of the person to whom you are talking. How to explain your legitimate reason for raising the matter? Is there anything you can say from your own experience that may help? For instance, I have found it helpful when a person challenging me says that she might have reacted or behaved as I did in a similar situation. Clearly this is not always possible: honesty is important!

> What will I do if things go badly? How can I keep calm? What could I say? It could help to imagine the conversation you may have and all likely negative responses and work out how you will respond in each case.

> How can I best conclude the conversation? How do I end on a positive note?

As in the congregation as a whole, so in the local community, much depends on the quality of leadership and the extent to which it elicits support and cooperation.

REFERENCES AND NOTES

1. Futrell, op. cit. (ref 31, p. 18) p.17. Sean Ruth talks of a group being paralysed if leadership is not clearly delegated: people hold back from taking initiative or are constantly alert in case someone gets upset with them for encroaching on their territory, in *Shared Leadership,* an unpublished paper.
2. I am grateful for this clarification to members of a conference on Small Religious Communities in Dublin, March 1997. Arbuckle, op. cit. (ref 1, p. 30) pp. 98-99, distinguishes between "transactional leadership" – the smooth running of the organisation – and "transforming leadership" – purpose, meaning and vision. In this he follows J. M. Burns in *Leadership* (Harper and Row, NY, 1978).
3. Arbuckle, ibid. p 101.
4. The word 'non-directive' was coined simultaneously by T.R. Batten and Carl Rogers, with a subtle difference of meaning. I am using it in Batten's conception explained in *The Non-Directive Approach* (ref 10, p. 31). A short book explaining the approach in the Christian setting has been written by George Lovell, *The Church and Community Development*, op. cit. (ref 10, p. 31).
5. Lovell, *Analysis and Design*, op. cit. (ref 5, p. 38) pp 197-8.
6. There are an increasing number of books and studies in the theory, theology and practice of collaborative or non-directive mininistry. Avec Resources publishes an annotated catalogue (ref 10, p. 31).

VII
Mission and Ministry

I use mission as the overall term for the apostolic work which is determined by the charism of a congregation. Each community is engaged in that mission but may well emphasise or highlight a particular aspect of it. Hence a community's own mission statement needs to be consistent with that of the congregation as a whole. Ministry describes the activities undertaken both individually and corporately. The mission is thus incarnated in and expressed by what a small community is and does.

This chapter has five sections: the decisions which need to be made by a small community when deciding on its mission and ministry; joining an existing area of work; developing a new programme or project; collaborative ministry; mutual support and work consultancy. The material covered in this chapter is depicted on the flow chart in Figure 7.1.

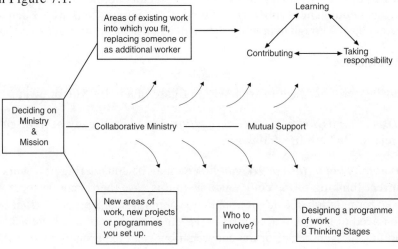

Figure 7.1
Ministry: alternative paths

1. A COMMUNITY DETERMINES ITS MINISTRY

This section applies to a new community, but some of the ideas may be of use to a community which wants to look afresh at its situation or make a fresh start.

Mission and ministry, both individual and corporate, have probably been in your thoughts since you first considered becoming a small community. You may have done no more than dreamt dreams and exchanged ideas informally. It is possible, however, that there are already some deciding factors, such as a particular model of community (cf. p. 34) or a predetermined focus, for instance, an option for the poor or racial reconciliation, or you may have been invited to the area to do a specific job, such as parish work; or one or more of you may be taking up professional work in the neighbourhood. Some or all of you may have articulated a first formulation of your purposes in setting up this new community (cf. p. 71). Once you are *in situ*, you can start clarifying and possibly amending and developing them. Having moved, you will begin to see local needs and opportunities, and be able to assess where you could make a worthwhile contribution. It is wise, early on, to have informal conversations together in order to exchange ideas and check out their compatibility, so that you have food for thought and are alerted to possibilities as you encounter them, gradually building up a common mind. In considering your future work, it is important to think together openly and creatively about mission and ministry and to avoid coming down too soon on one idea or another. Allow yourselves the luxury of dreaming dreams and seeing visions! Very gradually apostolic possibilities which are feasible and which begin to motivate and excite you, will emerge as strong contenders.

i. Factors to be taken into account

In exploring your mission and ministry, the four factors below are among those to be taken into account when you form criteria for decision making. Each will be considered in turn although in practice they will be intricately interrelated and overlap.

· Religious factors

The following religious factors are likely to figure in any list you draw up:

The charism and mission of your congregation. This has already been discussed on p. 74 in relation to both life and work.

The current thinking of the congregation. You may be considering new work as part of the current thinking of the congregation. In this case there may be some more or less explicit formulation of a mission statement or purpose or a proposal from a chapter which you need to take into account. On the other hand, you may have asked to try out something new on behalf of the congregation as an experiment to stimulate new thinking with a view to forming new, more open attitudes.

The signs of the times. Change is endemic if you are to be aware of and read off the implications of the signs of the times. Pausing to reflect on what is currently of significance in our world and our patch of it, is far more than a one-off activity. A way of doing this is outlined in a community meeting on p. 231.

· Needs

Clearly, whether you are considering the needs of the neighbourhood in which you live, or the wider needs of the Church or society, this is of primary importance. As you get to know the area, you will inevitably discover some of the more obvious needs of those who live or work in it. However, it can be useful to consider how you build up a picture of the area and what this is saying to you about those needs, before going deeper into those areas about which you may decide to do something. This will enable you to check whether or not there are unmet needs which are being ignored.

· **Purpose or statement of mission**

You may wish to reconsider your purpose or mission statement as you get to know the area and do further thinking about your ministry (cf. p. 71).

· **Resources**

Consider what resources you already have or could obtain.

Your individual and collective abilities, skills, training and experience. What are these things saying to you about areas of ministry? Are they highlighting some and cutting out others? What is particularly life-giving for you?

Physical resources at your disposal. These include your house, money, equipment and so on.

Your time and energy. This will vary with your age and health, and according to other commitments you may have in the congregation or elsewhere.

Availability and desire for training in new skills. This may or may not be the moment to take up some course of training which attracts you, is available nearby, and which has a bearing on a needed ministry in the locality.

· **Other factors**

Clearly you may want to add other factors or specific criteria which are important to you, including your predilections and hunches which need to be taken into account. It is important to listen to your feelings and desires, to acknowledge and own them, however much or little you allow them to influence your decision. I would suggest, however, that you keep the list short and pithy. Lengthy lists can become bland, boring and unusable.

ii. Exploring possibilities

As a community or as individuals, the focus of your ministry may be local, meeting the needs of the parish or neighbourhood, or regional, meeting the needs of the wider church or society. Various ways of exploring possibilities are given in Chapter Sixteen, *Meetings and Exercises* on pp 231-40.

iii. Making your decision

You will find ideas about decision making in Chapter Thirteen on p. 171. You may wish to consider some of the questions below.

How do we feel about starting up something new, or about co-operating and possibly developing what is already being done?

What gaps have we come across?

How do we ensure we do not duplicate work in progress?

How acceptable would doing (a particular activity) be to local people, to the parish clergy, ecumenically, or to other local workers, such as social workers, teachers, doctors etc.?

Once you have come to a decision about your mission and ministry and checked it out with those particularly involved locally and with those in authority in your congregation, you will be ready to start work.

2. JOINING AN EXISTING AREA OF WORK

If you are joining others in an existing area of work, be it parish or neighbourhood, local or diocesan, you may be replacing someone or be an additional member on the staff or work force. In both cases, there are three aspects to be aware of as you are inducted into the work. These stages overlap but it is worth considering them separately in order to be alert to their opportunities and pitfalls.

· Learning

Although you will be contributing and taking some responsibility from the start, being new requires learning from other people and asking for information and help. This is the time to listen, watch, ask questions, try things out, and generally fit into the situation as it is, rather than try to change things before you are familiar and conversant enough to see the implications of doing so. In so far as your attitude is one which is open and receptive and you are not defensive when you make some *faux pas*, then your very mistakes can make bonds between you and those with whom you are working.

· Contributing

There may well be a subtle change in your contributions as you gain experience and form good relationships. As time goes on you will be able to contribute ideas, make suggestions, provide information and raise issues without giving offence. Being tentative is a key to allaying any fears that you are criticising, judging or wanting to teach people 'how things should be done'. Avoid remarks such as 'in my last place, we always did such and such'. Obvious traps, but so easily fallen into!

· Taking responsibility

As your confidence and competence in handling the situation grows, so you will be in a position to do the appointment justice and bring to it your unique skills and abilities.

3. DEVELOPING A NEW AREA OF WORK, PROJECT OR PROGRAMME

This is a complex undertaking and needs thorough preparation alone and with others.

i. Who to involve?

To undertake this exciting but demanding task in a collaborative way, your first question is "Who to involve in thinking this out with me and in working out the first steps?". In principle, the earlier you involve those who will be affected by or involved in the project the better. You will both benefit from their local expertise and be more likely to make plans that are feasible and more widely acceptable. In some situations it may be fairly clear with whom you need to start the thinking process. At other times you may face a more difficult choice. Consider the examples below.

It may be that a job description has been drawn up prior to your appointment. In this case, it could still be useful to talk it through with those who will be affected, in order to learn about the situation and gain their co-operation in fleshing it out.

A question to be asked frequently is, "Is there anyone else we should involve at this stage to help, to whom we should give information, who could advise us on finance, technicalities or practical matters, or participate in other ways?"

Example 1
You are appointed assistant to a parish that has not previously had one.

Clearly you will be expected to begin thinking things through with the priest or parish team who are employing you.

Your objectives could be to form a good working relationship and ascertain where he or the team stand in terms of collaborative ministry (cf. p. 117). Depending on this you may work out together your role as assistant and what it will entail or you might suggest this is done in consultation with a parish council or a group of lay people.

Some of the questions such a group could start by asking themselves are:

1. How far do we clarify your role and function as assistant before testing it out and clarifying it further with other parishioners?
2. Who else can we involve in the parish and how can we best do so?

Is it useful to discuss with each parish group separately or at a general parish meeting? Which is most likely to encourage people to attend and contribute ideas?

If we go to each separately, how can we let people know what we are doing (in order to avoid one group resenting the fact that they were not first on the list!).

Are there ways of involving parishioners who do not belong to any group, through: informal conversations, a special evening to meet them and talk, an 'at home' on a particular day in the presbytery or parish hall, or a series of street meetings in different people's homes?

Example 2
You are setting up a project for homeless young people

Who to involve and in what order?

Local churches?

Local professional workers, e.g. social workers, probation officers, teachers, doctors, police?

Local organisations, e.g. Citizen's Advice Bureaux, etc?

Homeless people themselves?

Your objectives could be:

- to form good working relationships;
- to draw on their experience of the situation and learn what is not already being done;
- to gain the interest and commitment of two or three people prepared to think through the next steps with you.

It could be helpful to list the pros and cons of approaching each of the possible categories of people first. In doing this you are likely to see where the balance of advantage lies.

Before involving others you need to do a certain amount of private thinking, for example:
- what are your objectives for the first meeting?
- how will you approach those concerned to set up the meeting?
- how will you explain why you are seeking their participation?
- how will you prepare for and conduct the meeting?

The more carefully you do your private thinking the more fruitful is the involvement of others likely to be.[1]

These questions and ideas may seem complicated and no doubt a detailed and gradual evolution of a useful programme of work could be evolved without them, but they are included because the first steps in forming a collaborative and reflective working relationship are so important. Those involved are more likely to feel responsible for ensuring that you make good use of your time, and be committed to making their contribution. This process is one of developing community.

ii. Designing a programme of work

In *Analysis and Design* Lovell describes approaches and methods of designing church and community programmes[2] which were developed in Avec[3] in local situations from working with hundreds of people. The notes below draw heavily on this work and are based on Lovell's diagram (Fig. 7.2). As I briefly elucidate each stage, I hope to give sufficient information to whet your appetite for more, and to send you to the source.

Figure 7.2
Eight Thinking Stages

Stage 1: Depicting situations. background, context and how we see and feel about them

Stage 2: Depicting things as we would like them to be

Studying things as they are

Stage 3: Establishing points of reference such as purposes

Stage 4: Conceptualising, analysing, diagnosing, forming hypotheses and synthesising

Stage 5: Drawing up development agendas

Defining what needs to be done

Stage 6: Designing work programmes & means of evaluating them

Stage 7: Planning ways of putting designs to work and of evaluating them

Working out how to do things

Stage 8: Deciding, contracting and commissioning

Stage 1: Depicting work situations, background and context and how we see them and feel about them

This is where local expertise is invaluable in order to build up a picture of the work situation, with all its opportunities and problems: the key individuals and groups and the relationship between them; and the facts concerning everything which has a bearing on the project such as finance, resources, types of people, decision making, and who has power, responsibility, authority and influence. As Lovell says: "The art in all this is to depict these various realities about workers and their situations in ways that enable all concerned to grasp the essentials and to work at them. I say 'depict', rather than describe, because, for me, it conveys portraying things through graphics and possibly paintings as well as through the spoken and written word. The aim is to portray as clearly as possible the essentials of situations, the experience and dimensions of problems, the story-line of cases. Descriptive economy is necessary in what is essentially an exercise in profiling: too many words and fussy diagrams obfuscate."[5]

Sitting round a table with a large sheet of paper on which to draw diagrams or maps to show relationships or to note key items, facilitates the building up of a common picture. Before moving to Stage 2 ask yourselves, "Is there anything of significance we have missed out? Anything forgotten?"

Stage 2: Depicting things as we would like them to be

This is an important step: to share ideas, hopes, visions of how people would like to see the situation in order to develop a shared vision and articulate a common purpose. What are the changes for the better you hope to bring about through the project or programme of work?

Stage 3: Establishing points of reference

This stage is closely linked with the previous one. The main points of reference are:

Beliefs. The need to explore your beliefs is considered on p. 69. What is it that inspires you, keeps you going in the desert patches of life, enables you to make sense of life, burns within you, strikes deep chords for you, or makes you feel life is worth living? Lovell says "What is required is as honest a statement as possible of any beliefs upon which we believe we are operating in relation to a specific aspect of our work at a given time."[6] Ways of using beliefs in your work are outlined in Table 7.1a on p. 113.

Purposes. Formulating a purpose for the community has been considered on p. 114and some of these ideas are relevant here. Purposes are also considered in Table 7.1b.

Noxiants. Those things you wish to avoid have been considered on p. 71.

Resources. When estimating your resources in terms of people, time and energy, it is important not to allow your heart to run ahead of you, and over-commit yourself or allow others to do so – a danger of Christian ministry because the work to be done is endless. It helps no one if burnout is experienced. Other resources are to do with such things as finance, equipment and premises. In making an estimate of resources needed, you cannot expect to be as accurate as a quantity surveyor, but you do need to ask yourself, 'Is this feasible?', 'Are we in danger of over-stretching people?', 'Is there a weak point anywhere?'

Needs. It is possible that you will already have discovered something about the needs of local people which has led you to setting up the programme or project on which you are engaged (cf. *Discovering people's real needs* in Chapter Sixteen). It is worth remembering, and this links up with what was said about resources, that you and those with whom you work also have needs. Any programme of work, at best, meets the needs of those for whom it was conceived *and* those who initially set it up and are concerned with the organisation. This is about the mutuality of collaborative ministry in which all have much to gain and learn. It helps to avoid the danger of being patronising and arrogant. We all have needs and some of these are undoubtedly met through the work we do, even though that is not our primary motivation. The work must not constantly squeeze out more personal needs.

Table 7.1a
Notes on belief in church and community work[7]

In working with people for development, the freedom and ability to think creatively, to make good decisions and to evaluate work done, is greatly enhanced by having readily available reference points. These tables are about two such reference points.

Beliefs

Belief and theology are important factors in working with individuals, groups, communities, organisations and churches for human and spiritual development. There are several ways of translating this rather bland statement into the fabric of church and community development work:

1. by developing those attributes in oneself and others by which all are:
   – in touch with their beliefs;
   – able to examine them critically;
   – able to examine those of others;
   – able to modify and change their beliefs as they see the need to do so.

2. by getting over to others the vital importance of belief and theology in planning, and carrying out work;

3. by invariably stating and using belief as well as purpose in planning, programming and evaluating work;

4. by reflecting theologically on work and experience and promoting this practice among others;

5. by acquiring, and helping others to acquire, more skills in enabling people to reflect theologically;

6. by enhancing in oneself and others the ability to work with people of diverse beliefs and the ability to explore these differences with them.

All this helps to handle belief creatively in the processes of living and working, to keep up theologically with experience and insights, to become theologically more competent and effective in work, ministry, dialogue and mission.

Table 7.1b
Notes on purposes in church and community work[7]

Purposes

Purposes arise from the depths of individuals and groups, they are 'gut aims'. For Christians they point to what they feel will bring in the Kingdom of God. Associated as they are with motivation, drive, and thrust, they have affective as well as intellectual content. They energise and galvanise. Articulating them is a necessary prerequisite to assessing them critically and using them. They are useful as a guide in initiating action and in responding to it.

Formulating purpose is often a difficult thing to do. How does one get at it? It is possible to get at a statement of purpose:

- by specifying precisely what changes in oneself, others and the environment are felt to be key to real human and spiritual betterment;
- by getting at that which is cardinal in specific situations to human and spiritual development and to bringing in the Kingdom of God by way of change in people and environment;

- by expressing one's intuitions and gut feeling about what is needed;

- by differentiating between objectives and purposes, through asking 'why' or 'what for' of each successive objective until the most useful formulation of purpose is reached;

- by stating beliefs and purposes separately;

- by formulating statements which make clear that objectives are subordinate to purposes. This can be done by adding to a statement of objectives an 'in order to . . .' clause. It can also be done by adding to a statement of purposes a list of objectives, each one prefaced with 'by' or 'through'. This is particularly useful in sorting out objectives from purpose, and classifying them.

- by stating purpose succinctly and clearly in terms of:
  - people and their relationships rather than in terms of things and their relationships, the human rather than the material;
  - specific situations and people.

Stage 4: Conceptualising, analysing and diagnosing, forming hypotheses and synthesising

This is the stage in which you try to look beneath the surface to see what it is that is holding things together, and what may be drawing them apart, breaking down relationships, or causing things to malfunction. Essentially this is about taking apart in order to see what is working or not working and hypothesising as to what is happening and why. Much social analysis stops here. To be fruitful it needs to be coupled with designing realistic plans as in Stage 5.

Stage 5: Drawing up development agendas

This is a moment to pause and digest all that you have worked through, to mull things over and allow your feelings, hunches, intuitions and ideas to interact. It is a time of discernment. "Genuine development agendas emerge from this process which is soul-searching rather than brainstorming".[8] From this will come those tasks which you see to be essential if the situation is to become fruitful.

Stage 6: Designing work programmes and projects and means of evaluating them

This stage is akin to landscaping a wilderness destined to be a garden, or producing an architectural plan of a building. It depicts the result aimed at, the structures necessary, the relationship between the parts, groups and individuals that will be necessary if the action decided upon in the development agenda is to be realised effectively. This is an important activity before you plan who will do what, how, and when, in Stage 7. Figure 7.3 illustrates what is meant by designing: all the various groups who were involved in a project for the homeless are set out in relation to each other and particularly in relation to the community and the kind of interaction aspired to between them.

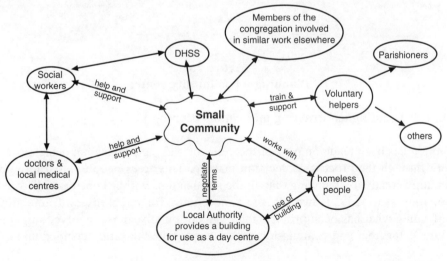

Figure 7.3
Example of a project design

I have often found that when I am faced with an impasse in a situation and am at a loss as to how best to move, to sort out the elements of the design in this way unlocks the door to the way forward. I take a sheet of paper and portray the various groups and individuals including my own place in the scheme of things, and the desired relationships between us all.

Lovell has written extensively and in a very practical way about this often neglected area in church and community work.[9]

Stage 7: Planning ways and means of evaluating and putting designs to work

This is the stage when you plan what to do, who will do it, when and how. It is likely to include seeing people, convening meetings, setting up groups, writing and telephoning. Some people find it helpful to make a flow chart so that the timing of the various actions can be depicted in relation to each other. For instance, the simple flow chart shown in Figure 7.4 below was the basis for more detailed ones on each aspect of building a community centre.[10]

It is also wise to make a decision as to when you will review and assess how the work is going. The date can always be moved earlier or later, but having decided on a date you are more likely to evaluate what you are doing rather than allow things to drift.

Reviewing and evaluating are discussed in Chapter Eight on p. 121 and some suggested methods are outlined in Chapter Fourteen on p. 180.

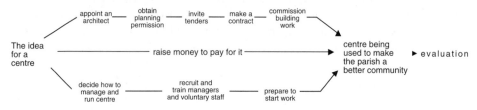

Figure 7.4
Planning a community centre.

Stage 8: Deciding, contracting and commissioning[11]

Mention has been made on p.41 of the value of making provisional decisions as you work through the process of decision making. This frees people to explore openly and think creatively, knowing that all the implications will be considered before final decisions are made. However, the time comes for checking and amending or confirming what has been provisionally agreed. Finally, those involved might make contracts together and commission each other to take the action decided upon.

While working through these eight steps, it is necessary to keep in mind and make full use of your key reference points: beliefs, purposes, noxiants, needs and resources.[12]

Small Communities in Religious Life

4. COLLABORATIVE MINISTRY

Working in a collaborative way has been briefly discussed in relation to leadership on p. 99.

i. The concept

Collaborative ministry is an essential element if your work is to be developmental rather than controlling. Since 1992, it has been the official policy of the Bishops' Conference of England and Wales.[13]

The current stress on collaborative ministry is rooted in the emphasis of Vatican Two on the church as the people of God. When on a pilgrimage through difficult and at times dangerous terrain, while leadership and some form of organisation is vital, everyone needs to work together if there is to be forward movement and harmony. Everyone is called on to help, to support, to encourage, to fill gaps, at times to take a lead and at others to follow, and always be prepared to contribute generously of their skills and abilities, and, when necessary, to question the direction being taken. On such journeys, people who constantly seek esteem, push to be first, tell others what to do, patronise, or collude with those who do these things, cause conflict or slow the journey down. Jesus, in his retort to the status-seeking of James and John, laid down the ideals of collaboration for his followers.

> 'You know that in the world the recognised rulers lord it over their subjects, and their great men make them feel the weight of authority. That is not the way with you; among you, whoever wants to be great must be your servant, and whoever wants to be first must be the willing slave of all.'[14]

Unfortunately, we human beings constantly fall short of such ideals. This has been and still is true of the church. The current emphasis on collaborative ministry is not being made before time.

ii. Working collaboratively

However, believing in and talking about collaboration is one thing; working to achieve it, after centuries in which the external hierarchical forms of church organisation and that of society, have both dictated behaviour and seeped into our very consciousness, is another. One essential element in working collaboratively is the non-directive approach. This has already been described when discussing leadership in the community on p. 101. What is outlined there is equally applicable to your attitudes and approach in ministry.

There are difficulties in working collaboratively. People in parish and neighbourhood are probably more used to solely directive action – and some may well be happier and feel more secure this way. For them, the responsibility of taking action based on their own thinking and decision making can feel daunting. Furthermore, those who have worked with them, and perhaps those who still do, may only have experienced and be skilled in being directive. In working with many priests and lay people who have found themselves newly committed to working *with* rather than *for* people, I have accumulated several useful guidelines:

Assimilate the approach yourself. This is a gradual process in which practice is helped by reading about it and reflecting or discussing what you have read. A glance at the bibliography on p. 247 may help you decide where to begin.

Avoid imposing collaborative ways of working and the non-directive approach on those who do not wish them, who fear them, or who do not understand and are confused by them.[15] To be directive or non-collaborative in introducing people to the non-directive approach is inconsistent and counter-productive.

Avoid the use of jargon such as 'non-directive'. Talk more informally about 'looking at this together' and 'sharing our ideas'.

Begin in a small way. For instance, to ask questions, to really listen to the answer and take seriously what has been said, will encourage people to participate, to give their ideas and to think about what is suggested or what could be done rather than passively accept it or unthinkingly reject it.

Explain to people what you are doing and why. This is particularly important with people who are unused to participating. "It seems to me, if we all pause and think about this, we will have more ideas to choose from", "Can you talk in two's and three's, this will give everyone a chance to talk this over".

Prepare well beforehand. How much you prepare or do not prepare for meetings and programmes depends to some extent on your temperament. When working in a new way with people, adequate preparation is enormously important. Some of the ideas suggested in relation to community meetings in Chapter Fifteen on p. 200 could also be useful.

Stimulate a group discussion on collaborative ministry. You could use:

- *The sign we give.*[16] This document, the outcome of a working party set up by the Conference of Bishops of England and Wales, has three discussion outlines helpful for those who are moving towards collaborative ministry, and three which are more appropriate for those with experience of it. These could be used as they stand or amended to suit your situation and group.

- *The Church and Community Development: An Introduction.*[17] This simple book explains the theory and practice of working *with* rather than only *for* people. It has a useful section on 'Deciding where one stands' and how to take the next steps.

The diagrams shown in Figure 7.5 differentiate between different approaches. These could be particularly useful with people with whom you have worked non-directively or leaders in the parish or neighbourhood who are interested in your approach.. Distinguish between these three different ways of working.[18] There are pros and cons to each approach, and each can be appropriate in different situations at different times.

Small Communities in Religious Life

In three groups, members could explore a different approach and share their ideas as to its strengths and weaknesses with others. Such a discussion would avoid the danger of imposing an approach on a group.

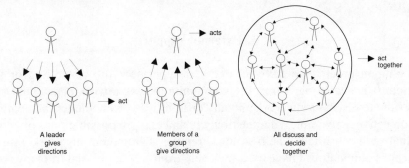

Figure 7.5
Different ways of working

5. SUPPORT IN MINISTRY

Any work with people in which we are seriously engaged, is extremely taxing. We need support as persons to keep our motivation and courage up, and as practitioners to increase the effectiveness of the work. Members of a community can certainly give the first kind of support and possibly the second, but you may well need to seek further afield for this.

i. Mutual support

As members of a small community you may be engaged in the same or different areas of work. In either case, it can be useful to spend time discussing how you will keep abreast of what is going on in the work and in each other in relation to it, so you are able to support each other, offer help or information and generally co-operate.

It is likely that much mutual support will be given and received from each other informally, but you may decide to ensure it happens on a slightly more formal basis as suggested below.

Commission each other. In order to emphasise the corporate nature of your ministry even when individuals are engaged in very different areas or work – it is important to publicly entrust each other or be entrusted by the provincial or her delegate, to the work you are each doing. Decide on when, where, and the format which will best suit you. Follow the religious event with a celebration!

Regularly include different aspects of the work in the prayer of the community.

Set a period or meeting aside on a regular basis to talk about your ministry. Share information and work on any difficulties you are facing. The problem tackling sequence in Chapter Twelve might be helpful. You could work throughout any event or situation which you see as a 'failure', using the case study method described on p. 169.

Act as ministerial co-consultants to each other. This could be done by taking an hour or two to concentrate on one person's work at a time. A procedure for this was developed by Lovell and myself in Avec.[19] This is described in *Work and life resumé* on p. 187.

ii. External support

It is common practice to have an external supervisor in counselling or spiritual direction. It is becoming increasingly common to seek a work consultant: someone with whom to discuss your work and any difficulties you encounter, and who, from a more objective viewpoint, will question you and explore possible lines of action. It is vital that such consultancy help is non-directive. Throughout my work with groups, teams, and communities I have used such help from T R Batten and from my colleague, George Lovell. I know it has enabled me not only to be more effective in the situation under discussion, but to develop professionally and personally.[20]

REFERENCES AND NOTES

1. Lovell, *Analysis & Design,* op. cit. (ref. 5, p. 38) pp 193-196.
2. Ibid. pp. 93ff. and pp.159ff.
3. Avec: A Service Agency for Church and Community Work was set up in 1976 by George Lovell and Catherine Widdicombe. It is described in *Avec: Agency & Approach* by George Lovell (Avec Publications 1996. ISBN 1 8717 0902 4). Unhappily it closed as an agency in 1994.
4. Lovell, op. cit. (ref. 1, above) p. 114.
5. Ibid. p. 117.
6. Ibid. p. 125.
7. This is slightly adapted from an Avec handout by George Lovell.
8. Lovell, op. cit. (ref. 1, above) p. 119.
9. Ibid. p. 159.
10. Lovell & Widdicombe, op. cit. (ref. 3, p. 93) p.86.
11. Lovell, op. cit. (ref. 1, above) p.120.
12. Ibid. pp121ff.
13. See *Reflections*, p.8. This is a paper on the 'Final Reflection' of this meeting of the Bishops' Conference of England & Wales, 24 September, 1993.
14. Mark 10:35-45, The New English Bible, New Testament (Penguin Books, Oxford University Press, Cambridge University Press, 1961, 1964) p. 74.
15. Op. cit. (ref. 10, above). This is a description of how Lovell and Widdicombe worked with a group of local churches to introduce the non-directive concept and enable them to make a decision as to whether or not to use it. pp 27-33.
16. *The Sign we Give* (see ref. 4, p.59).
17. Lovell, *The Church and Community Development*, op.cit. (ref. 10, p. 18) p. 65.
18. Widdicombe, op. cit. (ref. 2, p. 54) pp186-7.
19. Avec (ref. 3, above).
20. Lovell, op. cit (Ref 12, p. 93). In *Consultancy, Ministry and Mission: a handbook for practitioners and consultants in Christian organisations* (Burns & Oates 2000) George Lovell has provided a teach yourself book to help people to get and to give qualitative non-directive support and assistance in relation to their vocation and work.

VIII
Reviewing and Evaluating

This Chapter is addressed in the first place to members of communities, but is also relevant to those in authority or those facilitating a community review.

Chapters and visitations are two ways in which religious take stock of where they are as a congregation, province or community and how best to move forward. Individuals make annual retreats for the same purpose. Communities have a similar need. Although changes and adjustments to life and work will be made as you go along, there comes a time when the effectiveness and well-being of a community requires it to review and evaluate the situation and progress. This is best done as a collaborative exercise so that everyone living in the community and all those engaged in a programme or piece of work can both contribute their ideas and reactions, and learn from it.

This chapter considers the value of taking stock, when it might be done, and the process of evaluating. Chapter Fourteen outlines some practical ways of doing so.

1. THE VALUE OF TAKING STOCK

Some learning experiences occur with little reflection. Stock-taking is a more conscious process of learning from experience so as to live and work in a better way, both for ourselves and others. This can produce a shift from a 'blame culture' to that of a 'learning organisation'. Gillian Stamp writes, "In a blame culture the aim is not to review in order to learn from something that has not turned out as expected, but to find out who did wrong and blame them. Understanding what it means to forgive, frees people to learn from their mistakes."[1] Reviewing and evaluating contribute to on-going growth and development of members, individually and corporately. Ideally they do this in several ways.

It enables you to live more purposefully. Re-considering your goals and purposes in the light of your experience of trying to achieve them may reveal, for instance, that they are unrealistic, too general, not appropriate or not sufficiently challenging. You may find they have been unused and forgotten. However used and useful they have been, you may want to alter or rephrase them in some way or to work out how they will affect your life and work more deeply.

It encourages you through identifying all that has gone well. It is important in your struggle to live as a community, to pause and appreciate the positive effects you are having, the fruits of your work and life.

It challenges you to new effort. Evaluating may reveal and make you face up to what is not going so well and why. There is a great deal to be learnt from our failures, from those things which did not come up to our expectations, and from misunderstandings. Considering these negative aspects of your life and work can alert you to pitfalls and cul-de-sacs of which you are unaware.

It helps you to be realistic about your gifts, skills and limitations. Evaluation may, for instance, show areas in which you need help or support from others, skills or necessary information you need to acquire. You may realise you are not playing to your strengths and making maximum use of your particular gifts and graces, individually or as a group.

It alerts you to possible new directions. Considering what you are doing and not doing in relation to the needs of the situation may reveal new areas of work, new activities, or more effective methods. Through evaluating you may realise the time has come to close down some area of work or hand it on to others.

It enables you to design and plan our work more systematically. Through giving you an overview of all you are doing, you will be able to see the interconnections or lack of them and how one piece of work affects others or could do so with profit. Your future designing and planning can therefore be based on a more comprehensive picture.

It enables you to make what we have learnt available to others. Sharing the fruits of your evaluation, successes and failures, could help those about to set up small communities, those in authority who have oversight of such communities, those responsible for initial and on-going formation, etc. What you have learnt could be a valuable addition to the body of knowledge needed to help people work out how best to live religious life today.

It makes it possible for you to be pro-active. Evaluation may help you to take some control of your life and to take action in relation to that sense of 'divine dissatisfaction' which many Christian workers feel in relation to the gap between how they would like things to be and how things actually are.

Table 8.1 may assist you in orientating yourself to the evaluation process.

Table 8.1
Orienting yourselves to evaluating

A preliminary reflection or conversation before you begin to review your situation may alert you to hidden fears and dangers which otherwise might emerge suddenly. The questions below may help you consider some of the difficulties and pitfalls.

· What are my/our positive and negative feelings towards evaluating? Try to explore why you feel like this.

· What do I/we fear? What negative effects could it have?

· What do we want to avoid? How will we do so?

· Are we convinced we need to evaluate?

· Would it help us to be open if we agreed to maintain confidentiality between us until we decide, as we conclude, what we need to share with others? What else could help us?

Small Communities in Religious Life

2. WHEN TO REVIEW AND EVALUATE

It can be useful, particularly when a community is being formed or re-formed, to decide when you will review how things are going. The timing will vary with each situation. If you evaluate too often, it can be as unsettling as constantly digging a plant up by the roots and re-potting it. If done too infrequently, there is a danger of getting into an ineffective rut or forming habits which become increasingly hard to challenge or change. If you find it hard to decide when to evaluate, you might at least make a date when you will make such a decision.

There are certain moments in the life of a community which lend themselves appropriately to this task:

Visitations. A visitation is more likely to be a fruitful event if the community has done its own preparation and knows what it wants from this event. It can be useful, therefore, to engage in a process of self-evaluation beforehand, so that you know what issues you wish to discuss, what requests to make, what problems to raise, and what you wish to say about yourselves to the provincial team and province. Clearly the visitors will also have their own agenda to help them obtain the necessary information about the community and its relationships, both within the congregation and beyond it, in order to discharge their responsibility to the province, to the congregation, and to the church. Without an accurate picture of the community situation and without knowing how the community perceives the communications and directives from the provincial team, they are working in the dark. Ideally, therefore, a visitation is a combination of self-evaluation and external evaluation. 'Outsiders' are often in a better position to see things missed by insiders, be more objective and to enable the community to be. Visitations are discussed in more detail on p. 129.

Comings and goings. The community changes its shape and is, in a sense, a new community whenever a new person joins it or someone departs from it or dies. These can be useful occasions on which to review the basis on which the community operates and take stock in the light of the loss or addition of skills, gifts and personalities. More is said about comings and goings in Chapter Eleven.

Chapters. These are markers in the life of a congregation and are meant to have an influence on each member and community. It is more likely that this will be so, if you are able to prepare for a chapter and consider its outcome in relation to an accurate picture gained through reviewing and evaluating.

Beginnings and endings. The beginning or end of a project or piece of work, or of a term or year – whether academic, Christian or secular – also provide appropriate occasions for taking stock.

Community renewal. If a community is giving itself a time of renewal, as described on p. 241, review and evaluation could well become part of it.

3. THE PROCESS OF EVALUATING[2]

In the process of evaluating you need to consider those things which indicate the effect of an activity or project, how to obtain feedback about such effects, and ways of assessing the feedback as objectively as possible. Each of these processes is discussed below.

i. Indicators of change

In ministry, as in all work which aims to bring about change for the better in the lives of people, the information you are looking for in order to indicate how things are going is not easily measured. It is easy to count the number of people attending a certain activity or visiting your home. It is more difficult to assess whether these things have helped people to be more caring or courageous, more spiritually alive or more committed and outgoing. Yet it is this kind of interior change which is at the heart of Christian ministry, and which we hope for in ourselves and in the lives of those amongst whom we live and work.

Lovell defines an indicator of change as "a symptom of personal or social change which can be observed, classified, assessed and possibly quantified and which points to changes in people – in their attitudes, their ways of thinking and their relationships – which it is necessary to assess but which . . . are not open to direct observation."[3] For example, if people increasingly contribute ideas to a project or programme of work and are prepared to take other people's ideas seriously, it indicates greater commitment, self-confidence and openness to other people. The external change in behaviour points to inner changes. Determining indicators may well be done as a collaborative exercise with those concerned, when working out your purpose at the start of a piece of work (cf. p. 71). This can be a fascinating experience. Having a list of indicators will alert you to the kind of feedback you seek as part of your process of review.

ii. Feedback

Feedback is the information which tells you what you and others think and feel about what you are evaluating. The amount and reliability of the information you receive is likely to be influenced by your attitudes and relationships.

Your attitude. People are more likely to contribute honestly, not only if you assure them you really want to know what they feel and think, but show that you welcome what can be learnt from negative or critical comment. I find it helpful to tell myself and others that no-one and no work can be perfect, there is always room for improvement and something to learn.

The relationship between you and those giving feedback. There is a natural tendency to discount negative feedback from people with whom we do not agree or get on. Such feedback may, in fact, be more honest and accurate than that of our friends!

· Types of feedback

Feedback can be internal, unsolicited, or solicited.

Internal feedback. By its nature, this is subjective, more or less so according to our individual make up. Some people see all they do through rose-coloured spectacles, others find it hard to see the good in anything they have done. Jotting down both my positive and negative thoughts and feelings about the area of work I am reviewing and comparing it with feedback I am receiving from other people, helps me to be objective

Unsolicited feedback. This comes unsought through what people say, their body language or behaviour. It will be partial as only a minority may give direct feedback, and people may be more or less honest depending on their relationship with you and their motives for giving feedback. Unsolicited feedback may therefore be misleading; it needs checking.

Solicited feedback. This may be sought in a variety of ways: from casual questions in conversation, "how do you feel about things?" to systematic or scientific questionnaires. It may be done on a one-to-one basis or through group discussion.

· The effects of feedback

It is worth considering the effect feedback is having on you or the community (cf. Figure 8.1). If you are receiving positive feedback this may well give you the courage to continue but there is also the danger of it making you so over-confident that you become careless. Similarly, negative feedback can depress you, make you defensive, or cause you to give up; or it can challenge you, cause you to decide to learn new skills and spur you on to great effort.

iii. Evaluating purposefully

Evaluation is the critical assessment of the feedback you receive in relation to your purpose, reading off the implications and deciding what action to take as a result. Reflecting on feedback and evaluating it are two overlapping activities.

· Reflecting on feedback

The process is not a purely rational one. It engages both mind and heart: what you feel is as important as what you think. How you 'hear' what is being told you depends on a variety of factors: your mood, the source of the feedback, how it is said, and to some extent, your own perception of the work or activity. It is both rational and intuitive. It is important therefore, to do two things:

To consider it with a critical mind. Explore what is being said, if possible ask questions of those concerned or, if not, conjecture why people are saying this. Could they be projecting into this their feelings from something else? Is there any misunderstanding? Does other feedback you have received support this or not?

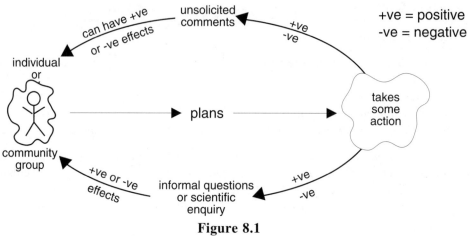

Figure 8.1
Effect of feedback[4]

To listen to it in a more meditative and reflective way. Allow it to speak to you over a couple of days. I find I am then far more likely to appreciate and accept what is being said, whether positive or negative, as it gives me time to assimilate it and it allows for mood swings: I will not be unduly influenced by excitement or depression.

We need time to reflect on the data, allow the detail to fall away, and give our intuition a chance to surface. Carl Rogers[5] was a great believer in people having confidence to trust their hunches enough to consider them seriously, and bring the more logical side of the brain to play on what has arisen from the feeling and intuitive side.

· Evaluation in relation to purpose

All evaluation needs to be done in relation to your purpose, what you actually set out to achieve (cf. p. 71). For instance, if a parish set out to build a more caring community through setting up a visiting scheme, it is not enough to evaluate success in terms of numbers of visitors or visits. Deeper questions need to be asked: What effect has the scheme on the lives of those visited and on the visitors themselves? What have they learned? Has it affected the other parishioners and the relationships between people? Have some visitors become possessive? Do people feel intruded on in any way?

REFERENCES AND NOTES

1. Stamp, Gillian: *The Enhancement of Ministry in Uncertainty,* BIOSS Occasional Paper (ref. 8, p. 31).
2. I am drawing heavily on the work George Lovell did while working in Avec (ref. 3, p. 120).
3. From an Avec handout drawn from Lovell's unpublished thesis for his doctorate, *An Action Research Project to test the Applicability of the Non-directive Concept in a Church, Youth & Community Centre Setting* (Institute of Education, University of London, 1973).
4. I am indebted to George Lovell for this diagram.
5. Rogers, Carl: *On Becoming a Person: A Therapist's View of Psychotherapy* (Constable, 1967, 3rd reprint 1972) p. 22.

Small Communities in Religious Life

IX
Community and Congregation

This Chapter is addressed primarily to local communities, but those in positions of leadership or acting as facilitators to communities may also find it useful.

The mission and ministry of the congregation is worked out, according to its particular charism, largely at local level: if local communities did not exist , there would be no need for councils or teams at provincial and congregational level. Those in overall authority are charged with servicing the communities, thus helping them to live according to their charism and constitutions. It is only possible to do this effectively if those at ground level help them by their attitudes and actions. Figure 9.1 depicts the relationship between those working on the ground in communities and those who are in positions of overall responsibility.

The relationship which is built up as new general or provincial councils come into being and as new communities are formed, is crucial to the well-being of the whole. Basic to this relationship is the theological insight that we are all part of the pilgrim people of God, stumbling forward together; all of us far from perfect; all of us needing each other's help, which comes by way of support and challenge; none of us more important than another in the sight of God, and each following our religious vocation – and our individual vocation within that vocation – as best we are able.[1]

Healthy attitudes between people at different levels in a religious congregation enable the whole to function well. It is up to both the local community and the provincial team to exercise co-responsibility in a mutually useful and enriching way. This chapter considers the contribution a small community needs to make by way of response and initiative towards the well-being and development of the province and congregation. Such co-responsibility may be exercised individually or corporately by the members.

1. CO-RESPONSIBILITY BETWEEN COMMUNITY AND PROVINCIAL TEAM

The following are some of the ways in which a community can exercise responsibility towards the provincial team:

i. Paint a realistic picture of your situation

Be open about your difficulties and problems as well as your successes, without necessarily expecting them to be solved for you. If your community is trying out some new mission or living in a radically different style, it is particularly important to keep those at provincial level *au fait*. It is information from the grass roots which makes any prophetic stance they take in the church or in society, authentic and grounded[2].

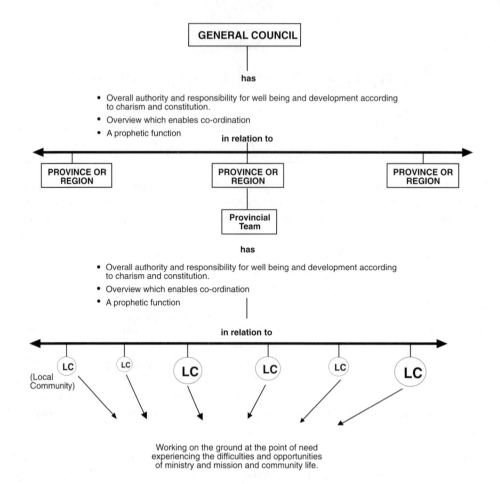

Figure 9.1
The various levels of responsibility in a congregation

ii. Raise questions and take initiative

Because you live cheek by jowl with people in need in your locality, you are in a good position to think out new forms of ministry to meet new demands and opportunities as they become apparent. The amount of freedom you have been given by the provincial team will determine whether you raise questions, ask permission, use the team as a sounding board, or go ahead and report later. Co-responsibility in this context calls on you to inform the provincial team not only about what you have been engaged in and why, and what happened as a result, but also about what you are learning from it. Being reflective communities in relation to your locality will be of benefit not only for yourselves and your work but for others in the province.[3]

iii. Let your needs and wants be known

Exercising responsibility towards all local communities is written into the task of the provincial team. This does not mean that you as a community have nothing to say. Unless you are clear and communicate what you need and want from members of your provincial team, you leave them guessing. With the best intentions, any initiatives they take are less likely to fit you or your situation.

There may be helpful and unhelpful ways in which the team can perform its function towards you. It may be inclined to do too much or too little or to be untimely. It is part of your responsibility, therefore, to think through and make known what you consider would help you. Clearly, discussion, negotiation and agreement will avoid misunderstanding and misplaced expectations.

iv. Prepare for visitations

Visitations provide an opportunity to sort out many of the above points and evaluate how both parties experience the working out of co-responsibility. The community may need to be pro-active in relation to the agenda if it is to make the most of the opportunity offered by a visitation.

Questions such as the following may help you to prepare.

What do we want from this visitation?

What has happened since we were set up as a small community or since the last visitation – both positively and negatively?

How can we best give the visitor a true picture of our community, how we live and our mission and ministry? Are there any things we are likely to omit or hide or ways in which we might misrepresent things?

Is there any particular issue or problem we wish to discuss with the visitor? If so, how can we prepare to do this?

Is there anyone locally we wish the visitor to meet? Why?

Is there anything we are uneasy about or find problematic in the way the provincial or general council relates to us? Have we any general requests or suggestions to help them function more effectively in relation to ourselves? How best to phrase this?

Is there anything we want to say to encourage the leadership team on its way?

v. Respond to letters, circulars and directives

In organisations, not just religious communities, those in authority frequently complain about a lack of response to written communications. Over recent years there has been a plethora of paper sent to and expected from local communities. Understandably, this has often caused negative reactions. On the receiving end, such communications may be unwelcome because:

– there are just too many of them;

– they appear irrelevant to the life and work of those who receive them;

– they are bland statements of the obvious in religious jargon rather than fresh insights communicated in a stimulating way;

– the community is expected to carry out some directives which they are unhappy or even deeply disturbed about;

– the community is already actively engaged in thinking through some other issues or following another plan which conflicts with what is sent to them;

– members of the community have different and conflicting responses to what they receive;

– some action is requested which is unsuitable or out of harmony with what is already going on in the community's parish or locality, so the directive is felt to be intrusive and out of touch.

Receiving honest feedback is an important way the provincial team is able to build up an accurate picture of what is going on in the lives and work of those at the grass roots of the province. Unless the team has such a realistic picture, it will be unable to serve the local communities, the task for which it was elected. Clearly, giving critical feedback to some provincial teams is easier than to others. Where it is difficult, it may help during a visitation to initiate a discussion about receiving and responding to suggestions and directives so that mutual understanding and trust is built up. Ways of responding to a directive about which you feel negative are suggested in Table 9.1.

You may find it instructive, after several months, to assess all the letters, circulars and directives you have received. A great deal of thought and energy will have been expended on them by those in authority, and it is only fair to let them know whether it is to good or bad effect and why some communications were especially helpful and others only marginally so or even unhelpful.

In deciding what action to take, you need to consider the likely positive or negative effects of any action on yourselves, on anyone with whom you work or are in contact locally, on your ministry, or on the authorities who sent letters or directives. In this way you are trying to hold together your own integrity, the well-being and development of your community and your ministry, your loyalty to authority, and the well-being of the province and congregation.

Table 9.1
Responding to a directive about which you feel negative

If as a community you find yourselves reacting negatively to any letters or directives, there are several steps you might take before replying to those who sent them:

Step 1: Consider why you feel as you do.

Give yourselves time for the real reasons to surface before exploring them objectively. Some of your negative reactions may be due to:

Personal factors: e.g., exhaustion; a general feeling of being 'browned off'; laziness; fear of becoming involved or taking on more than you can manage; temporary or permanent anti-establishment feelings (Why? What has happened to cause this? What have 'they' said or done or have you said or done?); a fear it will upset your cosy regime, etc. Some of these may be hard to face. Some feelings may be uncomfortable and hard to own (cf. *Dealing with feelings* on p. 140). To recognise them and own them are a necessary prelude to taking control and stopping your feelings from determining your reaction.

Circumstances: for example, heavy work loads; pressures which take all your time and emotional energy; local events in which you are heavily engaged; the suggestions just do not fit your community or situation.

The letter or directives themselves: for example, the way they are couched – over-spiritual, highly directive, abstruse, carping; length; insensitivity to your needs; and so on.

Those who have sent the communication: even if the community feels out of sympathy with those in authority, all they 'send down' is not worthless, nor does it relieve the community of responsibility to respond. As a community, the way you relate to those in authority will contribute either to the well-being or the reverse of all concerned: yourselves, the team, the province and the congregation.

Step 2: Consider various responses and how you could make them.

Unhelpful responses include ignoring the communication, putting off any request for action until too late, or giving it a token assent and taking no action bar the bare minimum. There are more positive alternative responses, some of which may well be more difficult to take but which are called for by those committed to co-responsibility.

Accept the communication. Take it seriously and, if it is asking for some action, implement it and try to ameliorate any negative effects. This may or may not be successful. Reporting honestly on the outcome, whether successful or not can be educative for all concerned.

Clarify the purpose behind the communication. Why has it been sent? Can you achieve this purpose in another way. You may need to explain the reasons for your unease to those in authority, and possibly suggest an alternative action you could take.

Explain your predicament. Let those in authority know that because of your current situation or programme you cannot deal with it adequately or follow its suggestions. Explain why this is so and possibly suggest you take it up at a later date. Ask whether this is acceptable or not. Perhaps those who sent it can see other ways round the problem which faces you.

vi. Respond to members being moved into or out of the community

How a community might deal with the inevitable comings and goings in its membership is considered in Chapter Eleven *A Change of Community Members*. The concern here is about the responsibility a community has in relation to the leadership team. With a community which has been in existence some time, it could be useful to let those in authority know the sort of people for whom this community would be a growthful experience and those for whom it could well be too stressful. It could also be useful to give some indication in relation to timing: there may be internal or external factors which would make it inappropriate to move people around for a particular period. Or you may need people with particular skills

vii. Seek help when necessary

Subsidiarity requires decisions and actions to be taken at the lowest appropriate level of an organisation. Your community, like every other, will occasionally meet difficulties, and ways of tackling these are considered in Chapter Twelve. As a community, when you have the information, experience and expertise to do so, you will learn more if you face and deal with those problems that you are able to tackle without recourse to others.

However, there are likely to be times when your community, particularly because of its size, needs help. Maybe you know a member in another community or an outsider who would be able and willing to facilitate discussion of a tricky issue. In some matters a community will need to seek the help of the leadership team.

2. CO-RESPONSIBILITY BETWEEN COMMUNITIES

In my experience this is an overlooked area. Other communities are often regarded as being solely within the purview of provincial and council. Often it takes a crisis to alert people to the needs of another community (cf. Table 9.2). However, in some congregations, communities create formal or informal links between themselves on a 'pairing and sharing' basis. In this partnership they undertake to support and help each other in various ways, such as:

- sharing ideas and experiences which have been useful: for example, ways of conducting a community meeting on a particular topic, rituals or celebrations, books and articles;

- responding, when asked, to plans and ideas as objective outsiders;

- facilitating a meeting of the other community or helping to sort out a difficulty;

- giving privacy and space or a holiday to a member from the other community;

- going out together, where distance does not preclude this;

- lending personnel for a few days when needed;

- having joint meetings or celebrations together.

This kind of activity makes for mutual well-being and development and is a way of building up a healthy infrastructure in a province.

Table 9.2
Considering co-responsibility

A simple exercise in raising community awareness of co-responsibility is to reflect on and discuss the questions below:

- In what ways have we benefited from co-responsibility? When has it been or not been working?

- What additional help or support do we look for or need from other communities?

- What have we experienced in relation to being co-responsible, as individuals or as members of a community?

- Are we convinced about the need to be co-responsible or is it something to which I/ we only give notional assent?

- What prevents me/us from exercising co-responsibility?

- What would help me/us to do so?

- Are there particular areas where we are or are not co-responsible?

---

3. CO-RESPONSIBILITY BETWEEN THE COMMUNITY
AND THE PROVINCE AS A WHOLE

How this is worked out will depend very much on the culture and tradition of the congregation and the situation of the local community. Where a small community is pioneering a new way of life or new form of mission or ministry, it may be written in from the start that it will report regularly to the province on developments. This enables new ideas to be considered, what is learnt to be shared, and support, encouragement, feedback and possibly other ideas or suggestions to be received. Doing this may spark off further initiatives. Apart from keeping the province in touch informally, there are other more structured ways:

- contributing to province newsletters or bulletins;

- writing a circular, newsletter or periodic report;

- having a slot in an assembly, area or province meeting;

- calling a special meeting or seminar;

- encouraging visitors from other communities or inviting people to special occasions;

- taking part in consultations and decision-making processes. If provincial decisions are to fit your small community and to be implemented in a way which is beneficial, as a community you need to have your say. This is particularly the case if you are a very different community from most of the others, through size or situation or ministry;

– taking part in assemblies and province-wide or area meetings: this is likely to include not merely physical participation but preparation beforehand.

A way in which one or several communities could share a picture of their life and work is suggested on p. 194.

4. CO-RESPONSIBILITY BETWEEN THE COMMUNITY AND THE CONGREGATION

One of the benefits of an international congregation is the enriching cross-fertilisation of ideas between communities in different provinces. Much that has been written about co-responsibility between community and province also applies to the relationship with the congregation. It is a more neglected area.

An exercise in raising community awareness of their relationship with others is shown in Table 3.2 on p. 51. It could be adapted.

REFERENCES AND NOTES

1. Schneider says, "The order at the global level, which is not dogmatic uniformity but deep unity in shared faith and spirituality, can be authentic only if it emerges from the lived variety and ferment at the local level, among the individuals and groups that make up the community." op. cit. (ref. 3, p. 31) p. 28.
2. When the Conference of Religious in the UK discussed and committed itself and its members to taking up a prophetic stance in 1989-90, they stressed that it was the kind and quality of local work which gave authenticity to any prophetic action they took.
3. Lovell, *Analysis and Design,* op. cit. (ref. 5, p. 38) pp 93ff. The Jesuit community setting up in Portadown, Northern Ireland realised from the start that, through their local experience, they would have a contribution to make to development through action to the wider church and other congregations.

PART FOUR

TRANSITION BETWEEN COMMUNITIES

X
Moving to Another Community

This chapter is addressed primarily to those moving in or out of communities but may also sensitise anyone else who is at all involved in the process: those saying farewell to or receiving members, those in leadership, or those facilitating a community or accompanying an individual member.

Moving from one community to another is a fairly common occurrence in religious life: it may be planned in advance or result from some crisis or traumatic event; it may be within the same area or country or between home and overseas. Some people appear to take it in their stride while for others it is a major upheaval. Whatever the circumstances, unless it is unexpected, transition is a long drawn out process: it starts to take place long before the actual moving out and moving in, and it continues for long after. It is an internal as well as an external process. The internal aspect is often neglected. Yet it is a time of potential learning and growth for all concerned, but particularly for the individuals going through it.

Because the process of transition is a personal one, it does not mean you have to struggle through it alone. Over the years I have worked not only with many people moving from one ministry and place of work to another, but with hundreds of missionaries returning from overseas to settle back in the British Isles.[1] Much of the work was done in groups in which people shared insights, supported one another and gained courage from realising they were not alone: others faced similar problems and shared similar traumas, excitement, hopes and fears. I am drawing heavily on what I learnt through this work and also on my own transitions from living and working from my community base in Pinner to living alone in a London flat, and, after fourteen years, my retirement from full-time work there and moving back to live and work in my community once more.

This chapter considers living in the present, reflecting on the past, and looking towards the future. Although set out systematically you are likely to find yourself going backwards and forwards, repeating, clarifying, deepening. Like life, transition is not a tidy process. Your journey is unique to you, as is its timing: you have a personal rather than a standard speed which is linked with your own inner clock.

As indicated already, people also vary in their ability to face change of any sort. For some, times of transition are traumatic: they are overwhelmed by feelings of uncertainly and confusion, and find the resulting chaos deeply unsettling. Whereas, others experience excitement and new energy in the challenge of re-ordering their ideas or way of life and work. For many, joy and sorrow, exhilaration and irritability jostle each other. The relief of finding a secure foothold can soon give way as it presents new problems. The excitement of glimpsing new insights and seeing a new pattern emerging can be closely followed by unsuspected obstacles. I have experienced liberation as some hitherto deeply held belief or practice about which, at some level, I have long felt uneasy, is suddenly recognised for what it is and can be discarded, indeed must be discarded if I am to live with integrity. Such wonderful times of clarity, certainty and vision are rudely interrupted by intrusive realities which can be as mundane as money needs or as hurtful as experiencing that what I have so painfully learned, is rubbished by those near and dear to me. More painful still is to realise some truth in what is being said and having to struggle with the new chaos this creates. However carefully you work at it, transition can still remain a difficult and painful process.

Knowing how you generally react to change can help you prepare and respond in a creative way. It can also enable you to help others in transition. Not knowing can lead to false expectations and misunderstandings.

1. LIVING IN THE PRESENT

A physical move from one community to another can hardly be accomplished without an inner movement of ideas and attitudes. It is certainly a time when these can be called into question and this may well be painful if such questioning is long overdue. At various times of transition I have found one or other of the things which follow particularly helpful.

i. Analysing and responding to what is happening

As an analytical aid, try drawing a more specific diagram of your situation based on that depicted in Figure 10.1.

Analyse the situation in which you find yourself. This may be done at any point as you move from A to B. You may prefer to work on your own or you may get more out of it with a confidante or friend helping you. In order to explore what is actually going on for you as you make this move from A to B, what is happening inside you, and the effects of your experience, consider the changes you are undergoing.

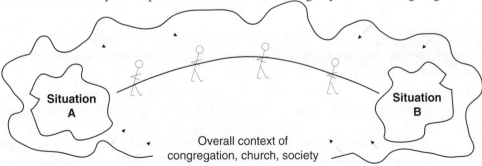

Figure 10.1
Moving from one community to another

Changing relationships. You may experience sorrow at leaving behind some people with whom you have a deep relationship. Acknowledging this together and working out what sort of relationship you wish to have in the future and how you will develop that, can help you to feel positive about it. On the other hand, there may be people to whom you are relieved to say goodbye. How you do this so that you end on a friendly note is also important for you and them. Forming new relationships can be a slow business and therefore your on-going relationship with the one person who will be moving with you – God – is invaluable. Ask yourself: Where is God for me in the process of transition?

Changing your perceptions. From the moment you know you will be moving, your perception of your external world changes. You see the situation you are leaving in a different way, maybe you find yourself valuing the known and familiar and the opportunities it has given you to develop. You are also likely to start distancing yourself from it, losing interest in things into which you had put your energy. What do you feel as you look ahead to the new situation?

Once you move to a new community, locality, and probably new work, your perceptions will change again, it will look different once you are in it, from when you saw it at a distance. You may be pleased or disappointed, surprised, shocked or depressed. What are your perceptions of your new situation? What effects are they having on you? Do you think you are seeing things in the same or a different way from others in the situation? Is this causing you to alter your judgement, to feel isolated, or to act in one way rather than another? How can you make use of your perceptions to gain a more realistic picture? How do you ensure that your perceptions have a positive rather than a negative effect on you, on others in the community, on others in the congregation, and on others in the locality?

Change of structures and procedures. These external changes call for a change in your habitual routine or ways of doing things. How do you feel about this? How easy or difficult do you usually find it to adapt or change your habits? You are uprooting from the known and familiar and challenged by the new and unknown. Ask yourself what effect this is having on you, both as you prepare to move, and particularly, when you have moved.

Cultural changes. These are very evident when moving from one community to another but they are also present when moving from one house or neighbourhood to another. It is better to recognise and name them rather than deny and ignore them. What strikes you about the way people behave, their customs, the way they talk, dress, think, what they like, their habits, and so on?

You may experience culture shock. From the experience of moving to an overseas community, missionaries identify several phases in the process of dealing with their culture shock and coming through it.

Reaction. All their senses are alert and their emotions are volatile.

Rejection. They are inclined to reject aspects of the situation they dislike or which are quite different from anything experienced before.

Regression. They are full of nostalgia and regret. They want to return home or they try to create a little UK ghetto where they are.

Recovery. They come through this period while still cherishing happy memories but these no longer pull them back to where they came from. They begin to accept and enjoy where they are.

During the middle two stages in particular they often feel quite depressed. You might consider whether this has anything to say to you during your transition.

There may well be other changes you wish to explore.

Becoming more aware of what is happening within you and others is likely to enable you to come to terms with your feelings, and to take some control over your life. As the changes you are experiencing can have a positive or negative effect on you depending on your response, it could also be useful to ask yourself:

- What is involved in responding creatively rather than critically? How can I help myself to do so? What help do I need from others around me, and from God?

- What are the theological or spiritual implications of these effects on me? What is God asking or expecting of me? How do I feel about this? How honest am I being in my response to God?

- What do I hope to learn from the process of transition? How can I help myself to do so? Would it be helpful to keep a transition diary, to journal, talk or write to a friend?

ii. Mindfulness[2]

The danger in times of transition is to be either so caught up in thinking about all you are leaving behind and making a tidy exit, or so pre-occupied by planning the future, that the present moment and what you are experiencing *now* is ignored. It is worth pausing in order to be in touch with what is going on in your life, what is happening to you, and how you are experiencing this in-between time. Mindfulness is an age-old Christian concept as well as a traditional Buddhist practice. It requires us to hold ourselves in stillness and be aware of this moment in which we are alive, the only moment we have. It asks us to be conscious of what is happening to our bodies and within us, to savour this moment of life which is unlike any other and will never come again. "This moment is really all we have to work with. . . . In every moment we find ourselves at the crossroads of here and now." Kabat-Zinn talks about pausing long enough to let the present moment sink in. "Instead, we fall into a robot-like way of seeing and thinking and doing. In those moments, we break contact with what is deepest in ourselves and affords us perhaps our greatest opportunities for creativity, learning and growing."[3]

Give yourself a little extra 'time out' to walk round the garden or park or just sit. This is a time in which we are "able to see things as they actually are and respond with the full range of our emotional capacity and wisdom." [4] This is not a luxury, we owe it to ourselves and to God to be conscious of who and how and where we are, far more often than most of us normally do.

It can help to find a phrase which appeals to you; one that Kabat-Zinn recommends is 'This is it.' [5] Or pause over some action such as walking upstairs, or before a particular task, or have an object on your desk or windowsill or in your pocket, an object which serves as a reminder of the value of *now*. You may find awareness moments in those times of waiting at a bus stop or for the arrival of a friend.

iii. Dealing with feelings[6]

Times of transition affect us deeply and all sorts of feelings and thoughts can surface unbidden and take us by surprise. We become more emotionally volatile than usual. Having strong feelings is a factor in the situation rather than a fault. They can, of course, be used constructively or destructively and it is only in how we use them that the question of morality arises. Feelings are indicators of need: for example, fear of the future points to the need for security and acceptance; will there be a place for me? Will I be able to cope? Below are four steps in managing emotions.

Step 1: Noticing your feelings. Become aware of how you feel, get in touch with your feelings, notice where they come from. Allow your hopes and fears to surface.

Step 2: Naming your feelings. Honestly acknowledge how you feel to yourself.

Step 3: Owning your feelings. Tell yourself you, not others, are responsible for your feelings, they are part of you, and it is all right to feel the way you do. Do not blame others for your feelings: others may have provoked you or triggered off your feelings, but you are responsible for them.

Step 4: Responding. Feelings can generate a lot of energy and motivation. You are responsible for using the energy, and how you use it may have a positive or a negative effect on you and on others in the situation. Some of the ideas which follow may be helpful.

Take time to express your feelings: you may do this alone by journalling[7] or with a trusted friend who will help you come to terms with them. One of the worst things we can do is to repress our feelings: they often fester out of sight and break out unexpectedly with the consequent danger of overwhelming us.

Analyse the reasons behind your feelings. This may help you come to terms with them. Try to trace the source of your feelings. They may be because:

– in the past you faced a similar situation, which you may or my not remember, and you are reliving old emotions which you may have been unable to deal with at the time, perhaps because you were too young or inexperienced;

– you are going into the unknown, in which case, you might tell yourself that the fear beforehand can be worse than the actuality. Try to wait until the unknown becomes the known and then assess things, or you might work out what you will do if your worst fears are realised;

– you know something of the people and situation to which you are going and foresee specific difficulties. Try to work out how you might pre-empt or deal with them. Perhaps you can pick up a few hints from having dealt successfully with such problems in the past or from having failed to do so. Failures are a great source of learning.

Build up your self-confidence by reflecting on past occasions when you have felt like this about the future. Were your fears justified? If so, how did you manage? Remind yourself that since then you have more experience and have developed in various ways. What helped you then which might help you now?

Try to move from fear of the future to hope and expectation by reflecting on the good things in the new situation, the opportunities and possibilities it opens up for you.

Ask yourself, what are the things I must avoid in order to prevent exacerbating my negative feelings or using them destructively? Ask yourself if your feelings are indicating that some change is necessary in the way you relate to people, how you see and treat others. If so, what do you want to do about it? I use the word 'want' advisedly because, in my experience, it is only when I really desire to make an inner attitudinal change that I have sufficient motivation to do so.

2. REFLECTING ON AND CONCLUDING THE PAST

The past can never be completely rounded off and finished with. It lives on in our memories, habits, attitudes and feelings – in fact in us as whole people. Although it remains a constant and rich resource from which we draw, at times it can come up like a rake handle and hit us unexpectedly. When in transition, we are particularly vulnerable to aspects of our past coming to the surface and demanding to be dealt with. It can be beneficial to do some reflecting on the more immediate past, in order to make the most of our experience and try this time to leave behind fewer frayed edges or unfinished business and therefore fewer and lighter rake handles to take us off balance in the future.

Moving house is one of the most stressful experiences we can have. It is therefore worth considering, as part of your personal preparation, what you are moving from and to, (cf. Figure 10.2). Doing so is likely to have positive effects on you and on others. Even if you are still physically in A the very fact that you are planning to move means that psychologically and emotionally you are on a path – which may feel like balancing on a tight-rope – between A and B.

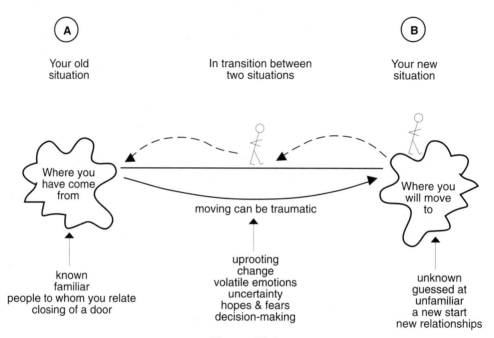

Figure 10.2
Walking the tight-rope of change

In reflecting on the past there are various aspects which can or need to be taken into account. What can you learn from it? What do you need to let go of? How can you celebrate it? These questions can be asked in relation to your immediate past or to several phases in your life and to different areas such as community life or ministry. All these aspects are complexly interwoven. In what follows it is as though I am inviting you to look into a room from different windows. The window you choose to gaze through will reveal much you may have already seen through another, but this time you see it from a different angle or in clearer focus. Each time you reconsider the past or reminisce you are making more sense of it for yourself, re-shaping or re-modelling it in some way. Even in looking through the same window you may see it differently, understand it better or re-interpret it. I have therefore differentiated between:

Learning from experience
Letting go
Celebrating the past
Withdrawing from your ministry
Preparing those with whom you have worked for your withdrawal

i. Learning from experience

Consciously learning from an experience is something which may profitably be done at any time. Moments of transition are natural breaks in the flow of one's life and make particularly good times for reviewing the past.

From the moment we first saw the light of day – some researchers say since conception – we have been learning. It is natural, habitual and in part unconscious. As children we learnt to cope with life by doing certain things which brought us rewards and by avoiding or suppressing things which had painful consequences. We all learn differently and various learning modes are appropriate or not according to circumstances: formal or informal learning, customary or crisis learning, systematic or ad hoc, learning alone, with another or in a group or crowd. We can concentrate in order to learn or we may be taken by surprise, the 'Aha-learning' which comes unbidden and unexpected.

Whatever is our preferred mode of learning, we all have a rich resource of potential insights stored away in our past experience. When older people reminisce, they are sorting out and making sense of their past lives: clearing things up so that they understand them and are at peace with them is one way of acquiring wisdom.

There are innumerable methods of learning from the experience of life. In no way is the list which follows comprehensive. Choose the way which appeals to you and use or adapt it. Maybe these ideas will spark you off to think of something which suits you better. I use the word 'appeal' because I hope this will be an interesting and enjoyable exercise in which you mine deep insights you never knew you had. Such exercises can be done privately or talked over with a friend or confidante.

· Reflecting on your previous transitions

You can call on past experiences of making transitions from your entry into the world, which is an unconscious memory, to transitions you do remember (cf. p.76). Think back to such times as moving house, changing schools, leaving home, changing jobs, joining the congregation, or leaving the noviciate. This is unlikely to be your first move as an adult. It may, however, be the first one which you make a conscious decision to think about and learn from. Go over one or more of these experiences, relive the departure and entry points. How were they for you? What were your feelings? Can you discern any pattern in them? What can you learn about yourself and the way you reacted to these events? How will any such insights help you in your present transition? What do you need to do? What to avoid?

· **Reflecting on phases of your life**

This may be done informally as you walk or garden or you may prefer to write the story of each key period of your life. Ernest Neal, a community worker from Jamaica, spent his working life in several different jobs and countries. When he knew he had a limited time to live, he wrote a slim book in which, having described each period, he ended with "what I learnt from. . .".[8]

In these he wrote some telling points, for instance:

- Village people participated in community projects as much for the attention received as for the value of the project.

- I learned that personal acceptance had to be achieved before technical assistance was acceptable.

- The function of a teacher is to teach and not fail students.

- Effective dialogue between different racial, economic and cultural groups is enhanced by beginning discussion on common problems.

You may want to focus specifically on the immediate past or on various periods of your life. You will find that articulating your learning from any stage in life makes it more available for use in the future.Whether you tell yourself your story in your head or on paper, it could be valuable to jot down what you learn from looking back.

· **Reflecting on past ups and downs**

De Mello calls these the joyful and sorrowful mysteries of one's life.[9] Through reliving some of these experiences we are likely to get insights into what we can learn from them to take with us into the future. It is particularly valuable to do this with aspects of our life which we feel we did not handle well or where we made mistakes and felt a failure. We often say things like:

"I'll never do that again"
"Next time I'll make sure that. . . ."
"That's something worth remembering"
"That changed my approach to people/work/things"

Learning from previous experiences, particularly the 'bad' experiences, we are likely to be able to come to terms with them. Looking back on your life what are the main things you:
- want to develop and build on?
- want to avoid?
- want to keep in mind?[10]

· Journalling

Progoff has a more stringent method of working on one's past and you may consider attending a Journal Workshop or reading his book.[11] The steps below are based on Progoff. They can best be done in a quiet spot so you can reconnect with the thread of your life.

> *Identify the key stepping stones in your life.* Gently think over your life, let things come to mind. There is no need to strain or search. After a while jot down a list of up to ten.

> *Explore each stepping stone period*, a process which may take several days or even weeks. Take them one at a time, not necessarily chronologically and describe them "It was a time when. . . ." What were your attitudes and feelings at this time? What were your beliefs, aims, hopes and fears? What did you achieve? Did you encounter failure, disappointment, difficulty?

> *Read over and reflect on what you have written.* What now strikes you as an important learning point or insight which you wish to take with you into the future? What have you learnt about coping with life, making relationships, working with people, or about anything else? What do you wish to avoid in future?

· Telling your story

When we tell our own story we do it in a way which makes sense of our experience, saying it as we see it at a particular moment in time. We often tell and retell past sequences of events until they are in a shape and form with which we are happy, so that we can live with our past. As we do this, we change our perceptions of events, and our feelings and attitudes alter – so the story comes out differently. This is a way of coming to terms with the past and of learning from it. You may like to talk your story onto a tape giving yourself an hour to cover its major aspects or taking time over each 'chapter'. Listen to what you have recorded, putting it on 'pause' to write down what strikes you as you go along. Perhaps you now want to alter it, as fresh thoughts come or you see things differently. What do you see now which you did not see at the time? Do you now construe things differently? At the end, read over your reflections and see what other insights occur to you. What is it telling you about yourself? Remember your story continues: you are in the middle of it. What do you want to take forward?

· Looking back at your cycles of life

Many aspects of our lives follow a cyclical pattern: we respond in similar ways to similar experiences. At times it can be necessary or advisable to endeavour to break the pattern. Looking back, try to recognise any recurring patterns of events and responses in your life. Ask yourself: what can I learn about myself from this? What is it telling me? Is my response helpful or dysfunctional? Do I want to make a change or try a new way of reacting? How else might I have reacted? What can I learn for the future?

· Drawing your lifeline

This exercise may be done alone but is more often done in a group. It is described on p. 215. If members of your new community also do it, it would have the added value of helping you to get to know each other at a deeper level.

ii. Letting go

Life is a journey and we are only too liable to increase our baggage as we travel. Times of transition provide an opportunity to make a fresh start, to leave behind certain things, or relinquish old habits, and let go of worries or pre-occupations. This is easier said than done and it can never be fully achieved: we always take ourselves with us. But in so far as exterior change affects us internally and vice versa, now is a time to encourage your personal growth in the way in which you want. Think of yourself as a vine and become the vine dresser who prepares it for the coming season.

**Table 10.1
An exercise in letting go**

Step 1: Do a private brainstorm: jot down everything you will be leaving behind – people, things, routines, experiences, etc.

Step 2: Read through what you have written and mark those things you are pleased to leave behind, and those you will miss.

Step 3: Mark those things you need to do something about, to reflect on, to say something about, to pass on to someone, etc.

Step 4: Differentiate between (a) things you will have to let go of and (b) things or relationships that must be maintained, but in a new way. You may find there are things on your list you have a choice about: customs or habits. If so, decide whether or not you will let go of them – or make a determined effort to do so.

Step 5: Now comes the hard part! Ask yourself: how am I going to let go of those things I must let go of and those I want to let go of? Is there anything I can do about those I will miss (Step 2)?

Step 6: Ask yourself: how am I going to maintain those things I will be taking with me?

Finally: Decide how and when you will review your decisions.

The exercise in Table 10.1 focusses on the personal factors which make up one's inner life. Aspects of your work situation are considered below. As in so many of these suggested reflections, this one may be done alone or in a group. Your departure may even be an opportunity to do this with some or all of those in the community you are leaving. It can be a useful exercise at other times. It may help you to take time over it or to do it quickly.

iii. Celebrating the past

To celebrate the past is to put into a festive form much of what has been touched on already: what you have learned and gained from your experience, the relationships you have made, the happy times and also the struggles and difficult times, in short all the richness that has gone into making you who you now are. There is much for which to thank God.

You may prefer to celebrate alone on a retreat or to do it in company with those whom you are leaving behind, or both. If it is done communally it can be valuable and heartening for you to name some of the riches from the past which you particularly value and wish to take forward with you into the future in some way. Others in the community, whose future will also be different without you, may like to do the same.

iv. Preparing to leave your ministry

This section is primarily for those for whom the move to a new community entails leaving behind some paid employment or voluntary work in which they have exercised responsibility. It could be adapted to include areas of responsibility in the community. Although leaving a work situation is a fairly common occurrence in people's lives, in my experience there is so much else to think about that some important aspects more often than not are neglected. What I have tried to do below is to span these and suggest various ways in which to work at them. I draw heavily on the work George Lovell and I did when people came to Avec to work at the transition they were about to make.[12]

· Reviewing the situation

This entails spending some time clarifying the situation and what you feel about it. Make a quiet uninterrupted space for yourself to review your time in the job, its ups and downs, what you have achieved and where you feel you may have been less than successful, the relationships you formed with various people or groups which were life enhancing – and those which were problematic.

The following questions may help you to take stock of this period of your ministry before you move to a new one:

How do I feel about leaving? sorry? glad? or . . . ?

What have I learnt in this job about:

– myself: for instance, my way of responding to and tackling situations, crises, problems, boring and routine tasks?

– relationships, especially the deeper mutually satisfying sort? What have I learnt to avoid? Are there particular types of people with whom I find it difficult to relate? How do I customarily cope: do I write them off, ignore and avoid them, or maintain a friendly exterior? What do I usually do after a row or upset with someone: avoid or ignore them or try to mend the fences?

– the actual work I have been engaged in: is it something which feels right for me to be doing or have I been a square peg in a round hole? What skills have I developed? How competent and confident do I now feel in comparison with when I first started?

· **Rounding off 'unfinished business'**

Ask yourself what still remains to be done? The immediate response may be in terms of actual tasks which are not completed, projects you started up and hope will continue. It may also be useful to include those things about which you are disappointed, events that went off at half-cock, areas of work or relationships about which you still have a pang or a niggle, and outright failures. Such things are a gold-mine for learning and insights but, as with all forms of mining, they need time, energy and hard work.

I remember an Anglican priest on an Avec course who told us about an incident in his past life. He had been chaplain in a psychiatric prison and after attempting to humanise the system he was severely reprimanded by the prison governor: "Padré, you have your area of work and I have mine, if you want to repaint the chapel walls I will not interfere. In future, you will not interfere with the discipline and running of this institution. Good day." He felt a failure and he knew he had made the difficult situation in which he had to work, even worse. That afternoon, years later, we spent a couple of hours going over the story, bit by bit, identifying:

– those things he did or said which contributed to the unsatisfactory result.
– those things which were going for him in the situation and which he could well have built on.

Then we replayed the incident in the light of what we had learned and we felt, at the end, that there was a good chance that, if he had done it in this way, he would have had some measure of success. Finally, we all pondered in silence, and then produced an amazing list of things we had learnt from this case. Afterwards the man gave a great sigh of relief and said, "Now I see what I could have done. This has been niggling me for fifteen years. After today I can put it behind me." This case study method was developed in Avec, based on the work of Batten. It is described in detail in books by Batten, Lovell and myself.[13] It can be done alone or with a group. The latter may be painful and you have to be determined not to be defensive, but it can be far more rewarding: a group of people are likely to have so many more insights into a situation than one person. The various steps in working through a case are described on p. 169.

v. Preparing those with whom you have worked for your withdrawal

What you do by way of preparing people for your departure and the advent of your successor or for carrying on without you, can have a critical effect on the on-going work.

· **Breaking the news**

How you break the news that you will be leaving can have a positive or negative effect on those with whom you work and the work itself. It greatly helps if you tell them about your departure well beforehand, so they not only have time to come to terms with any feelings they have, but are able to make any necessary preparations to bid you farewell, to ensure the work continues, and to welcome your successor, if you have one.

· Dealing with their feelings

In this section I am thinking of the most difficult case: that your departure is viewed with great sadness, distress or even anger. It is relatively easy to adapt the ideas below as appropriate.

You may well have picked up some of the feelings being experienced by the people with whom you have been working. I find it helpful, as a general rule, to try to stand in the shoes of other people in order to empathise with what they are going through, before I make any move towards them. I list below some of the feelings which may be around and suggest possible ways of helping people to come to terms with them.

Loss. Your departure may lead to a feeling of bereavement among people which is often accompanied by anger.[14] This may be directed at you or at your congregation. It may be that your departure comes at a time when several other things are happening in people's lives, and thus adds to their feeling of insecurity. It may be difficult to help them, especially if your own feelings are volatile. However, it is usually supportive to accept their feelings, even their anger, allowing them to express themselves, by listening to them non-judgementally and non-defensively. It could also be useful to help them through the various stages of managing their emotions outlined on p. 140.

Desertion. People may well feel let down: you may have been heart and soul in some project with them and suddenly you are withdrawing and leaving them to it. Consider taking the action below.

> Name the feeling openly and suggest that "We talk about it together, because if I were in your shoes I could very well feel that I was being badly let down. . .".

> Empathise with them by talking about your own feelings of 'sadness' at leaving the work: how difficult you are finding it to cut yourself off from all you have been involved in and found enjoyable and stimulating. (In doing this you need to keep your purpose in mind to help those you are leaving come to terms with your departure. You must avoid giving the impression that you are preoccupied with your own grief.)

> Suggest you need to support each other in your thoughts and prayers.

> Ask them at some future date to let you know how things are going.

You may well think of other helpful responses. Probably the most important thing is that people recognise and talk openly about how they feel: this is half the battle when trying to come to terms with feelings.

Inadequacy. However much you have promoted participation, people know that they will be unable to bring your unique contribution to the work and that, in this sense, the likelihood is that it will be the poorer and they will be the poorer without you. However, your absence could challenge their ingenuity and call forth abilities they never knew they had. Some of the ways suggested below may help encourage them and build up their self-confidence.

Go over the various tasks which you have performed and see how they will pick these up. 'Tasks' can include anything from the welcoming smile to locking up.

Get members to enumerate the gifts and abilities of those remaining. This could be done in the context of a prayer service: often people wait until a person is about to leave them, but more often until someone has died, before they articulate all they have been and have given to others. Obituaries come too late to help the person concerned! You might ask people to spend time now writing what they would like to put in the obituary of one or more of the others.

Provide a lot of photos, pictures or objects from which individuals choose one to give to each of the others to represent what that person has been for them. This may or may not be accompanied by words.

Talk to individuals informally about what they are already contributing and try to boost their self-esteem and their appreciation of others in the group.

If there is a skill which will be needed once you have gone and which is clearly not in the group, try to think how someone with that skill might be recruited on a long- or short-term basis. Perhaps a member of the group could develop the skill. Remind them that your successor will also bring new skills and abilities to bear on the situation.

Lead a guided meditation emphasising how each been given gifts by God from the start of their life, helped to develop those gifts through experience, and have arrived in the present situation through the God'sprovidence. God values what they have and knows what opportunities they will have, through which to grow to be the person God wants them to become. (cf. p. 206 for hints on leading a meditation.)

Negativity towards your successor. It is natural to compare the person who takes over a job with their predecessor. At this stage such comparisons may be based on knowledge of your successor, or surmises from vague hints or on imaginary fears. Nevertheless, negative feelings can be very real and if allowed to remain can have a bad effect on the relationship. A sensitive person picks up feelings of this kind. In fact being near a person who has negative feelings about us is probably something we are all sensitive to and affected by, whether we are conscious of it or not. People find different ways of coming to terms with negative feelings. The ideas below may enable you to suggest how people could do so as steps in a group process, or they could be adapted for private use.

Step 1: Accept your feelings. Feelings arise in us and we need to accept and own them if we are to deal with them in a positive way. We are not to blame for feeling negative, but we are responsible for what we do about it. To exacerbate the feeling, as said above, can harm another person or the situation; to disown or repress it can harm ourselves and it may show itself in various ways or burst out unexpectedly.

Step 2: Allow people to talk about how they feel. It may be that an individual has a conversation with you, but where negative feelings are around in a group, it can be helpful to discuss them openly together. In this case, it is important that people understand and agree to the reason for the discussion: to help them come to terms with their feelings so that they are able to give a genuine welcome to your successor.

Step 3: Help people to think about and explore their feelings by asking questions such as: why do you think you feel like this? Can you remember feeling like this before in your life? When can you first remember feeling like this about someone? What do you usually do when you feel like this? What happened? Were your fears borne out?

Step 4: Suggest people stand in the shoes of your successor and picture how she is feeling about starting a new job in a new place. Give people time to quieten or centre themselves with closed eyes. (cf. p. 206 for hints on leading such a guided meditation).

(a) Slowly talk them through the situation of being your successor. (You are leaving work in which you have been engaged, saying goodbye to it and to people and places you are familiar with. How do you feel about it? As you look ahead to your new job, what are your hopes and fears? When you think about the people you will be working with, how do you feel? What do you hope for from them? What would you find difficult to cope with?)

(b) When the moment is right, ask people to slowly come back into being themselves, but keep their eyes closed. Tell them "You are meeting my successor for the first time. There are just the two of you. What would you want to say to her, now you know how she might be feeling?"

(c) Ask them to open their eyes when they feel they are ready. Without putting pressure on people, have a discussion about the experience or how they now feel.

This can be a very powerful exercise in changing attitudes.

· **Preparing for your successor**

The purpose of preparing for your successor is several fold: that the work continues in good shape, that the people with whom you have been working experience a smooth transition and make the most of the change-over, and that your successor gets as good and helpful a reception and start as possible.

Reviewing and handing over the work. This is probably the easiest part. Reviewing with the people and colleagues concerned would achieve three further results: you would hear how other people view and assess your ministry, together you would build up an agreed picture of the current situation, and others who are to continue in the work would most probably gain new insights as they review the past. It may also be that people see aspects of the work for which they could take more responsibility.

A review of this sort with others can be useful in giving you feedback which, although some of it could be painful, could prove invaluable as you move forward to the next stage of your ministry.

Various methods of reviewing work are suggested in Chapter Fourteen. Evaluating historical developments, set out on p. 185, may well be appropriate so people can picture the flow of change and development over a period of time. Step 3: "Looking to the future" may be more appropriately renamed "Implications for us now" with questions such as:

What are the immediate implications:
– for the future of the work?
– for handing over to a new person?
– for what we need to say about any aspect of the work or alert the new person to?

Welcoming your successor. How those concerned welcome your successor is very much up to them and, although this is probably something best left to them to think about on their own, you may feel it right to raise the question with them. Situations vary so enormously: some call for a welcoming prayer service and celebratory meal, others for no more than introducing the newcomer to the key people and groups, explaining about the work in progress, showing her round, and offering what help and support is appropriate.

· **Withdrawing when you have no successor**

It may be, of course, that you have no successor, there are no funds to employ someone, the job is coming to an end, or other ways of continuing the work have been decided upon. In this case, in addition to many of the ideas already mentioned, the following exercise could help to ensure that the work continues after your withdrawal.

Personal reflection. Ask yourself the following questions below; others may well occur to you.

> *About the work:* What needs doing? What is my specific contribution? What is likely not to be done when I am no longer around? Is there some work which is best not carried on once I have left?

What is of key importance which I feel must be continued? What alternative ways are there of doing some of these tasks? What about job-sharing?

Are such things as purpose, policy, underlying principles and assumptions clear? Are they stated anywhere? Do they need checking?

About the people and the work. What dangers do I foresee? Have people the necessary skills, abilities and gifts to carry on the work? What is missing? Could someone be trained or recruited to help?

Are people sufficiently committed to carrying on? Have they enough self-confidence and trust in their corporate strength and experience to do so? Are they likely to feel uneasy or happy when expected to shoulder responsibility?

Is there any danger of conflict arising? Are there personality difficulties which are likely to come to the fore when I have left? Who is likely to take a lead?

Help the group prepare to go it alone. The above reflection will have alerted you to much of the ground to be covered as you help people think ahead and decide how they will organise themselves when you have left. It could be useful to consider the following:

Job-sharing. For a variety of reasons people often baulk at taking over a job from someone, but would be prepared to do part of it. Suggest dividing up the different facets of the work between two or more people. This could be a sensitive and difficult area but an open discussion about how people will organise themselves and who will take a lead in what area would probably be more easily done with your help, than on their own. List any tasks or overall functions which need to be taken on. This could include the leadership functions of having an overview of the work; being a central person to whom people can refer when difficulties arise or absentees have to be replaced; convening meetings for planning and problem solving or reviewing; and keeping a pastoral eye on the well-being of individuals. People may well think of others. Taking on these responsibilities could be done by one person or a small group or committee. It may be that the leadership functions outlined on pages 96-9 are appropriate.

Recruiting. Help may be recruited in a variety of ways:

– have an 'open meeting' at which the function and activities of the group are explained and displayed.

– issue an open invitation through the organisation's outlet (write in newsletters or magazines or speak about it at a function or gathering) or through a local press advertisement for community groups.

– list all the groups and agencies and people who might be approached. Ask the group to brainstorm their ideas. Brainstorming works best if certain 'rules' are adhered to (cf. p. 203).

– using registers and lists, review by name everyone members can think of in the locality to decide who to invite to the group.[15]

Training. People may be prepared to do a specific task if they are given an adequate opportunity to learn about it and develop their skills. This may be something you are able to do for a period before you leave, or there may be someone else locally who would induct them, or a course on which they could go.

Facing problems. A useful question to get people discussing is "What will you do when problems arise, as they inevitably will?" The problem-solving sequence on p. 194 may be helpful, but ideas and commitment are also necessary. For example, "We will work through problems together", "We will not ignore them until they grow and we are landed with an explosive situation", "We will always ask the question 'any problems?' at our regular meetings", and so on.

Reviewing again. Suggest setting a time for a future review of how things are going. You may want to leave them with some ideas as to how to set about it or suggest where these could be found when needed (cf. p. 185). An outside facilitator could be useful to help them review.

3. LOOKING TOWARDS THE FUTURE

There are a number of intangible aspects to moving out of one situation and into another, not all of which call for specific action. However, being sensitive to them and reflecting on what could be going on beneath the surface, is likely to help make a smooth entry for yourself and others as you move forward. This section is about the internal and external personal and communal preparation necessary immediately prior to moving in.

i. Anchorholds

Everyone responds to change. We have an inbuilt resistance which serves us well in so far as it guards us against uncritically embracing everything new, and does us a disservice if it dominates to such an extent that we are always closed to different ideas and ways of doing things. However we personally react to change we need anchorholds. The function of an anchor is to tether a ship to the ocean bed, to stabilise it so that it is not driven before the wind onto rocks or lost at sea. Whether we are aware of it or not, we probably all use such anchors when we are faced with a major change whether it be a bereavement, moving house or a change of ministry. Such anchors are those things to which we return over and over again. They may be spiritual, emotional, physical or mental.[16] Most probably they are a combination of all four, so

I make no attempt to categorise them. I list a few examples from my own experience which I, or others I know, have found helpful.

Relationships with family or friends: maintaining these by such things as visits, phone calls, letters, photos, pictures. Friends may be living or dead, saints and sinners!

Routine: this may include taking the dog for a walk, one's method and time of prayer, the eucharist, a daily walk, a siesta, a hobby. . . .

Exercise: swimming, walking, Tai chi, gardening, yoga. . . .

The written word: a book, poem, passage, quotation, saying. . . .

Objects: a picture, crucifix, prayer book, paperweight, icon, photograph, fossil, crystal. . . .

In reflecting on what the anchorholds are in your life, remember you are a physical as well as a spiritual being, in fact, the spiritual in us is often stirred into life through some material object or activity. Ask yourself: what will keep me in touch with who I am when I move into a new place with new people among whom it will take time for me to feel at home? What will give me security when so much of my life is shifting around me? What is it that will ground me, comfort me, and hold me when so much is new and strange?

ii. A change of culture

Cultural shock has already been mentioned (cf. p. 138). Missionaries often talk about being better able to cope with it when they went to a foreign land because they were expecting it, than on their return home. Home had changed in the interim, and they experienced a culture shock all the more painful for being unexpected. The difficulty returning missionaries face in trying to 'read' a culture they think they know, but do not, can be akin to your experience of moving to a new area of the country, or moving from a house in a suburb to one on a council estate. Cultures differ in overt and subtle ways in such things as terminology, customs, perceptions, expectations and food.

Unconsciously our whole being has learnt to fit in and feel at home where we came from. Whether we liked it or not, we knew what was expected of us and responded unthinkingly: in many ways, we were largely on automatic pilot. Being in a new situation can therefore be a jolt to the system and without realising it we expend energy in learning new ways, becoming aware of new verbal and non-verbal signals.[17] In addition, there is a danger of reacting unfavourably to new ways and patterns simply because we are unused to them.

iii. Guide posts

I have found that it is when many changes occur simultaneously in my life, that I experience symptoms of stress. Carolyn Potucek, who studied the effects on missionaries returning to their country of origin, has found several ways in which they could help themselves.[18] Those below are particularly apposite in moving to a new community.

· Create a structure in your life
This puts some order into the chaos created by change and helps you to feel more in control. It could be a daily , weekly or monthly structure: whatever it is you will find it a stabilising influence in the necessary flux. Remember it is provisional and can be changed or discarded as you need. Avoid it becoming inflexible or a burden.

· Form relationships
Close friendships may have been disrupted, yet, for our well-being, we all need people with whom we can talk openly about ourselves. "Regular communication of inner thoughts with at least one person is a necessity in maintaining mental health."[19] Deep relationships of this kind may take time to develop in the new situation, and until they do, you will need to rely on a friend or a support group already in place, both of which are still available by letter or phone if too distant for face to face meetings.

· Develop hardiness
This refers not only to physical hardiness maintained through regular exercise, a balanced diet, and adequate rest and sleep, but inner hardiness which enables you to view life creatively with humour, imagination and a certain playfulness. "Persons who exhibit hardiness are committed to the activities and individuals in their lives, they have a share of control over events; and they view changes as challenges."[20]

· Cognition and coping
The key to coping with a situation and not becoming over-stressed by it is the way we see it. Our perceptions, the way we interpret life and events, informs the way we cope or do not cope. Potucek's advice is for people to reflect on their view of things, their attitudes and feelings, and to focus on what is energising, motivating and enabling, recalling past successes.

· Self-efficacy
By this concept Potucek is talking about expecting to be able to do what is required to bring about some outcome. It is about having positive expectations, self-confidence and determination which persist in the face of demanding and difficult situations.

iv. Reconsidering your apostolic vocation

By 'apostolic vocation' I am referring to that inner urge or commitment that you have, or which burns within you, to work for a particular cause or in an area of need. It may be something that has grown over the years as a result of training and experience, or something which comes at a stage in mid-life or later, after being exposed to certain people or circumstances. It is that strong inner call to commit your personal resources to a particular area or work. For many people, I believe this call develops as a result of the process of being missioned to a task or place, but for others it appears in a flash of insight, or again as an increasingly persistent inner voice, almost akin to divine nagging.

In whatever way we have experienced this in life, there may well come a stage, with retirement or with a change of personal or external circumstances, of which a move to a new community may be one, when it is useful to reflect on and question this inner call. A period of transition provides a God-given opportunity to give yourself time and space to reconsider your apostolic vocation and check if God is still calling you along the same path or asking something different from you. Possible ways of approaching this are suggested below.

· **Explore your motivating beliefs**

Beliefs have been discussed on p. 68. The inner convictions that move you deeply and which are particularly meaningful to you can change or vary in intensity at different periods in your life. They inform your activity. At one extreme we have seen them at work in people like Oscar Romero, Martin Luther King, and in his namesake Luther, who is reputed to have said "For this I stand, I can do no other."[21] While most of us feel we are not called to such heights, we are equally as loved and important in the eyes of God, and within each of us is that particular call at every stage in our lives to believe strongly enough about something to commit ourselves to it. We are each called to put our hands to some apostolic plough whatever our age, circumstances, ability, health or condition.

Ask yourself questions such as:

- What are the real springs of my motivation?

- Are there things that I believe in so strongly that I am driven to take action?

- Do they still call to me, demand things of me in the same way?

- Are they spent forces in my life? If so, what is it that I now believe and about which I feel strongly? Where am I to put my thrust in this next stage of life and ministry?

- What are my beliefs saying to me about my basic purpose in life (cf. p. 71 for a discussion about purposes).

· **Try an ignatian retreat**

Whether this is a full thirty-day retreat or a far shorter one, Ignatian-guided retreats follow a path of reflection and prayer which lead you to examine and explore the inner direction of your life with a view to hearing what it is *now* to which God is calling you. Other types of retreat may well fulfil the same purpose for you.

· **Finding your providential way**[22]

The chart in Figure 10.3 lists some questions and gives some suggestions for a personal discernment process.

'Finding My Providential Way'

What are the key factors to take account of when making 'big' decisions?

others — do things for me / decide for me

God — makes some decisions for me (that I exist)

some key life/death decisions I have to make for myself

When I have a decision I alone can make, people tend to leave me to it or to push me into it. A third way to help is to stay 'with' the person, to raise unloaded, searching questions, to help them think openly and critically about the alternatives and their effects i.e. work *with* them (non-directive approach).

Factors to do with Time
Do I want to make a short term or long term decision? Do I usually live moment by moment or plan in stewardship of time?
How soon must I/should I decide?
Would it help to make a time/date by which I'll decide?
Take time, don't rush.

Factors to do with Discipleship/vocation
What is my vocation in life?
What do I feel called to do?
What are my motivating beliefs?
Which do I feel most strongly about now?
How committed am I to - my profession?
- ......?
- ......?

Factors to do with other people/community
How is my community going to feel? be affected?
Would it have negative effects on them, their health? or our relationship?
How much weight should I/do I give these factors?
What advice would my community/people who know me well give?

Factors to do with me

Qualifications, talents, abilities, experience
What am I qualified/able to do?
What can I do well/best?
Where is this relevant and needed? and possible?

Preferences, interests, commitment
Where is my heart?
What do I want to do, enjoy doing?
What am I interested in?
What do I get some deep satisfaction in doing?
What am I committed to? who...?

Practicalities, security, profession aspects
What financial remuneration, security do I need?
What other security? What about my health?
Do I need further training, first or after?
What effect on my professional life?

Effect on me
What effect would doing X or Y or Z have on me?
What do I think and feel about it?
What should I do about it?
What weight should I give to these effects?
To what am I saying No?
What doors closing? temporarily/permanently?
What might I feel like afterwards?
Is there a pattern or thread running through my life?

Factors to do with opportunities, needs
What is needed in the world, 3rd world, society in UK, locally etc.?
What opportunities do I see?
What possible openings are there?
Who could help me find out?
What organisations might help?
What do I feel strongly about or attracted to?
What motivates me?
Careers advice from anyone?

HINTS on ways of deciding

• Look at several alternatives
  - pros and cons
  - effects of choosing each one
  - 'make' the decision and live with it for a day or week and see how it feels i.e. 'trial decisions'.
  - work your way through each decision - what would it actually entail and mean?
  - pursue to a point where decision comes clear - e.g. go for an interview for job/place.

• Think about it, feel your way through it, pray about it.

• Write things down, work it out on paper. Have a dialogue with the opportunity or decision you are seriously considering

• Look at ways you made past decision and effects of them. Will this decision be irreversible or not?

• Talk things over with people (ask them to help you think and not push or pressurise you).

• Consult all who might be affected. Be open to and critical of what is said.

• Keep hopeful - God will show the way if you work at it.

• Periodically sit in God's presence with the thoughts you have jotted down. Read them over quietly. Do not think about them but gently allow thoughts and feelings to surface should they do so.

**Figure 10.3
Finding my providential way**

Small Communities in Religious Life

REFERENCES AND NOTES

1. Courses for returning missionaries were organised annually from 1976-1994 under the auspices of Avec (see ref. 3, p. 120) and the Methodist Church Overseas Division. George Lovell designed the first courses and for many years we worked together on them.
2. I write intentionally about 'the practice of the present moment' from the Buddhist perspective because I have found that learning about this old practice in a new way has made a fresh impact on me. Undoubtedly many followers of the Buddha have developed this practice to a remarkable degree, as it attested by William Johnston SJ in his epilogue to *Be Still and Know: Meditation for Peacemakers* by Thich Nhat Hanh, p25 (Pax Christi & The Fellowship of Reconciliation 1987. ISBN 0 9506 7575 X). Another excellent book is *Mindfulness Meditation for Everyday Life* by Jon Kabat-Zinn (ref. 17, p. 93).
3. Kabat-Zinn, ibid. p xiii.
4. Ibid. p119.
5. Ibid. pp 16 & 37.
6. I am indebted to the Reverend Gerard T Burke for a helpful conversation on this subject.
7. Progoff, Ira: After studying with Carl Justav Jung, he developed journalling as 'a tool for life'. This is described in *At a Journal Workshop* and *Process Meditation* (Dialogue House Library NY, 1975. ISBN 0 87941 006 x).
8. Neal, Ernest: *Hope for the Wretched* (Agency for International Development 1972) pp 53, 40, 8 and 9. Sadly this book is out of print.
9. de Mello, Anthony: *Sadhana a Way to God* (Image Books, Doubleday & Co Ltd. ISBN 0 385 19614 8) pp.71-75.
10. These questions come from work done by George Lovell. Ways of coping with failure are described in *Meetings that Work,* op. cit. (ref. 2, p. 59), pp 28-30. See also *Analysis & Design*, op. cit. (ref. 5, p. 38) for a detailed account of a seminar in Liverpool on the subject, pp. 51f.
11. Op. cit. (ref. 7 above). Journalling courses are conducted throughout the world. Information about current journalling workshops can be obtained from William Hewett S.J, Campion Hall, Brewer Street, Oxford OX1 1QS (Tel: 01865 286 100) Hewitt has now developed his own scheme.
12. Avec, op. cit. (ref. 3, p. 120).
13. Batten, T.R: *Training for Community Development: A Critical Study of Method* (O.U.P. 1965) pp 39-40 and 113-120; and *The Non-Directive Approach in Group and Community Work* (O.U.P. 1967) pp. 96-100. *The Human Factor in Community Work* (O.U.P. 1965) and *The Human Factor in Youth Work* (O.U.P. 1970) contain examples of actual cases and discussion of them by a group. Lovell, *Analysis and Design,* op. cit. (ref. 5, p. 38) pp. 43-48; Widdicombe, op. cit. (ref. 2, p. 59) pp. 129ff.
14. Elizabeth Kubler Ross, who has done so much work on bereavement and change, has a hypothesis that, in the face of all categories of personal change we experience the emotions of denial, anger, bargaining, depression and acceptance, usually in this order. cf. *On Death and Dying* (Tavistock 1970. ISBN 422 73510 8).

    Ronald Lippet in *Phases of Organisational Change* talks about shock, defensive retreat, acknowledgement, adaptation and change.

    G. Lewin uses the concepts of 'unfreezing' from old habits or views, 'moving' from them and 'freezing' into the new ones. See also *Conduct, Knowledge and the Acceptance of new Values in Resolving Social Conflict: Selected papers on Group Dynamics*, G Lewin (ed.) (Souvenir Press, London, 1973).

    David Coghlan SJ has an excellent chapter 'Understanding Change ' in *Reviewing Apostolic Religious Life* (Columbia Press, 1996. ISBN 1 856 0717 7 4) p. 59.

    Rashford, N.S. & Coghlan, D. in *Human Development,* 1988 have four categories: Denying: "This doesn't affect us"; Dodging: "Ignore, don't get involved"; Doing: "This is important. Got to do it now"; Sustaining: "We have a new way of proceeding".

15. Widdicombe op. cit. (ref. 2, p. 59) pp 29-30
16. An interesting example of an 'anchorhold' occurs in *The Moonstone* by Wilkie Collins (1968 Penguin Classics 1994). Beveridge turns to *Robinson Crusoe* whenever events threaten to overwhelm him or he is faced with a difficult situation. There is a telling hymn by Priscilla Owens "Will your anchor hold in the storms of life" in *Hymns and Psalms: A Methodist and Ecumenical Hymn Book* (Methodist Publishing House 1983) No. 689.
17. A fascinating and revealing book is *Manwatching: A Field Guide to Human Behaviour* (Jonathan Cape 1977) by Desmond Morris.
18. Potucek, Carolyn: *A Community-Based Approach to the Re-entry Process* (Columbia Biblical Seminary & Graduate School of Missions, Columbia, South Carolina May 1991) pp. 32f.
19. Ibid. p.34.
20. Ibid. p.32.
21. Diet of Worms, 1521.
22. A phrase borrowed from Charles Wesley

XI
A Change of Community Membership

> *This chapter is written for communities that are gaining or losing a member and those with one or more members living elsewhere.*

A community is responsible not only for helping and supporting the members who are on the move so that it becomes a creative experience for them, but also for its own well-being. Both are taken into account in the three aspects considered in this chapter: gaining a new member; losing a member; and the relationship between a community and a member who is living elsewhere. How an individual might prepare for moving from one community to another is considered in Chapter Ten. The responsibility of a community for its composition is considered in Chapter Nine, *The Community and the Congregation*.

1. GAINING A MEMBER

Just as communities prepare for the advent of a novice or newly professed member in order to give the person a good experience of religious life, so it needs to prepare for whoever joins it, be they young or old, healthy or sick, coming as a superior or as an ordinary member. This is a critical moment for good or ill, not only for the individual but for the community as a whole.

· Feelings and attitudes

Your feelings will colour your attitudes and both will inform your behaviour and be picked up consciously or unconsciously by a new member. It could clear the air to face your feelings alone and possibly together, in order to gain some control over them. Dealing with feelings in general is discussed on p. 140, but there are some questions that may help you to identify and consider your own feelings in relation to this situation:

What are your hopes in relation to the new member? What might he bring by way of new or different ideas, outlook, gifts, experience and so on?

What are your fears? How might your hopes and your fears cause you to act or react unhelpfully? What do you want to avoid?

The newcomer, as happens in times of transition, is likely to have volatile feelings during the settling in period. His move may come after living in a community for a number of years and he may well feel bereaved and cut off from friends and all that has felt like home for so long. In addition, he is faced with adjusting to new people, new routines and life style, a new place, and possibly facing a new ministry. Sensitivity and support will be called for. Reflecting on times of transition in your own life will help you to stand in the shoes of the newcomer.

· Becoming a new community

To realise that with a new member, you will in fact be a new group which needs to go through the process of becoming a life-giving and effective community, is probably better than thinking in terms of 'integrating' someone into your community. This may require a change of attitude and be a challenge to radically re-think the *status quo*. However, it may not be realistic to have a formal review because of the pressure of work and the fact that a new member needs time to settle in. The process of becoming a new community does not happen overnight. The questions below could be reflected on individually or discussed communally before the newcomer arrives.

What do we think about the idea that we are a new community because a new member is arriving?

> How much are we prepared to change or give up with the advent of a new member? What is non-negotiable? What can we afford to be flexible about? How far are we prepared to have our life-style or habits questioned? How open are we or do we want to be to new ideas? Are there any obvious changes that need to be made to accommodate the newcomer?

· Welcoming the new member

There are various actions you could take before the new member arrives which would help her to feel wanted and welcomed, for instance:

- making a phone call or letter, perhaps, accompanied by some information about the community;

- inviting the member to come and look around or to join in a special event or celebration;

- one or more of you visiting the prospective member in the community she will be leaving;

- helping with practical arrangements regarding luggage or enquiries about any special facilities she will need;

- considering what you want to avoid, such as too many conversations in which the newcomer could feel excluded, in-jokes, or talking too much about a member she may be replacing;

- deciding how you will induct the newcomer, both into the community and into the neighbourhood and parish;

- preparing some sort of welcoming ceremony, however informal.

2. LOSING A MEMBER

All members of a community will be affected in some way by the departure of one of their number. Some may feel bereaved, others relieved. To have a farewell event is more than a kindness to the one who is leaving, it can mark in a fitting way the end of a phase in the life of the community: a phase which will have had its ups and downs. It therefore provides an opportunity for celebration – perhaps of reconciliation and healing. It is advisable to check out with the person concerned what sort of event would be helpful or unhelpful.

A simple celebration might include an opportunity for:

- each community member to say what of value she will miss when the person leaves them;
- the person who is moving out to say what she is taking with her from the community which will be valued or of use in the future;
- asking forgiveness of each other and sharing the sign of peace;
- prayers and a blessing for the one who is going and for the community remaining.

On the practical level there may well need to be a re-shuffling of tasks: it is often when a person is no longer present that one realises all she did!

It may also help the one departing to have people from the community to which she is going invited for a meal, and for a promise to invite the member back for a visit or special celebration. It is often such small and obvious things which can easily be overlooked but which can make all the difference to one's feelings.

3. LIVING APART FROM A COMMUNITY

Increasingly, there are religious who live apart from a community for shorter or longer periods. In some instances, these members are attached to a small community; in others, a group of them form a non-resident community in which people keep in touch with each other in various ways: meetings, correspondence and so on. Members may live on their own, for instance, because they are on sabbatical, attending a course, experiencing an alternative life style, working in an area where the congregation has no house, caring for an elderly relative, or for some personal need, such as exclaustration for a year.

Religious life has been lived in a variety of ways down the ages. Residential community is the most common form but for community to be genuine communion it does not necessitate living under one roof. Religious community and common life are not to be equated: community can exist between people who are separated from one another geographically.[1] Religious community has its own peculiar characteristics and these have implications for members who are temporarily living away from the majority (cf. p.88).

Exercising co-responsibility is essential if communion is to be authentic between those living singly and those living communally. For it to be effective, both parties need to receive from and contribute to the other. How this can best be done, needs to be agreed between those living alone and any community to which they belong, or with other single members with whom they form a non-resident community. This will vary according to the individuals concerned and their situations, the congregation and its communities. There can be no uniform pattern. Ways have to be worked out which are mutually life-giving and do not put too much of a strain on one or other party. Negotiating what sort of relationship will be beneficial both for the community and for the member living elsewhere is something that all those concerned could well do together. A suggested way of doing this is given below.

Table 11:1
Negotiations between a community and its absent members

The aim of this exercise is to work out the conditions under which both the community and any individual who is away for a lengthy period or lives singly could deepen the communion between them. Both parties need to be present and do it together. Sufficient time needs to be given for people to surface their feelings, especially those that are negative, as far as they feel able and to work through them together.

Step 1: Talk about the situations in which the absent member will be living and working, so that everyone has some idea of what it will be like.

Step 2: All put yourselves in the shoes of the absent member. Picture your situation. Jot down your feelings, both positive and negative. What are you looking forward to? What fears have you?

Step 3: Now, as an absent member, jot down what you would like from your community? What would help you to feel you belong? What do you *not* want?

Step 4: Share as much as you wish of Step 2 and list the results of Step 3.

Step 5: Now all put yourselves in the shoes of the members who will be living in community. Jot down what you need and want from your absent member. What would you want her to contribute to the well-being of the community? What do you expect of her?

Step 6: Share and list the results of Step 5.

Step 7: Looking at both lists, discuss what would be mutually beneficial and what would be feasible. Come to some agreement and set a date to check whether or not these arrangements are satisfactory, or decide what you will do if one or other party is finding the arrangements impractical or unsatisfactory.

REFERENCES AND NOTES

1. The 1917 Code of Canon Law equated 'community' with common life. This is a historical development and has not always been a characteristic of religious life.

PART FIVE

TOWARDS EQUIPPING
SMALL COMMUNITIES

This Part contains ideas for tackling difficulties, making decisions, evaluating life and ministry, and for running community meetings. It also suggests various exercises, reflections and discussion outlines which I have used or which have emerged as I worked with communities and groups.

They will be more effective if you adapt them to suit your own community and situation: they are not blue prints for success. They can be used in a small community or with a cluster of communities. Clearly, in most cases it will be helpful for one or two people to act as facilitators. The suggestions for encouraging participation on p.199, and particularly for reflecting and sharing together on p.202, are most important in order to avoid imposing exercises on people or pressurising them to share more than they are ready or wish to share.

Reflecting on how the the exercises were designed, I have discerned an underlying pattern for many of them. This is outlined in Table 15.1. It can be used as a check list for reference when preparing to use a particular exercise and it may enable you to adapt it more easily to your situation – or better still – design your own. More detailed consideration is given in Meetings That Work *(See Selected Bibliography).*

The exercises are classified but there is much overlap.

XII
Problems and Problem Solving

This chapter deals with a practical aspect of life which no community can escape: the occurrence of difficulties, problems and failure.

Wherever there are human beings, problems will arise. Where people have high ideals and purposes the problems will be greater: you face greater difficulties in tackling Everest than in climbing Snowdon. I use the word 'face' in order to emphasise that a problem is something to be worked at, not something to be clutched to oneself and bemoaned.[1] I also try to avoid talking about a 'problem person' or an 'awkward group': it is harder to be objective and loving about those so named, than if you objectively consider the difficulties you, the person concerned, and the community face.

Lovell[2] clearly differentiates between those problems which result from past mistakes or failures over which we may or may not have had control, and those which are inherent in the situation if we are going to achieve our visionary purposes. In either case we are faced with a challenging opportunity through which we are likely to learn much, whether it issues in a 'solution', warns us how to avoid a similar problem occurring, gives us deeper understanding of human nature – our own and other people's – or helps us get a more realistic picture of how things are.

When there is nothing which can be done 'out there' towards improving the situation, it could well be that an interior change of attitude is called for in order to live with the difficulty, realising that in this way we are being called to work out our salvation. Many people have been surprised by joy on finding themselves capable of such interior movements, which are truly moments and movements of grace. However, such moments are not everyday occurrences and there is need for practical and seemingly more mundane ways of facing problems which arise in community life.

1. PREPARING TO TACKLE PROBLEMS

Tackling common problems as a group has the advantage of drawing on diverse insights and ideas and of sensitising members to other view points. There are, of course, some personal problems which cannot always be dealt with publicly by the community. For instance, someone in the early stages of altzeimers or who has obsessive behaviour which affects everybody. It may well be, however, that at some stage the community does discuss these things, with or without the person present, much as a family would do, in order to support each other and the individual concerned.

Although you can learn from past experience of something similar, each problem is unique. It does not do to be mechanical in applying the solutions which have been successful before: this time they may not be. Some problems may be avoided if they can be foreseen.

Considering questions like: "What is likely to happen if. . ?", "What is the worst than can happen?", "How are people likely to react?", can help you to prepare for or avoid some difficulties which may arise. Working through problems as they arise will often enable you to forestall similar difficulties in the future. There are various practical methods and techniques of proven value in tackling difficulties in community life.[3]

Decide what you will do when facing a problem. Lovell puts the choices starkly: "Problems of one kind or another stand between us and the achievement of anything of value in church and community work. Avoiding them contributes to their destructive power; owning them begins the process of controlling them; tackling them starts to give us power over them; dealing with them purposefully enables us to seize the opportunities they block off. Moving from the avoidance of problems to dealing with them is releasing, creative and satisfying".[4]

Problems avoided usually re-appear, often in more difficult circumstances. A wise community makes provision for working on those difficulties which are best tackled together: this can include a tacit agreement to raise and work at problems when they arise, rather than ignore or repress them. This can be particularly helpful when inter-personal difficulties arise, as they surely will. To agree beforehand, that rather than allowing negative attitudes to build up and fester, you will talk to each other openly and work through them, can be enormously helpful when the moment comes.

Stand in other people's shoes. This may give you a clearer insight into how another person sees or experiences things. It can also be a great help when working for mutual understanding between people in opposing positions.

Journalling.[5] I find this particularly useful both in sorting out my general feelings and in tackling my negative feelings towards another person or situation.

Consider when to tackle a problem. Like the birth of a baby, there is a before, a during and an after to be considered in relation to problems. "The life of a problem has three stages: the latent period, when the difficulties are incubating, the active and disruptive period, and the post-active period".[6] What is appropriate and what you are able to do varies with each stage.

Prayer. this may seem like stating the obvious, as prayer clearly needs to accompany the tackling of any problem, but I have found the actual holding of the problem before God to be effective. For a space of time I forgo analysing or thinking about it. I just hold it there before God, handing it over while I remain quiet. At times, in the same way, I will hold a person with whom I am experiencing difficulties, before God. After a while, I listen for any thoughts or feelings which may or may not come into my mind or heart.

Find a confidante. Talking confidentially to a trusted friend or counsellor who is outside the situation and more objective can also be extremely helpful.

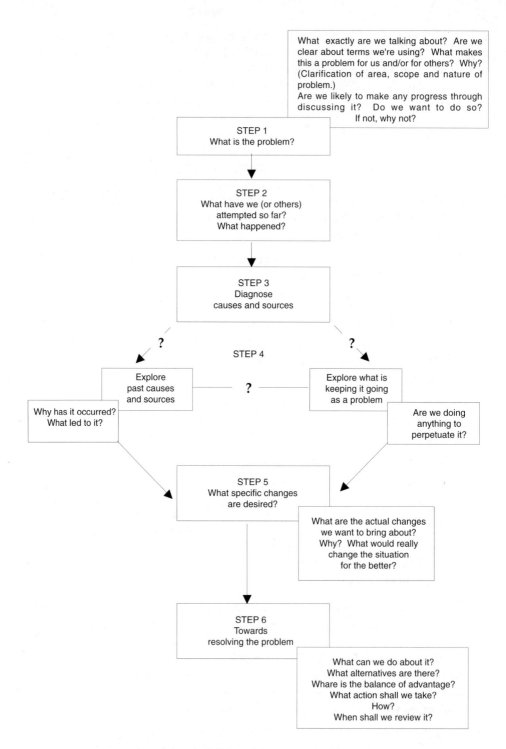

**Figure 12.1
The Problem-Tackling Sequence**

Small Communities in Religious Life

2. THE PROBLEM-TACKLING SEQUENCE

The notes below refer to the steps depicted in Figure 12.1.[7]

Step 1: What is the Problem? Clarification of the difficulty and of the terms used can help to ensure not only that people are talking about the same thing but that the *real* difficulty is discussed. When a team leader sought my help, he said, "The problem is Pat who dominates our discussion." A few questions elicited the clarification that the real problem was that other team members were not contributing their ideas and insights because Pat contributed so many, took up so much time, and generally sapped the energy of the group. This was re-phrased: "How to enable everyone in the group to make their contribution?". This widened the problem leading people to consider not only Pat's participation but that of the other group members.

Step 2: What have we (or others) attempted so far? Investigating what people have already done and what happened as a result, can throw additional light on the difficulty, and lessen the likelihood of people becoming defensive or you becoming exasperated as suggestion after suggestion is turned down because "it didn't work when we tried it before".

Step 3: Diagnosis of causes and sources of the problem. There is a difficult choice between exploring the initial causes and sources of the problem or focusing on those which are keeping it going. Reviewing the history of a problem may be necessary if it helps people to understand it and points towards what can be done about it. But it can prove demoralising and paralysing; rehearsing old arguments can re-activate painful emotions; complex factors and analyses may be more than people can handle and can inhibit fresh thinking and distract from the search for a way forward. On the other hand, the discovery of what is keeping the problem alive is likely to provide clues for future action.

Step 4: What specific changes are desired and why? It can be difficult but rewarding to try to identify specifically the key change that would improve the situation. Again, it will be a pointer to future action.

Step 5: Towards resolving the problem. It is only useful to discuss a problem from the point of view of what one can do about it *oneself.* It is no good deciding the problem would be solved if X did such and such, unless there is a way to approach X on the matter. Use imagination and lateral thinking to get out all the options and explore each one in turn.[8] Considering the pros and cons and possible effects will increase objectivity and therefore the likelihood of agreeing on a way forward which is realistic and feasible.

3. DEALING WITH FAILURE

The case study is a way of working through a specific incident or activity that has failed to achieve its target. It is a structured method developed by Avec based on the work of Batten.[9] It may be used individually or as a group exercise. It will reveal how and why actions taken in good faith caused a negative reaction. Using this method can often have a positive effect on your feelings as well as enabling you to identify what can be learnt for the future. There are several steps:

Step 1: Briefly write down the story: your objective or purpose, your initial assessment of the situation, what you did, how you did it or what you said, and what happened.

Step 2: Go through the story identifying the things you did or said or omitted to do or say that contributed to the unsatisfactory outcome. If you are doing this as a group exercise, and there is disagreement about certain things, put them down with a question mark.

Step 3: List those things which are 'going for you' in the situation: these may well be elements on which you can build in future.

Step 4: Determine the implications. There are two possible ways forward: (a) This may be done by working out in specific detail just what you would do *now*, if you were to start again avoiding the mistakes you have identified; or (b) If the incident is a recent one and the negative effects are still being experienced, you may well wish to work out just what you can now do to redeem the situation in the light of the steps above.

You could do (a) or (b) in the following way:

 – list all those involved or affected.

 – consider possible actions you could take in relation to individuals or groups rather than taking the first that comes to mind. This will give a wider choice and may alert you to pitfalls. Be specific about the methods you might use, how you could set up the first meeting etc. These details can be crucial to the success of the encounters.

 – decide, in the light of the above, what you will do and the best order in which to approach each person or group. As you work through what you have decided to do, you may well need to amend your plans in the light of the outcomes of earlier meetings.

Step 5: Draw out any general implications or conclusions which will be useful as guidelines for the future.

This may appear a painstaking exercise, but it can be enormously enlightening and cut through seemingly hopeless situations. I have also discovered I can work through the steps far more rapidly now that it has become my usual way of coping with failures.

REFERENCES AND NOTES

1. Erich Fromm talks about 'facing' rather than 'having' a problem op. cit. (ref 2, p. 92) p.21.
2. Lovell, *Analysis and Design,* op. cit. (ref. 5, p. 38) p. 67.
3. Ibid. pp. 58-66. See also *Meetings that Work,* op. cit. (ref. 2, p. 59) pp. 74-76.
4. Lovell, ibid. p. 51.
5. Progoff, op. cit. (ref. 7, p. 159).
6. Lovell, op. cit. (ref. 2 above) p. 58.
7. This draws heavily on the workof T.R.Batten op. cit (ref. 10, p.31) and George Lovell's elaboration in Chapter Two 'Working on Problems' in *Analysis and Design* op.cit. (ref. 2 above). See also p. 82 in Widdicombe, op. cit. (ref. 3 above) p. 75.
8. de Bono, Edward: *The Five Day Course in Thinking* (Penguin 1967).
9. Again I am drawing on the work George Lovell and I did in Avec (ref. 3, p. 120) based on the work of Batten (ref.10, p.31). This description of the case study method is based on that in *Meetings that Work* (ref 3 above) pp. 129-130.

XIII
Decisions and Decision Making

Decision making is the stuff of life and this book is all about making decisions of one kind or another. This chapter provides a check list for decision making and an Ignation model of a discernment process adapted for use by a group.

There will be some matters about which you may not have the authority to make a decision but which you wish to make a proposal to higher authority. The questions below are relevant to these, as well as decisions you are able to make yourselves. At times it may be useful to work through the procedures systematically, at others just to work on a particular section, particulatly relevant to you.

If the question as to whether or not everyone needs to be involved is asked early on, the making of minor decisions can often be delegated to one or two people thus saving time and energy. In this case, as a community, you may want to formulate some principles or criteria to guide a particular decision or an area of decision making.

1. WHAT SORT OF DECISION DO WE WANT TO MAKE?[1]

This is an important but frequently neglected question to be considered beforehand.

· Consensus

In a small community it is likely that you will want to work towards consensus: time-taking but more unifying. Obtaining genuine consensus can be a painstaking process with the accompanying danger of the minority feeling under pressure to conform. This can happen if two or three members speak forcibly, making it more difficult for others to express another view point or listen to one. It is worth spending time discussing this before embarking on a major decision. This is important if it is a difficult decision about which you are very uncertain, or which has far reaching implications, or one on which you are likely to have opposing views. Prior discussion can prepare you interiorly to take seriously any unease you or others may experience, explore the pros and cons of the various options before you, and help you to face the costs of seeking consensus and commit yourselves to it.

There is, however, the possibility that genuine consensus will be impossible. This may be due to the time factor: there just may not be time to work through to consensus, or someone on principle cannot agree. It is good to be aware of the fragility and complexity of seeking consensus, and you may have, in the eventuality, to opt for something else. In this case one of the suggestions below may be of use.

· A *Runyararo* Process

I have found this helpful when working with religious communities. It is only subtly different from consensus. The term *'runyararo'*, meaning 'for the good of the tribe', is borrowed from an African tribe, which uses it in settling disputes over which two parties cannot reach agreement through discussion. One of the two will eventually say with genuine commitment, *'runyararo'*, that is, 'for the good of the tribe I will go along with what the other party wants'. It is not lightly arrived at. Working for *'runyararo'* in decision making recognises realistically that not everyone will feel the same about the outcome: some may be wholeheartedly enthusiastic, others moderately so, and some be prepared to live with it 'for the good of the whole'. If a vote is taken – and this is often called for in the constitution of a group – it allows individuals to vote against the decision favoured by the majority, while committing themselves to support the outcome. The process leading up to this, if it is to be a genuine solution, is likely to require much time, energy and patience, but again, as with consensus, it makes for the unity and development of the group.[2] It is important not to put people in a corner: their agreement to live with a decision they do not favour must be genuine. If they are not able to say *'runyararo'*, and if you are all committed to this process, you will need to think afresh and defer the decision.

· Procedure used by the Uniting Church of Australia [3]

This church has developed detailed procedures for making decisions by consensus. The early steps are concerned with seeking full information, and open discussion about the issue. Eventually the chairperson asks whether or not consensus has been reached. If it has, well and good, if not, it may be that further discussion is necessary. However, there may be strong but not unanimous, support for the proposal. In this case, and in order to understand the strength of opinion, the chairperson may ask questions such as:

– Who supports the proposal?
– Who does not support the proposal but is prepared to accept it?
– Who is not prepared to accept the proposal?

After this, if there are people with misgivings, they are invited to share them, and discussion continues until the chairperson checks once more whether consensus has been reached. If after thorough discussion there are still dissenting voices the chairperson asks two questions.

(a) Do those of you who are unable to support the proposal, and are not prepared to accept it, agree that your point of view has been listened to, even though you do not agree with the proposal and are not able to accept it?

(b) Do those of you who support, or who are prepared to accept this proposal agree that you have listened to, and have heard what the others of our council are saying?

Small Communities in Religious Life

Given the assurance that the dissenting views have been both expressed and understood, the chairperson asks if, given the degree of support and opportunity for dissenting views to have been expressed, the minority agree to stand aside so that the council can agree to proceed with the proposal. If not, it is necessary to seek an alternative procedure such as deferring the decision or deciding by majority vote.

· Deferring a decision

If the decision is to be deferred because you are unable to reach consensus you may decide to let the matter drop for a period. In this case it is wise to make a note as to when you will re-consider the matter. You may ask one or two people to do further thinking and bring it back for later discussion or you may decide you all need to do further thinking, reflecting, studying, or discussing around the subject. I know of a community which was asked to allow a lesbian couple, whom they knew well but who were not Christians, to hold a small commitment ceremony in their chapel. After long discussion and despite feelings of sympathy for the people concerned, the community could not reach consensus: some were all for it, others were confused as to the morality of it, and others worried about what it would be saying to outsiders should it become known. The community members decided that they could not 'say yes' to the request because, on such an issue, it was necessary to be fully agreed, and convinced that their action was right whatever the consequences. They ended by saying "We all need to think more about this whole area of sexuality and discuss it thoroughly. If we have a similar request in five years time, we may be in a very different position".

2. HOW CAN WE BEST PARTICIPATE?

What is said about participation in community meetings on p. 199, and about the non-directive approach on pp. 101 is relevant here. Further points are mentioned below.

Keep in mind the purpose behind the decision to be made. Why do we want to make this decision?

*Differentiate between **the what** and **the how** of a decision.* If you succumb too quickly to saying "but that wouldn't work", you do not allow yourselves sufficient freedom to explore the idea or proposal. Having explored it, if you are convinced it is a good one, now is the time to see how you could make it work. With really good ideas, there are generally ways and means!

Provisional decisions. When you need to make a series of decisions about a plan or project, try making provisional decisions about each step or area as you go along. When you have completed the cycle, you can go back and check them. This can be very releasing and allow you to encompass the whole, while dealing carefully with each part before confirming them by a final decision. You may well find earlier decisions need slightly amending in the light of later ones.

Be aware of the danger of 'group think'. Irving Jarvis has coined this phrase to describe errors of decision making based on group conformity thinking and misplaced loyalty to a leader or institution. The thinking of the group becomes 'frozen' and members resist outside pressure to re-examine their views. New information is ignored or used in such a way as to reinforce rather than challenge their stance. If this is a real danger in the group, a discussion about the phenomenon and the symptoms of 'group think' outlined by Jarvis and Mann could be useful beforehand.[4]

Clarify areas of agreement and disagreement. Have a series of 'straw votes' to give some indication of how much unease remains in the group. You need to be on the look out for what members are agreed about and where there are still areas of disagreement or uncertainty. It may be useful periodically to remind the group of the criteria and purpose on which they agreed at the start, and work from there towards a solution which honours these.

3. WHAT QUESTIONS MIGHT WE ASK OURSELVES BEFOREHAND?

There are various questions which may help you to think openly and critically about the decision and enable you to avoid some pitfalls.

· **In relation to time**

How much time are we likely to need? When shall we work on this decision? Shall we set time aside in our diaries?

Are we likely to need reflection time *en route*?

Pause periodically for thought. People need time to check where they now are. Remember head and heart are both engaged in decision making and for most people one is usually ahead of the other. A pause allows integration of thought and feelings. Brendon Kennelly emphasises the value of such patient waiting: "How easy it is to maim the moment with expectation, to force it to define itself."[5]

Has the decision to be made by a certain date or do we want to fix a date to aim for? There may be penalties in terms of time, energy or money in taking a long time over a decision. It is helpful to face these openly and decide whether or not you are willing to pay them. One community had to make a decision about some radical alterations to its building. It was in danger of not thinking them through sufficiently because the builder warned them that prices would rise after a certain date. When they realised that their choice was between paying several more thousand pounds for a building which would really suit the needs of their ministry or saving that money and having unsatisfactory premises which would cause constant regret and difficulties, they felt released and justified in taking the necessary time to think and decide.

How to keep up momentum?

· In relation to information

Good decisions are made on a basis of sufficient and accurate information presented clearly and objectively so that all can consider it openly and critically. Information includes facts and feelings and both need to be taken into account. Ask yourselves:

Have we got all the information that we need? If not who will get it? From where?

Do we need to talk to experts? Are we clear enough in our own minds to do so now?[6]

The use of an outside facilitator may occasionally be useful or even necessary in a small community but, generally speaking, if you are able to work things through on our own, you will develop the skills you need to manage without one. If you decide to use a facilitator, it is important:

– to be agreed that you want outside facilitation: one person's unease or negative attitude could render a meeting useless.
– to be clear why you want it and what you want a facilitator to do.
– to ensure you retain control and that the facilitator does not take over or exert undue dominance in the discussion.
– to brief the facilitator well beforehand.
– to ensure confidentiality so you feel free to discuss openly.

· In relation to feelings

Is this likely to be an emotive topic for us? If so, what will help us:

– to discuss objectively?
– to be open about our feelings (cf. p. 161)?
– to stand in the shoes of other people who will be affected – or in each others' shoes?

What will we do if any of us feels very uneasy during and even towards the end of the process?

If you have a strong emotional involvement about an issue it can be difficult to participate in such a way that your feelings, while being taken into account, do not unduly pressurise other people. Try to face your feelings beforehand: there are dangers in allowing feelings free rein, in hiding them and the consequences, or in using them to manipulate the group. Manipulation may appear to pay off in the short term but there is likely to be a longer term, though possibly hidden, cost.

· In relation to particular factors

What particular factors need to be taken into account? What issues impinge on your decision? There may be some general facts to do with your specific charism, or practical issues.

What are the criteria for checking this is a good decision?

Are any of the community absent? If so, do we need their views and how will we get them?

Do we foresee any specific difficulties or areas of disagreement? If so, what could we do to avoid or ameliorate them?

· In relation to other people

Who else do we need to involve in the process:
- those affected?
- someone to give us information?
- a facilitator?
- anyone in the congregation?

4. WHAT ARE THE STEPS WE NEED TO TAKE?

The steps below provide a systematic way of thinking through a decision.

Step 1. Ask yourselves: What are the possible options before us? Think creatively around the subject in an exploratory way before listing the various options.

Step 2. Examine each option. Too often people focus on the first proposal without surveying the field and thus do not see another and better choice before them. Consider the pros and cons of those options about which you are serious. Take time to list the pros and cons of each item in turn, remembering that any idea however 'good' or 'bad', has both. It is also important to realise that feelings and hunches may be listed as advantageous or disadvantageous to a particular choice. What are the likely effects, including negative side effects, on you, others, the situation?

Step 3. Ask yourselves:

- Where is the balance of advantage? Can we ameliorate any disadvantage?
- Where are we agreed? Where do we disagree? Why?

Possibly have a series of 'straw votes' to give some indication of how much unease remains in the group. You need to be on the lookout for areas of disagreement or uncertainty. It may be useful periodically to remind the group of the criteria and purpose on which they agreed at the start, and work from there towards a solution which honours these. See what changes you might make which will bring about agreement.

Step 4. Come to a decision:

- to make the decision/recommendation.
- not to make it.
- to postpone making it for the time being (cf. p. 173).

As you work through Steps 3 and 4 the procedures suggested by the Uniting Church of Australia outlined in p.172 may come in useful.

5. WITH WHOM DO WE NEED TO SHARE OUR DECISION?

Ask yourselves who needs to know about it:

- – in the locality?
- – in the congregation?
- – any others?

How do we tell them? What is the best order in which to tell them?

Whether or not you decide to make or postpone a decision, there may be other people who need to know about it: those in authority in the congregation, church, or secular sphere; those likely to be affected by it; those with whom you have close relationships; and others who could be offended by hearing of the decision in a roundabout or casual way. Often the order in which you inform people affects their response. The same applies to the way you tell them: how you phrase it, whether it is by word of mouth or a written communication, your reasons for the decision and why you want them to know.

6. HOW TO IMPLEMENT THE DECISION?

However 'good' a decision, it remains barren if not implemented and, if badly implemented, may cause harm. How it will be translated into effective action needs careful attention *before* the decision is made. Questions such as those below may well be woven into the decision making as it proceeds.

What action needs to be taken? In what order? What needs to be done first? What can be done concurrently?

When shall it be started and when completed? It can be useful to make a flowchart of the work to be done in stages and with dates.

Who will be responsible for carrying out the various aspects? Have they got the necessary skills and abilities? Do they need help or support of any kind, whether from other group members or outside people or groups? Do these people need any preparatory training? Have they the necessary resources or do we need to make arrangements to get them? Are we and they clear about their brief?

How and when will they keep us informed?

What dangers or pitfalls do we need to avoid? Are there any safeguards we should build into the implementation?

What is to happen if a problem arises? It can be useful to make contingency arrangements in case of crises, or to prevent undue delay through people getting stuck and struggling with difficulties on their own. Those responsible for implementing the decision may find it impossible, in which case they would need to report back and say why.

With some decisions you will only know how good they are, by trying them out over a period of time. Give them a chance to work for you, but if they are not working, review them and make others.

7. WHEN TO REVIEW OUR DECISION?

Reviewing and evaluating decisions are considered in Chapter Fourteen.

Table 13.1
A discernment process[7]

This is based on the Ignatian model of prayerful reflection in order to discern the will of God. It can be used on its own, in preparation for discussion or in conjunction with it. The conditions necessary for discernment are that:

– sufficient information is available with opportunity for questions. It is important to give time to this before the process begins;

– a genuine commitment to being open to seeking what is best by way of a decision: this means avoiding argument or pressing for a particular alternative and being willing to change one's views if and when one becomes convinced.

The process itself has three threefold steps in relation to any particular way forward.

Step 1: Seeking the reasons **for** *going a particular way*

a) Everyone meditates privately about this in relation to the situation and circumstances and writes down their ideas.
b) All share, by reading what they have written down, and listening. Depending on the size of the group this could be done in sub-groups. There is no discussion at this stage.
c) Everyone goes off to reflect and meditate about what they have heard, and make further notes if they wish.

Step 2: Seeking the reasons **against** *going in this way*

Follow the same threefold process as in Step 1.

Step 3: Weighing the reasons **for** *and* **against**

Follow the same threefold processes as above taking into account the reasons for and against. Where sub-groups are used they may put their thoughts together and present them to the total group after Steps 1 and 2, or only after Step 3. Discussion follows. The process or part of it may be repeated at any stage.

REFERENCES AND NOTES

1. Widdicombe, op. cit.(ref. 2, p. 54) pp. 161-6 where fuller details are given of various kinds of decision-making processes.
2. Ibid. p. 162 where it is described in more detail. I am indebted to Reverend Peter Russell who learnt of this as a missionary in Rhodesia (sic.).
3. In what follows I draw heavily on *A Manual for Meetings in the Uniting Church of Australia,* 1994, p. 17ff.
4. Irving Jarvis and Leon Mann list the symptoms of groups adopting this defensive behaviour: an illusion of invulnerability, rationalizing to discount warnings of error, unquestioned belief in a group's inherent morality, stereotyped views of rivals and enemies as evil, pressure against dissenters, self-censorship of deviants, a shared illusion of unanimity, and self-appointed mind-guards. Cf. *A Psychological Analysis of Conflict, Choice and Commitment* (Free Press, 1977) pp. 129 ff, and *Group Think* (Collier MacMillan 1977).
5. Kennelly, Brendan: Unfortunately I have been unable to trace the source of this quotation.
6. Widdicombe op. cit. (ref. 1 above) pp. 173-5.
7. Ibid. p. 166.

XIV
Ways of Evaluating Life and Ministry

Theoretical aspects of reviewing and evaluating have been considered in Chapter Eight. Some practical methods and exercises for personal and communal use are outlined below.

Evaluation may be done in relation to the life of the individual, to community life, and to ministry. Reviewing any area will affect the total life and work of a small community and therefore ideas are given on all these. You could do a systematic review over a period of time, working separately and together, beginning with your personal lives and going on to community living, and ending with your ministry. Alternatively you could focus on one of them and then decide where to move from there. You may feel personal reviews are taken care of in annual retreats.

Whatever you decide to do as a group, it is important that the way of doing it fits you and is acceptable to everyone; that it is feasible and not an irksome burden or squashed in among your other activities. Considering the various models and methods suggested below will help you to create a process which is tailored to your needs, is stimulating and appropriate. No method, however good in itself, will work if people react negatively. Evaluating can be interesting and enjoyable. Going away for a day or more, in order to concentrate on the task in a different and attractive setting may be helpful.

1. INDIVIDUAL EVALUATION OF PERSONAL AND COMMUNITY LIFE

How you set about this depends very much on what you, as an individual, find most helpful. You may do it alone or seek the help of a spiritual director, work consultant or review partner (Table 14.1). The ideas below could be used as they are, adapted, or they may spark you off to think of some method which is better for you.

· Loving God and others

What is God expecting of me now in relation to:

– loving myself?
– loving others?
– loving God?

In relation to each of the above ask yourself the following questions:

How am I currently trying to do this?
What do I feel about how far I am succeeding, and failing?
What am I struggling with, or finding most difficult? Why is this?
What could help me? What can I do to help myself?

What help could I seek from others, from books, or from other sources?
How do I expect God to help me?
What would be a realistic decision to make for the future?
How *could* I keep myself up to it? How *will* I?

· **Change and Growth**

Keeping in mind the two quotations: "For me to live is to change, and to be perfect is to have changed often",[1] and "To be a Christian is a process of becoming",[2] ask yourself the following questions:

Who am I?	*Who do I want to be?*
– as a fully alive, fully developed human being?	– as a fully alive, fully developed human being?
– as a member of my community?	– as a member of my community?
– as a person aware of the goodness, truth and beauty of God?	– as a person aware of the goodness, truth and beauty of God?
– as a person in love with God?	– as a person in love with God?
– as a person in love with God's people?	– as a person in love with God's people?

· **Your religious vocation**

This reflection may be done over a few days or even longer. It may help to journal[3].

(a) Look back over the time since you entered religious life. You could highlight and examine the peak moments and the troughs. What brought you into the congregation? What is keeping you in it?

(b) Older People	(b) Younger People
You are at a time of life when you have a lot of experience behind you and hopefully will have gained in wisdom and self-confidence.	You are at a time of life when you still have energy and possibly half or more than half of your life ahead of you.
How do you now see yourself living out your religious vocation: – within the congregation? – within the wider church and for society?	How do you now see yourself living out your religious vocation: – within the congregation? – within the wider church and for society?

(c) Ask yourself: how will this affect the way I live and work in the community and outside it?

· Your community life

Ask yourself the following questions:

How far am I 'a sign' to the rest of the community?
Who are the people I push to the margins in my community?
Am I merely scratching the surface in my community relationships?
In what ways do these people in the community need me?
What do I see as my chief contribution as a community member?
What do I do which has a negative effect on community life?

· Specific areas

You may wish to review such things as your prayer life, your reading, your awareness of God, your relationships, how far you take time to reflect on life and what is happening to you. In relation to any area it can be helpful to start by listing all the questions which will help you to explore what you have been doing, how you have been doing it and with what result, and what you have *not* being doing.

Table 14.1
Review partners[4]

Review partners undertake to help and support each other as they review their life and work.

As a review partner, your task is to help your partner to think clearly and objectively and to express what she thinks and feels. Your basic attitude is one of being 'for' her. You can best do this:

– by listening intently and sympathetically;

– by accepting the thoughts and feelings expressed as valid rather than being critical or judgemental of them;

– by asking questions to explore what she is saying. For instance if you do not understand or automatically disagree, you could ask "Why do you say that?", "Can you explain that a bit more?", "I'm not sure I see why you feel like that about it, can you help me?". This will help your partner to explore thoughts and feelings and be more fruitful than appearing shocked or disapproving.

– by summarising what she is saying and clarifying together the picture which is emerging. This is harder to do. It may help to draw diagrams, or to classify the different areas in which she works, or the people she works with or different feelings about the work. I find that to ask myself "what strikes me about what is being said?" helps me to identify things of central importance.

Your second task is to help your partner decide if there is anything she wants and needs to share with the community and how she can best do so with an economy of words while giving an accurate picture. The most important part to present clearly is the final section on how she sees the future and any concerns she has about it.

Small Communities in Religious Life

2. EVALUATING COMMUNITY LIFE TOGETHER

Reviewing and evaluating community life will be most fruitful if:

- personal preparation precedes community discussion;
- you are honest and open with yourselves and each other and develop that great skill of 'speaking the truth in love' in a way which builds a person up rather than puts them down;
- you keep your purpose as a community in mind (cf. p. 71);
- you recognise and face conflict and struggle to work through it. (You may need an outside facilitator to help you.)

As has been said earlier, it is imperative that you find the way of reviewing that is acceptable and appropriate to your community. Consider the following alternatives.

Identify key areas. Browse through Chapter Five, *Living as a Small Community* and pick out five or six areas to review. Glancing through the questions below may help you to identify questions you need to ask in your situation.

What helps us to persevere when the going gets hard?

How have we used our failures – or not used them?

What energises us? What drains us?

What pulls us apart? What draws us together?

What have we found problematic, unhelpful, a hindrance, hard to tackle, or dysfunctional?

What have we struggled with?

What doubts or hesitations do we have?

What do we feel uneasy about, and confident about? What are we doing well, and not so well? What gaps are there?

What are our strengths and weaknesses, our gifts, skills and limitations?

What do we find life giving, individually and as a community? What builds up our morale?

Strengths and weaknesses. Identify and share the key things you are good at as a community striving to live in real communion, and the key things you are not so good at. Discuss and decide what you could and will do about them.

Helps and hindrances. Each of you list and then share what helps you live happily in the community and what hinders you from doing so. It is important to stress the need to put the latter courteously and objectively. Read off the implications and make decisions for the future.

Characteristics of religious. David O'Connor identifies characteristics of religious and clergy.[5] It might be helpful to begin by individually considering each in turn. When you discuss them together, remember that co-responsibility within the community means that help, support and challenge need to be forthcoming between you. Characteristics include:

– a tendency to neglect basic human needs for rest, recreation, supportive relationships, affirmation, understanding and acceptance.

– a danger of over-identifying with your vocational role, depending on it for all feelings of self worth.

– perfectionism, narcissism, a tendency to be self-absorbed, be success oriented, or 'workaholics', to deny humanity and its limitations, to allow people to put you on a pedestal, to repress feelings and sexuality.

– a stressful life-style: pace, demands, cutting back on recreation and prayer, etc. and having no support group.

– the danger of addiction: smoking, drink, drugs.

– lack of developing maturity.

As you consider these, beware, because it is often easier to see them in others than in oneself!

Practicalities list. List a few practical areas to consider which could reflect the health or otherwise of your community life:

– meals together, conversation and laughter.
– tidiness and cleanliness of the house (over tidiness and dirty mugs on draining boards both speak).
– callers: number, attitude towards them, what they say and how at home they feel.
– giving a hand or standing in for each other.
– grousing and gossiping.
– answering the phone or door.
– days or time off separately or together.
– state of the fridge: is it clean or frozen up, over full or nearly empty?
– use of the car or bicycles; TV; bathroom; or. . . ?
– handling day-to-day feedback, positive and negative, both giving it and receiving it.
– decibels in the house.
– replacing items which get worn out or used e.g. light bulbs, soap, etc.

3. EVALUATING MISSION AND MINISTRY

In order to decide what and how to evaluate your mission and ministry you may be attracted by one of the methods outlined, or a combination of them more appropriate. In all of them evaluate what has or has not been achieved in relation to your purpose (cf. pp. 152-4).

i. Some general methods

· Evaluating historical developments[6]

This involves getting a picture of the flow of change over a period of time.

Step 1: Getting the picture

The situation (5) years ago	The situation now	What are the key changes?	Areas of no change
Describe what it was like (5) years ago	Describe it as it is now		
....	....	....	....
....	....	....	....
....	....	....	....
....	....	....	....
....	....	....	....

(a) Under headings list key characteristics of the situation 3, 5 or 10 years ago; of the present; of the key changes; and areas of no change, use succinct phrases if possible.

(b) Mark those changes which are positive changes for the better and those which are changes for the worse. This could be done together or in sub-groups.

Step 2: Reflecting on the picture.

Reflect individually, in pairs or small groups, on what has gone well or badly; what you feel satisfied or uneasy about; what have been the good effects; what gaps occur to you? Why did these things happen? Does anything surprise you? What is it saying to you about what you decided to do, how you did it, the timing and so on? Is the overall development in line with your purpose?

Step 3: Looking to the future.

Read off the implications for the future. What do we need to continue, draw to a close, or start doing? Are there different approaches or methods we would do well to use? What do we want the picture to be in 2, 3 or 5 years time?

· Evaluating process

In some ways this is similar to the method above. Draw out the life-line of the community and its activities: when it started, major events or changes of direction, how it linked with other work or groups, the various outcomes, blockages, etc. See Figure 14.1.

When you arrive at the present moment, pause for a few minutes, and then ask, "Is there anything of significance we have omitted?".

You could then follow steps 2 and 3 of the previous model.

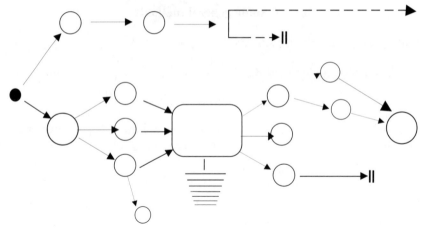

Figure 14.1
Flow Model

· Evaluating decisions

In this you need to plot and explore the key decisions you have made as a community over the time span you are reviewing, why you made them and what happened as a result.

Key decisions	Options (List them)	Why we chose X? (reasons)	Outcome? (Describe)	What we think about it now? (Describe/discuss)
....	....	....	....	....
....	....	....	....	....
....	....	....	....	....

Ask: What are the implications for us? What do we wish to do for the future?

· Evaluation of problems and issues

List the problems and issues which have arisen and work through them, possibly using the method outlined in Chapter Twelve *Problems and Problem Solving*

· Using a board Display

This has several steps:

> *Step 1.* On large sheets of paper write headings of various areas which you decide to review and put these up on the wall.

> *Step 2.* Give everyone individually or in pairs twenty minutes or so to go round them and write comments on each sheet.

> *Step 3.* Give each sheet to a person or pair to summarise and prepare to introduce a discussion of the points raised.

ii. Work and life resumé

This is a way of informing each other about your ministry, how you feel about it and how it relates to your life in community. It is based on an exercise developed over the years for Avec consultancy sessions and courses.[7] Members were given an outline from which to prepare a working paper of not more than 2000 words. This was read beforehand by participants of the consultancy group. Below is an abbreviated and adapted form. Before any session it is important to discuss and agree on confidentiality (p.190).

Step 1: Personal Preparation

Reflect on your work and life with the help of the questions below. Different questions are suggested for those who are actively engaged in a field of work, those who maintain the home base, and those who are retired. Clearly these categories may overlap. Select those appropriate.

Reviewing as an active participant in a field of work

Your current work. What am I hoping to achieve through what I am doing? What needs am I meeting? How do I live out our charism and mission through my work with people?

Yourself. What particular gifts/experience/training do I bring to this work? Do I enjoy it? Do I give myself adequate time to relax, study, read, and relate to others working in the same field? What new learning or training would I value?

The state of play. What is going well? What do I feel happy about? What difficulties am I up against? What concerns have I got? How far does the work depend on me or on a team of people? Is there any aspect of the work I would like to develop but have been unable to for various reasons? Why? Do I see any gaps? To what extent is it meeting the needs it could meet? Are there areas I would like to drop? Why?

Your community and congregation. How do I see my work relating to my community? How do I feel about this? How do I think others feel? Am I supported enough from above and by community members?

Looking to the future. (Be realistic, taking into account not only your gifts, training and experience, but your age, health and the resources available). Over the next five years how do I see the work I am doing and my involvement in it expanding, developing, diminishing, being phased out, changing or. . . ? Is there any way I could involve lay people more in my work? Could I see lay people taking it over? Should I ensure the work continues when I am no longer able to do it, and if so how? Can I see ways in which the work could develop without me and/or without the community's direct involvement? Is there any way I could be training someone to take over some or all of my work?

Reviewing as a member engaged in maintaining the home base

Many small communities will not have such a person, as the work is shared between members, but it could apply to the superior even if she has other work. The questions could be adapted for everyone to use. List the work in which you are currently engaged. Ask yourself: How does my work help to keep my local community going? What do I think and feel about this work in general? What parts do I enjoy doing and find satisfying? What do I gain from it? What parts do I find difficult to cope with? In what way? Are there ways in which I think it could be done more effectively with less time and effort? Have I all the help I need? What do I do with any time left over, or don't I have any? How long have I been doing this work? If I were not engaged in it, what could I imagine myself doing? Have I any particularly aspirations?

Reviewing as a retired member

Make a list of the work you do and note whether you do it alone or with someone else. This could include the work you do in the house to keep things running smoothly, or work you do which supports the apostolic work of others, or visiting people, or anything else which brings you in touch with people outside the community.

Mark those parts which happen every week, and things which are spasmodic. You could ask yourself these questions: Which parts of the work do I enjoy doing, find rewarding, find tedious or difficult, feel are too much for me, not enjoy, actively dislike, or find exhausting? Do I feel I am overstretched with far too much to do? Do I have enough to do? Do I make enough time for myself? How do I use personal time? Am I being constructive and creative or allowing myself to vegetate? How do I feel about activities going on in the house in which I am not involved, for instance, if a parish group meets here?

Having done this personal exercise, work out how much you need to share and feel you can share with others in the community. The fuller the picture you are able to give others of what your life and work means to you and what you feel and think about it the better, but clearly some things will be personal and private. To present it, in the first place, in written form, although often found to be difficult, usually proves enormously rewarding and helps clarify the situation and the issues. This could be circulated beforehand.

Step 2: Exploring the situation together

It helps to sit round a table with a large sheet of paper, on which to draw diagrams or maps and note key issues.[8] The person concerned describes his work, highlighting the main areas or key concerns. If he talks at too great a length people may not be able to concentrate. It is better to be brief and devote most of the time to exploring it through questions. Other members listen and ask questions in order to understand the situation and how the person thinks and feels about it.

Small Communities in Religious Life

The task of the member who is sharing his work is to help the group feel and think its way into his situation, to see it through his eyes, and to give people as true and complete account as he is able and willing to share.

The task of the group is to try to get a picture from the perspective of the member concerned, 'to stand in his shoes', and get an understanding of how he thinks and feels about things, his concerns and his hopes. To do this:

– listen with 'fresh ears' as though to a stranger. (The danger for people in a community is to think they know everything about each other.)

–ask questions. Try to ask questions which help to get to the heart of things, clarify what is being done, and which the member is stimulated to answer, rather than questions which put him on the spot, make him defensive or which appear judgemental. A useful question to ask is "Are there any other significant areas of your work not yet mentioned?"

– explore and analyse the situation and its underlying dynamics. Then ask the person concerned questions such as: What are the relationships between the various parts, groups or people? What is working well and what less well? What part of the work do you most enjoy, feel most concerned about, feel is progressing well, or is causing difficulties for you? What gaps are there? What are you up against? What are you hoping to achieve? What ideas and hopes do you have for the future? What would you like to happen?

Step 3

Next, look objectively at the situation, as you have come to see it, and read off the implications in terms of any key issues, difficulties, opportunities or points of development. Focus on areas which the person concerned particularly wants to think through as he looks towards the future. This could be a difficulty he is facing, a project or programme of work he is about to start, or be to do with his personal life in terms of some new field of study, or work or interest he wants to develop, or it could be about the relationship between his work and the community and its mission. Assist him in working out what he might say or do, by asking questions, putting ideas forward tentatively, helping him to think about alternatives. In doing this it is important that any action decided upon:

– is something he feels happy about and able to do rather than some action *you* might take if you were in the situation;

– fits him and his situation, that is, that it is likely to be feasible and acceptable to others involved;

– is in line with his basic purpose and objectives.

Finally, spend the last few minutes sitting back from the situation, scanning the picture as a whole and asking yourselves: what strikes us about all this? What do we want to say to him about it?

You may wish to divide the exercise into two with Steps 1 and 2 in the first session, taking anything from half an hour to an hour or more, and Step 3 in the next session.

The attitudes of the participants are key to an open sharing; everyone must be free to share what they want and feel able to. You are being invited to hear something of a person's vocational story: it is holy ground. In this way the whole focus of a session is on one person. This takes discipline and sensitivity.

Four ground rules facilitate the above steps.

No anecdotes. Everyone is asked to concentrate on the situation before them and not to bring in examples and stories from their own work situation. Instead, let these lead you to ask questions. This 'no anecdotes' rule is a hard but worthwhile discipline.

Avoid judgemental remarks. Comments such as 'you should not have . . .', or 'that was a mistake', are out. Instead, ask gently explorative questions such as 'Why did you ..? This process is described by Lovell in *Analysis and Design*[9] and *Avec: Agency and Approach*.[10]

Observe confidentiality strictly. What this means in your particular situation may well need clarifying. You may need to ask what may or may not be repeated to others or outside the sessions. A person may need reassurance that what he has revealed will not be brought up on another occasion or used as evidence against him in a moment of frustration or anger.

Make a contract. Agree that should major difficulties arise, you will seek each others' help to sort them out. This means making a contract to give each other time when necessary, even though inconvenient.

Remember

When anyone talks to you about their life
and its significance you are treading
on holy ground.

"Had I the heavens' embroidered cloths
Enwrought with golden and silver light
The blue and the dim and the dark cloths
Of night and light and the half-light
I would spread the cloths under your feet:
But I, being poor, have only my dreams;
I have spread my dreams under your feet;
Tread softly because you tread on my dreams."

W.B. Yeats[11]

---

iii. Reviewing specific areas

Ideas for focusing on some areas or aspects are given below together with a few questions which are merely starters. The list is by no means exhaustive. Choose those areas relevant to your situation. The questions point out the need for feedback (p. 124-6).

· The use of your home

How far is it or do we want it to be an open house? What people and groups use it and with what effect? What do they like about it? Any ways it could help them more? What witness value does it give (hospitality, care, option for the poor, community etc.)? Are there any other ways in which the house could be used to meet local needs? Remember your own needs for some privacy and peace, cf. p.80.

· Sharing your charism with lay people

How far are we doing this consciously or unconsciously? What sort of relationships do we have with lay people? How do they view us? How do we want to be seen by them? What do they share with us? Do they use our prayer room or pray with us? Are we sharing our charism with a selected group or with everyone?

· Relating to people of other denominations and faiths

What sort of relationships do we have and with whom? What do we see as the purpose of these relationships, and to what extent is it or is it not being achieved? How do we want to be seen by people of other faith traditions? How do we think they see us? Are there any key individuals or groups with whom we could be in touch and are not? What has been the most successful joint event or activity together and how do we view our part in it? What has been the least successful? What might we have contributed to make it work?

· Work with particular groups of people

What are we doing, for instance, with retired, sick, elderly, mothers, parents, children, teachers, clergy, handicapped, or young people? What is going well? What less well? What more could we be doing? How do those concerned feel about it? Are they passive receivers or pro-active collaborators?

· Visiting people in the neighbourhood

How much visiting are we doing? How is it received? What do we see as our purpose? Are we covering all those, house bound, bedridden or in hospital, who need visiting? Do other people help us or could they do so? Are we able to put those we visit in touch with each other in any way? How do people make use of us? Do they take advantage of us? How far do we meet their needs – physical, emotional, intellectual, or spiritual? Is there anything else we could be doing to make our visiting more creative?

· Preferential option for the poor

What are we actually doing in relation to poor and marginalised people in our parish and neighbourhood?

Are we making the best use of our present personnel, using fully the gifts and potential of each person? Do we help each other to be aware of the contribution we each have to make to the community? Are we making undue demands on any one of us or expecting anyone to do more than she should be doing or is able to do? (Have we the physical energy, training, skills etc.?) Could we organise our time and talents better so as to give more to those who are marginalised? Are we over-ambitious in what we are trying to do, given our present personnel?

Who benefits most from our resources? Could we help finance parish or other work? Do we hear comments on our apparent wealth? How do they affect us? Are we using our money to best effect? Do we spend too much on anything, such as travelling or telephone? In what way are we using our present buildings to help people who are on the margins? Are we sharing our facilities enough? Does our building in any way isolate us from people on the margins? Is our property – all of it – necessary, fully used? Could any of it – 1 or 2 rooms or more – be used in any specific way by, with, or for people on the margins, or by others to help such people? Some community exercises focused on having an option for the poor will be found on pp. 225-9.

· Witness

Diamuid O'Murchu writes that in religious life the "real decline is more in the area of witness. Religious fail to leave any marked influence on the moral fibre and spiritual character of the Christian community in general."[12]

What sort of witness, positive and negative, do I/we give through:

- any apostolic work in which we are engaged individually?

- all we do together, for example, hospitality, praying with people, joining in parish liturgy, attending meetings?

- the way we talk to people, for example, when questioned about religious life, or giving hope to people in crisis and difficult situations?

- our common vision, our similar attitudes and loyalty to each other?

- through our vulnerability, for example, when a member is sick and we are in need of help and support from outsiders?

- through our unity amidst our diversity?

· The way you work

It is necessary for you to work collaboratively as a team if you are to work collaboratively with others in parish or neighbourhood. Collaborative ministry is considered on p. 117 and the non-directive approach on pp. 101.

Working together. The sort of relationship existing between members of a team can make or mar any work they do together. Ask yourselves:

– How would we describe our working relationship? What has caused bad working relationships between us? What has inhibited good team work? What can we do to improve an unsatisfactory working relationship? What have we done when relationships have broken down? What can we do in future towards maintaining good working relationships or restoring them when necessary?

Working with others. These questions may enable you to explore how you are working collaboratively with others beyond the team.

– What are possible negative effects of being a team engaged in ministry? How inclusive/ exclusive are we? Are we promoting team work in the work we do beyond the team? How do people view us? How do we want to be seen: efficient leaders? enablers? partners? colleagues? or friends?

– How far are we making maximum and appropriate use of the different skills, gifts, training and experience of different people in the team and beyond it? Do we value some skills more than others? Are we in danger of expecting the same talents from everyone?

Futrell singles out four key features which are required by members of a team ministry. Explore what you do under each heading and whether it is adequate:

(a) "Faith-sharing and mutual support in faith and in commitment to your community as a ministry team. . . .

(b) Developing human inter-personal relations of mutual understanding and love. . .
.

(c) A corporate awareness developed in each person of always being sent to do my work as a member of this ministry team, as *us*: the whole community responding to *our* call to do this task through me.

(d) A corporate awareness of mutual accountability for carrying out these corporate commitments." [13]

iv. An overview

The aim here is to help a community to look realistically at its overall situation and the work it is doing; make as objective an evaluation as possible of its strengths and weaknesses; and to think imaginatively of possible future alternatives.

The following steps may help you to do this:

Step 1. Summarise briefly the total picture of the apostolic work and activities in which members of the community are engaged. Try to put this in some sort of visual or diagrammatic way showing what people are fully or partly involved in and any significant facts and feelings which have emerged.

Step 2. Sit back and scan it quietly. People could ask themselves: What strikes me about this? What questions or concerns do we need to discuss?

Step 3. On a large sheet list and discuss what strikes people. Ensure that people are clear about what is being said, and see how much agreement or disagreement there is about the total picture. Note any questions and try to group them. Then work through them in the most appropriate order.

Step 4. Decide how you, as a community, evaluate the work you are doing and how you see the future.

What do we think we should continue doing? Why? What changes do we see necessary as it continues? Can we streamline anything? Do we need extra voluntary or paid help?

Is anything we are doing being done by others, or no longer needed?

What do we think we should gradually phase out? Why? When and how do we think this could be done?

How does the fact that we belong to a national/international congregation affect our work? Do we put the energy and insights we derive from this, at the service of those with whom we work?

Is there anything we think we could well stop doing very soon or immediately? Why? How could we do this?

v. Drawing your conclusions

Evaluation is done for the sake of the future. What decisions do you now want to make about your mission and ministry? Who will take action? See *How to implement the decision* in Chapter Thirteen.

vi. Sharing a picture of your community and its work with the province

Co-responsibility exercised between communities requires them to share with each other what they are learning, and any insights into what works and does not work, thus contributing to the body of knowledge and experience on which all can draw. This is particularly true if a small community is a new venture in the province.

As a community you may be asked to give some sort of picture of your life and ministry at a province gathering. Below is one way of doing this which I have used with several communities responding to this request.

Stage 1: Building up a picture

Our community and our home: Under this heading can you, in a few sentences, give information which will help other people to picture you as a group and the house or flat in which you live.

The area and parish in which we live: Describe briefly the sort of area in which you live and the sort of people who live there.

What sort of parish are you in? What is your relationship with the clergy and parishioners?

What do you see to be the needs, opportunities and problems of the area and parish?

The work we are doing: Describe the work and activities in which you are engaged – together, separately and with other people. You may find it best to start by making a list of your activities. Try to classify them so you can see the underlying shape of your work. Asking yourselves "What are we trying to achieve through these activities?" may help you to group them according to purpose or objectives.

Problems or difficulties we face in our work: The harder the task one is trying to do, the more problematic it is likely to be. Have a go at stating any key difficulties. To identify two or three generic problems can be harder and far more useful than a long list.

Reflecting on where you are: Prepare to describe as far as you are willing to share them, your positive and negative thoughts and feelings; the needs you are meeting and any results of your work; how your work expresses your statement of purpose or mission or any other formulation of your vision as a community or as a province; and what you have learnt.

Stage II: Presenting your picture to others

Decide how you can best do this in words, spoken or written, diagrams, pictures, photos, other visual aids, through drama, or in some other imaginative way. You know your province and those to whom you will be giving your picture of yourselves: what will best communicate what you really want to share with them? Are they more likely to appreciate some creative presentation or a more factual paper?

vii. Reporting to your provincial team

As a community you may be required to give formal or informal reports, on an annual basis or during visitation, to your provincial team.

Drawing on the findings of any evaluation you have done, will enable you to give a realistic picture of your life as a community and your mission and ministry.

In preparation for this, try to put the key aspects of your community evaluation on paper in a way which will be clear and communicate what you now think and feel about the apostolic work and activities of your community. Are there alternative suggestions or specific proposals concerning the future of your community and its work which you wish to put forward to the provincial team to discuss and decide about? Some do's and don'ts of writing community reports are listed in Table 14.2.

Tables 14.2
Do's and don'ts of community reports

What to aim for:	What to avoid:
– honest portrayal	– blanket statements
– a balanced picture	– stating the obvious
– feelings as well as facts	– over-emphasis on generalities
– connoting things positively	– exhortations
– creativity	– lengthy quotes
	– boring people

REFERENCES AND NOTES

1. Newman, John Henry: *Essay on Development of Doctrine*, p.40. See also *Meditations and Devotions*, (ref. 16, p.93) pp. 508-9. He also wrote, "My unchangeableness here below is perseverance in changing".
2. I have been unable to pinpoint the source of this saying of Schillebeeckx, but it is certainly a strong assumption underlying *Jesus in our Western Culture,* Edward Schillebeeckx (SCM 1986 ISBN 0 334 02098 0).
3. Progoff, op. cit. (ref. 7, p. 159).
4. This was formulated when working with the Pallotine Sisters in 1992.
5. O'Connor, David F: 'Dysfunctional Clergy & Religious' in *Human Development,* Volume Two, Number 4, Winter 1990.
6. I am indebted to George Lovell for this model which I have used to great effect on many occasions.
7. Avec, (ref 3, p. 120).
8. An enlightening description of the use of diagrams and how to develop the facility is given by Lovell, *Analysis & Design,* op. cit. (ref. 5, p. 38) pp. 179-184.
9. Ibid. pp. 71-90.
10. Lovell, *Avec: Agency and Approach,* op. cit. (ref. 7 above) pp. 42-4.
11. Written in 1899 and published in *The Wind Among the Reeds: W B Yeats: Collected Poems* (McMillan 1970 ISBN 0 3333 4211 9).
12. O'Murchu, Diarmuid: op. cit. (ref. 2, p. 31) p. 38.
13. Futrell, John Carroll: in an unpublished paper *Forming the Team as an Apostolic Community of Love,* p.3.

XV
Making Community Meetings Work

Community meetings are an integral part of community life. They can be deeply life-giving and enjoyable for the individual and for the community as a whole. This Chapter discusses the practicalities of trying to make them so.

Meetings, whether formal or informal, are needed if people are to build up a sense of corporate identity, deepen relationships, exercise co-responsibility towards each other and make decisions. They can be a means of growth as members take responsibility for and a proper control over their lives. They are not an optional extra either for individual members or the community as a whole.

Many books can help you run group meetings.[1] In this chapter I address those difficulties which are particularly acute in community meetings, outline various types of meetings and consider issues to do with time and setting, facilitation and participation. Below is a quick list of points to refer to when running meetings.

Approaches to working with people, pp. 29-30, and 99-101.
Brainstorming rules, p. 203.
Check list for preparing exercises and meetings, p. 200.
Encouraging participation, p. 203-4.
Guided fantasy: hints on leading one, p. 206.
Sharing together, pp. 92 & 202.

1. DIFFICULTIES AND DANGERS

On the whole community meetings are not popular. Out of a group of thirty-six religious who were asked "How do you react when you hear the words 'community meeting'?" twenty-seven responded negatively. This response may be due to several factors: badly run meetings which allow some people to dominate or waste time, preoccupation with other things which seem more important, and past experiences of conflict or hurt. To these may be added the specific difficulties of meeting with people you know well and with whom you will continue to live after the meeting is over (cf. p. 33). Members of a community can all too easily fall into a pattern of responses, hear what they expect rather than what is being said, and stereotype each other. Meetings on some emotive issue may bring out the worst in people who use them to justify themselves or to get their own way. There may be a confusion of roles and relationships: you may be dealing with work matters which require a rigorous business-like approach, yet you are members of a community with relationships more akin to a family than to work colleagues.

2. TYPES OF MEETINGS

There is a clear distinction between what might be called a 'nuts and bolts' meeting which deals with those every day practical decisions which have to be made communally, and a meeting to deepen your spiritual life, or to get you thinking more widely. One community identified six types of meetings.

(a) Spiritual: way of life type of meetings (making the rule and constitutions come alive), preparing for some feast or liturgical season, a faith-sharing or prayer workshop type of exercise.[2]
(b) Life-style meetings.
(c) Input of a broadly educational nature from an outsider or prepared by a member.
(d) Informal sharing of books, stories, happenings, etc.
(e) Policy or major practical issues.
(f) Information and discussion related to work issues, mission and ministry.

These are not taken in strict rotation, but over a period the community aims to include one or more of each type. Over and above these, this community dealt with the small practical decisions by a weekly session labelled 'A.O.B.s'. If such a 'nuts and bolts' meeting is to be held alongside another type of meeting, it is usually best to finish rather than start with the practicalities, which can be emotive and drain group energy; and it is wise to have a break between the two.

3. TIME AND SETTING

In deciding on the time which best suits you as a community, one factor to be taken into account is your ministry. It is advisable that the timing of a meeting does not disrupt or cut into prime work time, nor yet be relegated to a time when people are spent and in need of relaxation and rest. If you believe in the value of community meetings, you will want to give them quality time.

Having a regular weekly or fortnightly time for meeting not only enables you to plan ahead but allows you to give notice to those who might otherwise be calling on you or your services. For a community engaged in a parish apostolate, it can be important for others to realise your meetings are sacrosanct – which does not preclude flexibility when necessary. However, it may suit some communities better to decide when to meet at the start of each week.

Such a seemingly small and obvious point as beginning and ending a meeting at the agreed times can avoid much frustration and anxiety.

The degree of formality and informality needs to be tailored to your community. For some, gathering around the kitchen table works well, whereas others find sitting in comfy chairs more helpful. It is worth trying out various venues and settings. Different types of meetings may need different settings.

4. FACILITATION

It is more important that meetings be well run than for everyone to take a turn in facilitating them. To expect someone who is inexperienced and nervous to lead a meeting can be a recipe for disaster. On the other hand, to have the same member leading every meeting can become dull and monotonous, and it does not give others a chance to grow or develop their skills. There are various ways of helping people who are unused or unable to run meetings. For instance, they could partner a good facilitator, or two people might plan and run a meeting together. This can be particularly useful if they observe each other and have a frank discussion afterwards about what each did which was helpful, anything which was unhelpful, and what they might have done when a particular difficulty arose.[3] Some types of meetings are easier to run than others and therefore better for beginners.

5. PARTICIPATION

The non-directive approach, an essential requisite for promoting fruitful participation, has been considered on pp. 99-101 and again on pp. 202-4. Below are some general guidelines to encourage participation and a number of practical suggestions. A check list when preparing for meetings and exercises and which will encourage participation is give in Table 15.1.

i. General guidelines

Community meetings are more likely to work if people are committed to them and expect to find them fruitful and enjoyable. Using a non-directive approach is of key importance in encouraging and enabling people to participate actively in a discussion.

The points below may also be useful:

Ensure that everyone has a say in everything that really matters. This includes the agenda, where and when meetings will be held and who will run them. Try setting time aside to list types and subjects of meetings for a few months ahead. Decide who will facilitate each one; some may need preparation by everyone, and while some may be run by one of the community, for others you may wish to invite an outsider in to take or lead a discussion. For the practicalities type of meeting, everyone will need to be able to add to the agenda a day or so beforehand.

Be inclusive. If you have elderly or sick members for whom a meeting is too much of a *tour de force*, think up some other way of including them. For example, one person could have a talk with them beforehand, feed in their ideas at the meeting and then share the outcome with them.

Prepare your opening gambit. Make sure the meeting opens in a stimulating way which raises rather than depresses people's expectations. Avoid being bland and platitudinous as in the following example of a meeting which opened with a quotation

Table 15.1
Check list for preparing exercises and meetings

Aim: You will need to formulate this in response to some felt or unfelt need in your situation or community.

Preparation: Sometimes, it can be useful to ask people to do some thinking or work beforehand.

Introduction and checking for acceptability: Explain the aim and structure of the meeting and check that the topic is relevant and the structure and method acceptable.

The steps and stages of the meeting: It is important to check that the tasks are clear and people understand what they are being asked to do. Check that visual aids and any other material you need for the meeting is to hand. Questions need to:

- be open rather than loaded,
- stimulate real thought,
- be clearly worded,
- avoid being unduly emotive or likely to cause defensiveness,
- be ones which you yourself would like to explore,
- be in the best order to lead people into the subject.

Implications: Towards the end, find some way to help people read off the implications for themselves and/or for the community as a whole. This may be done as personal or communal reflection and result in a community decision to take some action.

Conclusion: Be clear how you will draw the meeting or exercise to a close. One helpful way is to pause while people consider what has struck them or what they have learnt. After a couple of minutes let them share. End on time or re-negotiate the ending time if you are running late or suggest continuing at another time. Ensure that people are clear and agreed about any decisions or follow up tasks they have undertaken.

Notes or minutes: Will you need any sort of record of the meeting and if so how will this be done and by whom?

Venue: Where would be most suitable? How will you arrange the room?

from a book: "A community must see itself as a milieu where, thanks to prayer and fraternal love, the religious must be supported, enlightened and comforted". Although true, this did little to stimulate interest.[4]

Encourage people to listen to each other. It is particularly important for people who live together or are very different from each other to listen with 'fresh ears' as though they had never met. So often people do not expect or allow other members of their community to change or move in their thinking or attitudes. Methods of sharing are given in Table 15.2.

Prepare for emotive issues. Most communities have some topics that are emotionally highly charged. There are some pitfalls you need to avoid when discussing tricky issues; for example:

- trying to persuade or argue someone into changing their views: this includes preaching and proselytising. Changing one's deeply held opinions is a slow, painful, personal process. No one can *make* me change them. I can't *make* or *force* myself to change things I believe in or hold strongly. So we need patience with ourselves as well as with each other.
- judging, denigrating or criticising someone else's beliefs .
- being afraid to state one's own view in case it is harshly and hurtfully demolished. This means becoming vulnerable – and it has been said that Jesus was the most vulnerable person.
- becoming defensive about your own views or beliefs.
- closing your mind to the possibility of change or being so open that you change without giving real thought.
- pretending to believe something just for a quiet life, to curry favour, or keep in with someone or the community.

There are some things you need to do when tackling emotive topics:

- listen with the heart as well as with the head.
- try to stand in a person's shoes and understand what he is saying from the inside. It has been said that unless you can put an opposing viewpoint as well as the person holding it, you are not ready to argue with it.
- believe in the other person's integrity, respecting and trusting their sincerity. There are responsible positions on the different issues – no one must think he holds the high moral ground.
- be open to those things which challenge your own views and be prepared to think about them and take them seriously.
- explore what another person is saying and why he feels that way about it: thus help to clarify his position to himself and the rest of you.

Face the problem when community meetings are unpopular. Try to face this problem together and discuss what you can do about it. To plough on when most people dislike meetings is not a recipe for fruitfulness. As with most problems, it is possible to exacerbate or alleviate them. What can you do to make meetings more acceptable? Look at this from the point of view not only of the more obvious things to do with the topic, timing, venue, and so on, but what a person can do within herself, to try and change her attitudes: no one will ever enjoy community meetings if they are determined to dislike them. Up to now they may have done so, but maybe the future holds out more promise? Of course there will be times when a meeting is frustrating or boring: this is part of the ups and downs of life.

Table 15.2
Methods of sharing

As sharing is a necessary part of community discussion, it is important to have some generally accepted norms or ground rules. Several have been suggested in Chapter Five under *Reflecting and sharing together* on p. 92. Below are a variety of hints and methods that can be used with individuals, pairs or small groups in mind.

Have a short pause to allow people to think and possibly jot something down before opening up a topic or question for general discussion.

Give each person an opportunity to have his say while being listened to in silence before having a general discussion.

Suggest people limit their contributions to one or a limited number of key points.

When groups are reporting back on a number of points:
   – ask one group for their first point, then see if any other group has something to add, before discussing it.
   – for the second point ask another group to contribute first.

Without actually sharing their reflections, members could discuss the implications for them, personally and/or communally, of this reflection.

Afterthoughts: After a group has spent some time discussing a topic, it can be useful to ask people to pause, reflect for a moment or two on what has been said, and see what particularly strikes them. What takes place then is often on a different and deeper level of insight and learning.

ii. Practical exercises to promote participation

In addition to the four exercises outlined below, the use of such things as visual aids, flip charts, role play and imagination as well as the mundane but nonetheless important factors such as seating and room arrangements, help promote active participation.

Formulating ground rules.[5]

Formulating your own ground rules for the conduct of meetings will help them to run smoothly. One simple procedure for doing this is to ask each member to jot down one or two things that help them to participate in a meeting, and one or two things which hinder them from doing so. These could be pooled and read out or each person could read out her own. Deal first with the positive and then with the negative. From this a more formal code of good practice for the group could be drawn up. This can be added to periodically. Doing this is particularly useful when you want to help a group that does not function well to improve its performance. It gives everyone an opportunity to stand back and reflect on how they both help and hinder each other. It could be a useful review meeting in itself.

Table 15.3
Rules for brainstorming[6]

(a) Allow people a minute or two to think.

(b) List all points on a board or flip chart. This is done as quickly as possible without any discussion except to clarify a point. Above all there must be no criticism or denigration of any point at this stage.

(c) When ideas run dry, have a further pause while people reflect on the total list.

(d) After this any of the following may be appropriate:
  – start at the top and discuss each point;
  – get agreement on the 'two' or 'five' most important points and discuss those;
  – cross out points which are clearly not feasible in the situation;
  – divide into sub-groups and get each to discuss, assess or list pros and cons of one or more points.
  – listen to each report and discuss in plenary.

Encouraging participation: a method

Have what I call a table-cloth discussion.[7] This maximises participation and uses the resources of everyone to get out the aspects of a subject on which people want to work, or to form an agenda of questions. This is best done in groups small enough to sit round a sheet of paper on a table. Write down the topic or issue for discussion in the centre of the paper. Then ask everyone, using their corner of the 'table-cloth', to write down "the questions we need to discuss in order to tackle this issue". The next step is to ask them to number their questions in the order in which they could best be considered. Each reads out her first question and you decide which it is best to start with. Gradually work through all the questions. Notes of the discussion can be written on empty spaces on the 'table-cloth'.

Openness to people and ideas

Introduce the meeting by explaining that it is based on the premise that at times we all are or have appeared to be intransigent and closed to some idea or other. We can therefore learn from reflecting on our own experience.

Step 1: Ask everyone privately to reflect on and jot down what prevents them from being open to and thinking sensitively about some ideas. Assure them they will only be asked to share as far as they wish. These blocks may be:

things in myself which hinder or prevent me from thinking seriously about an idea or suggestion: (e.g. to do with my physical well-being, pre-occupation with other matters, my own expectations of sound ideas coming from certain quarters, or it may simply be that I cannot take on so many new ideas at once);

due to the person presenting the ideas (for instance, someone with strong mannerisms, or who is reproving or over-enthusiastic; whom I may suspect has ulterior motives or is not as committed to the ideas as he sounds; is dominating, hostile, or aggressive; or whom I dislike, etc.);

in the way the ideas are presented (e.g. in a confused way or so dogmatically there seems no room for moderation or addition; the use of jargon or emotive language; I may be given no time to reflect on what is being said and feel pressurised to agree or accept a 'complete package');

in the ideas themselves and their relevance (they may not relate to my experience or current thinking; they may be based on different premises from those I hold and call my whole mental framework into question; they may not appear relevant or appropriate);

in the situation (the environment may be uncongenial, or the timing wrong as far as I am concerned).

Step 2: Ask people to share their ideas as far as they wish.

Step 3: Read off the implications together by each person asking themselves: What can I do to help people be open to me and my ideas through my attitude and approach, the way I present the ideas, timing, venue, etc.? What can I do to become more open to other people's ideas? Some of the implications may be:

- to take time to listen to other people's ideas and explore why they hold them. As well as providing me with a deeper understanding of how and why they think and feel as they do, I may then be in a better position to ask them to consider my ideas.
- to agree with any of their ideas with which I can agree and build up as much common ground between us as I can, thus developing a relationship of trust.
- to ensure they realise that I am distinguishing between them and their ideas: in disagreeing with any of their ideas, I am not personally hostile to them.

iii. Learning from meetings

A meeting or a series of meetings could be reviewed and evaluated in order to learn ways of making community meetings come alive, be more effective and enjoyable.

The questions below are for personal use over a period of time. Rather than producing a lengthy list, try setting them out on a work sheet.[8] For example, take a piece of A4 and fold in two. On the front page write:

Making community meetings come alive

This worksheet and questions are intended to help us each think about what we have learned from the way a meeting was led: things which will be of help to us in the future. We may pick up practical ideas and hints of things to do when leading a discussion, or become aware of things we need to avoid. Jotting them down can focus our thinking.

With the remainder of page 1 and on other pages 2 and 3, divide up the spaces and write questions such as those below, so each has an inch or more of space. Each person decides on the areas she particularly wants to consider and writes in suitable questions, for example:

What am I learning:

 – *about starting a discussion?*
 – *about concluding a discussion?*
 – *about responding to what people say?*
 – *about what sort of questions to ask and how to ask them?*
 – *about what helps/hinders participation?*
 – *about starting the meeting so we work systematically?*
 – *about. . .?*

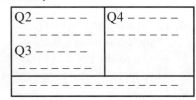

Additional questions, such as those below, could be put under a line across the bottom of the two inside pages.

Additional questions to help you think:

 Were you interested? What caught your attention?
 Did you become bored at any stage?
 Could you follow the discussion? Did you get lost?
 Did the discussion go round in circles?
 How did you feel about the person leading the discussion? How did you feel about the other members? What made you feel like this?
 Did anything put you off?
 What do you think the facilitator did best? What was she least good at?
 What did you like most about the discussion? What did you like least?

On page 4 whoever is leading the meeting could put questions such as:

 What I am learning from leading a discussion?
 About particular difficulties I faced?
 About my strengths?
 About . . . ?

A few minutes at the end of a community meeting might be given for people to fill in their work sheets. At some stage it would be valuable to spend part of a meeting sharing together as much as people wish about what they have learnt.

Table 15.4
Hints on leading a guided fantasy

The guided fantasies suggested in this book are simple ones. More sophisticated ones need to be used with care as they can evoke strong emotional reactions and are best used by those professionally competent.

Briefing for the guide

1. Get people to sit with eyes closed in a relaxed way and take a few slow deep breaths, becoming aware of their body as it touches the chair.

2. Invite them to use their imagination as creatively as possible to heighten the impact of the narrative. At the same time avoid pressure or directives of any kind.

3. Proceed with the guided fantasy.

4. Terminate the narrative with a 're-entry' routine: ask people to say farewell to the person they were with and the place they were with in, and slowly return to the present time, to the room and to the group; to open their eyes; alter their position, and maybe stretch a bit.

5. Begin the sharing session as soon as appropriate, allowing people freedom to share only that which they wish to share.

This is based on work by Esther Gordon.[9]

REFERENCES AND NOTES

1. See Bibliography p. 247.
2. Gordon and Soons, op. cit. (ref. 30, p. 94).
3. Widdicombe, op. cit. (ref. 2. p. 59) p. 192.
4. Ibid. "Ideally, the introductory remarks will not only put members at their ease but quicken their interest and stimulate them to participate. Some people find it helpful to draft their opening remarks and to check them out with a colleague or by mentally standing in the shoes of those who will hear them." p. 86.
5. Ibid. p. 189.
6. Ibid. p. 98.
7. Ibid. pp. 71-2. Other methods for taking meetings are outlined in this book.
8. Ibid. p.71. A worksheet is a questionnaire consisting of a few questions with space for people to jot down their replies. Clear instructions and unambiguous questions are necessary. Imaginative ways of setting out the questions on folded paper vertically and/or horizontally will add to its interest.
9. Gordon and Soons, op. cit. (ref. 2, above) pp. 131-4.

XVI
Meetings and Exercises

This Chapter contains practical suggestions for exercises, reflections and meetings which I have used or which have emerged as I worked with religious congregations and groups.

They are not blueprints for success, and will be more effective if you adapt them to suit your own community and situation. They can be used in a small community or with a cluster of communities. In most cases it helps if one or two people act as facilitators. The suggestions for encouraging participation given on p. 203 and particularly for reflecting and sharing together on p. 202 are important in order to avoid imposing exercises on people, or pressuring them to share more than they are ready or wish to share. Key reference points for working with groups are on p. 197, and a note about using questions in Table 16.1.

An underlying pattern for many of these exercises is outlined in the Table 15.1 on p. 234. It can be used as a check list for reference when preparing to use a particular exercise and it may enable you to adapt it more easily to your situation – or better still – design your own. The exercises are classified but there is much overlap.

1. WORKING TO FORM COMMUNITY

Several of the suggestions below pick up ideas considered in Chapter Five.

i. Characteristics of religious community

Aim: to stimulate reflection on living in community.

Introduce the meeting by explaining the steps below and either get people's agreement to them or their help in amending them to fit your situation.

Step 1: Explore the characteristics of religious community.

The characteristics mentioned on p. 32 could be written on a flip chart. Check whether there are other characteristics which occur to you. Explore each in turn. According to the number of people, this could be done one at a time with the whole group, or by individuals, pairs, or small groups, each focusing on a different characteristic.

(a) Explore the meaning of the characteristic. What are its implications for community life?

(b) Make lists of:
   – the challenges or demands inherent in a particular characteristic;
   – the opportunities or rewards inherent in it.

It may be helpful to write the findings on large sheets of paper for discussion.

Table 16.1
Questions – questions – questions!

As you will see there are many lists of questions throughout this chapter. They indicate the sorts of areas I would be wanting to ask about, were I facilitating a group exercise or doing it myself. Reading them in print can make the task of exploring an issue formidable, particularly when working on one's own. It is also true that we vary in how systematic or intuitive we are in considering our thoughts and feelings. There are times when we want to go deeply into something, and times when we want a lighter touch. To plough your way through a list of questions is not the only or always the best way to work.

If, when you come to an exercise, you find the list of questions unhelpful, you might try reading them through, not in order to answer them, but to let them sink into your subconscious. Follow this by doing your own reflecting on what emerges for you. In this way, some areas which would not have occurred to you, may do so. In doing this, you would be using the questions more as a consciousness-raising exercise than as a questionnaire.

Searching, objective and unloaded questions are key to penetrating beneath the surface.

The key question to any thinking process is: What are the questions we need to ask ourselves in order to explore. . . ?

Step 2: Private evaluation of your personal response

Take the findings of each characteristic in turn and reflect on your personal strengths and weaknesses in its regard. This could be done as a purely private exercise over a period of time. However, community members could support each other by deciding to do it at the same time, whether during a day of recollection or by selecting one characteristic for a week at a time to reflect on.

Step 3: Share your community response (cf. Sharing, pp. 92 & 202)

What does this exercise say to you? What are the implications for your community?

Long standing communities could evaluate their communal life by considering the challenges/demands and opportunities/rewards of each characteristic in silence for 2-3 minutes before discussing it and deciding how well or badly they live up to it.

ii. A salvation-struggling community

The concept of a salvation-struggling community is discussed on p. 88. If this concept does not appeal to you as a community, you could focus on those things which enhance community relationships and those which hinder them, or on what a Kingdom or Gospel-centred community would be like. People are often more realistic and practical if the discussion uses either an unfamiliar phrase or secular terms: they need to be explained and be acceptable.

If it is true that your human and spiritual growth and development lies in your struggle to live as Christians and as religious, then it is important to recognise the essential features of such a community and those things by which individuals support the struggle to live in this way or hinder it.

Step 1: Introduce the concept of a salvation-struggling community (or whatever concept you decide to use) and discuss it. What does it mean to you? Are you agreed about its meaning? Is it acceptable? If not, be prepared to change to one you are happy about.

Step 2: List the characteristic signs (a) by which a salvation-struggling community can be recognised and (b) of one which is 'asleep' and not engaged in the struggle. This could be done in groups, some working on (a) and others on (b). Pool and discuss, possibly marking those characteristics which are key. It may be helpful to classify them.

Step 3: Allow time for personal reflection on the following questions. This could take anything from 15 minutes to a week.

What could I myself do to promote a salvation-struggling community?
What would help me to do these things?
What makes me tend to avoid them?
In what ways am I in danger of forgetting or hindering our struggle?

These questions may seem mirror images of each other, but different ways of asking the same question often throw up different insights, and some people are helped by the positive and others by the negative question. Share in pairs or small groups (cf. pp. 92 & 202).

Step 4: Ask: What would help us to be more of a salvation-struggling community? Give people a minute or so to pause for thought, before pooling ideas and then asking: "What, if anything, do we do as a result of this meeting, individually and/ or as a community?" (cf. Sharing, pp. 92 & 202).

Step 5: Finally it can be enlightening to ask what has struck people from the discussion, allowing a pause for thought before people contribute ideas.

iii. Dealing with contentious issues[1]

The shadow side of our richness and diversity as human beings is our propensity for conflict, whether on a global scale or in small groups and communities. Dealing with it is one of the more challenging aspects of community life, and there is no infallible way of doing so, certainly not through the written word. There are, however, ideas and suggestions which are more likely to reduce than exacerbate conflict, and at times and in the right hands, could help to work through it satisfactorily.

Contentious issues can often be left unattended in a community because members have not developed the skills to deal with them, without taking an inordinate amount of time and emotional energy. A community which can tackle conflicting opinions on important matters in a creative way is a strong one. When embroiled in a heated conflict it may be useful to seek the help of a neutral outsider, but the more adept a community can become in handling its own problems, the better. If you decide to work at the contentious issue on your own, some of the ideas below may help you to decide if and how you will tackle things.

(a) **Agree to tackle the issues:** It is important to state the issues clearly and objectively, so people are agreed on the conflict between them. Bring as much as can be handled of genuinely polarised views out into the open and stated as objectively as possible. Try to ensure that discussion is about the real issues and not spurious or superficial matters. Avoid emotive terminology. State it as a joint problem: it is something which causes division between you. Agree to try to tackle the troublesome issue – not each other, though you may need to be forthright in talking together. Do not minimise the effort, time and emotional energy which may be needed. Check if everyone is committed to having a go, and make a contract to stick with it, even when you seem to reach an impasse. On these occasions people often have an untapped store of ingenuity if they really want to achieve something.

(b) **Review your attitudes**: Believe that your joint commitment and determination are likely to see you through to a satisfactory solution. To this end, listen carefully for anything that has a positive ring to it and as you listen, constantly ask yourself, 'What would help here?' It is important to keep calm, relaxed, and to be patient with yourself and with other people as you try to surface everyone's thoughts and feelings. Think in terms of reaching a 'win-win' rather than a 'win-lose' solution. This may involve moving from discussing the issues or causes of the conflict, to the sort of outcome wished for. Be concerned for the common good and well-being of the community and congregation.

(c) **Build in some safeguards**: Agree to certain safeguards should your discussion begin to exacerbate the conflict. For instance, you might agree that, if this happens, you will postpone future discussion until emotions have cooled down or people have had time for further thought. Or, you could put the actual discussion of the contentious issues on hold, while you consider what is happening and why things are going wrong. Clearly this would have to be treated extremely sensitively so it does not become an occasion for apportioning blame. Or you might think of another way of working at the issue, or consider obtaining outside help.

(d) **Work for mutual understanding**: As has already been said (cf. p. 90), until you can argue convincingly for the opposite viewpoint to your own, you are not able to appreciate it or ready to discuss it with those who hold it. Below are some ways of engendering mutual understanding:

– get group X (or X) to explain its position to group B (or B) so that group B is able to state it to group X's satisfaction and vice versa;

– help them to stand in another person's shoes. It can be a hard struggle to get people to do this but once experienced, people's attitudes can change radically;

– get out the essentials which each must find in the final solution. Encourage compromise and give and take on the non-essentials;

– get opposing groups to note the positive things about the other viewpoint;

– act as an objective 'go-between': interpret one group or person to another, avoid taking sides; and work for a solution or amelioration of the problem which is mutually satisfying and which does not compromise the beliefs or integrity of either person or group;

– struggle to formulate statements which incorporate the different nuances of all concerned;

– avoid solutions which fail to take account of all the factors and feelings and minority views;

– depersonalise the issues: where appropriate, keep discussion off personalities, and on issues;

– don't dismiss something as 'only emotional'. Feelings count.

(e) Towards a solution (cf. Sharing, pp. 92 & 202): Affirm and reaffirm common ground, and then explore areas of difference; establish what is agreed and gradually enlarge this, keep returning to it when differences threaten to divide. Help people to realise that agreement on some points does not mean people have to agree on all points.

Understand basic needs. Try to settle differences in a way that respects the need we all have for safety, security, love, knowledge, a sense of belonging, and self-esteem. Get people in sub-groups to work at a possible solution which meets both their own needs and those of others.

List alternative solutions and work on their pros and cons. Allow time for people to mull these over and to pray about them.

As appropriate, summarise and try to formulate a solution and check it for genuine agreement. Success in this may call for a celebration. In situations where the conflict has been deep-seated, when agreement is reached it may be helpful to seal it with some action, such as exchanging the sign of peace or a reconciliation service. It is important, however, to ensure everyone is ready for this: an imposed sign of peace can be disturbing, offensive, hypocritical and deepen the conflict.

iv. Living in a community where there are significant differences[2]

Introduction. This meeting follows from the consideration of living with difference, on p. 89. It can be obvious in community how people's different personalities, gifts and abilities are beneficial, but at times differences cause difficulties. As Christians, religious are committed to building up communities of love, yet you have probably not chosen the individuals with whom you live. You may be faced with a situation where the differences between people cause difficulties: hurt, conflict, jealousy, etc. The exercises below may help you consider such difficulties with a degree of objectivity and decide how to improve matters.

Step 1: Give people a sheet of paper on which the questions below are set out with an inch or so between each one, so they can jot down their thoughts. Work through the questions individually or in pairs.

(a) What are the significant differences between members of our community?

(b) When do any of these differences cause or present difficulties?

(c) What kind of difficulties are caused by them?

(d) What can we do in relation to the differences
  – when they are *not* causing difficulties?
  – when they *are?*
  – after they *have caused* difficulties?

Step 2: Come together to pool your findings. Discuss and possibly agree on some implications for action, individually or as a group. You may want to raise supplementary questions in the discussion e.g. why do we tend to be afraid of differences? When are they useful? (cf. Sharing, pp. 92 & 202).

v. Needs, wants and expectations

This exercise follows from the consideration of individual and community needs on p. 73. Every member has personal needs which to a great extent he expects to be met by or through the community. Bringing these to the surface of consciousness, individually and corporately, may well enable people to see to how far they are realistic, whether or not they are being met, and how they might be met more effectively. Our needs vary in kind and in degree at different ages and in different situations and because we are very different people. Something which would be superfluous for you, might make all the difference to someone else's well-being.

Step 1: A time for personal reflection on the questions below could be given either at the start of the meeting or well beforehand.

What are my personal needs and wants: physically, emotionally, socially, intellectually and spiritually? How different are my needs from my wants? What do I hope and expect of the community? What do I *not* expect of the community? How realistic am I being?

Small Communities in Religious Life

Step 2: Meet and allow time for everyone to share as much or as little as they wish while the others listen without comment. (cf. Sharing, pp. 92 & 202).

Step 3: Together, identify the issues or key areas of need and expectation you wish to discuss. Check how you are trying to meet these needs both as individuals, and as a community group. How realistic are people's hopes and expectations of the community? Are you doing too much or too little to meet each one's needs? How can you ensure each one's well-being without becoming over-indulgent?

Step 4: Decide what action to take individually and communally.

vi. Privacy and togetherness in community

This topic may arise in the above discussion, but it could well be the subject of a meeting in itself. The above method suggested for *Needs, wants and expectations* could be used with the questions below or it could be the topic for a table-cloth discussion (cf. p. 203).

Privacy. How much privacy do I need? How do I know this? What do I need to use it for? Why is it important for me? What practical arrangements could I/we make to enable me to have such privacy? Once I have it how can I safeguard it? When should I forgo it or allow it to be interrupted? How am I likely to invade my own privacy or allow others to do so? When is that legitimate? What are my perceptions of other members' needs for privacy?

Companionship in community. What are my needs for being together in community? How do I hope or expect these to be met? Are they fairly constant or do they fluctuate? Are there times when I have more need of community companionship? When?

In relation to meeting my own needs:

- do I look to my own community to meet them or beyond it?
- what arrangements do I find most helpful?
- when am I in danger of over-indulging or of ignoring my needs?
- what is my perception of the need for companionship and the friendship of those with whom I live?
- how far am I meeting or prepared to meet the differing needs of others for *koinonia* companionship, and friendship?

vii. A free day

One small community experienced many problems as members had different ideas on the subject. Variously individuals thought:

- everyone should have one free day a week;
- people had sufficient *ad hoc* free time and did not need a designated day;
- everyone should have the same day to allow for going out together;
- people should choose their own free day which they could alter week by week;
- when free, people should still attend communal prayer.

What are your views? What pattern would best fit you as individuals and as a community?

viii. Theological reflection on community

Reflecting theologically on community, can deepen your realisation of what you are about and be a strong source of motivation. Below are various alternative starters for personal reflection or group discussion.

Which scriptural texts are significant for you in relation to your small community?

E. F. Schumacher coined the phrase 'Small is beautiful'. Another common tag is 'There is strength in numbers'. What are the advantages and disadvantages of (a) small communities? (b) large communities? (c) a province or congregation consisting of both? Arbuckle has often said "The new belongs elsewhere",[3] meaning that new ways of living religious life need new situations in which to try them out. What truth do you see in this?

What do you see as the main links between a small community and:
– the theological concepts of the church which were emphasised in VaticanTwo?
– the renewal of religious life called for in *Perfectae Caritatis*?[4]
– the ability to witness?
– the gospel imperatives?
– the charism of your congregation?
– your mission statement?

Pope John Paul II has stressed the primary apostolic importance of small communities of religious women in a parish because they work with small numbers, build up community, and are a feminine influence[5]. How true do you think this is?

ix. Improving communication

For this exercise to be fruitful, it needs to be done by a fairly mature community where people are used to being open with each other. It needs to be treated objectively and with sensitivity. The danger is that it could lead people to blame each other or to become defensive.[6]

Step 1: In pairs take a scenario involving quite a bit of communication: an incident in which things have gone wrong because of a lack of or bad communication between you. Try to use a real, relatively recent scenario. You are free to change it a little: you may need to extend it or run two examples together.

Step 2: Pinpoint the breakdowns/trip-ups
Ask yourselves why? What happened?
If it happens again how could you manage better?
What could you learn from your mistakes?
What would you like to tell or pass on to the rest of us to help us?

Step 3: Come together to share scenarios. Do this by treating each like a case study which you have analysed. Either just describe your case study factually and say what you have learned; or do it as a role play, say what you have learned and ask the rest if they picked up anything else from it.

Together make a summary of points raised in terms of guidance or do's and don'ts. Points may arise in relation to one or two issues which need more detailed discussion at a later date.

x. Getting to know each other

Getting to know each other is an on-going process and a pre-requisite for deeper *koinonia* between you. Two possible exercises for helping the process are suggested below.

· Drawing your lifeline

You will need sheets of paper and pencils, perhaps also crayons or coloured pens. Give people the instructions below:

Find a quiet spot in which you will not be disturbed. Begin by sitting quietly to centre yourself and become conscious of your breathing. Now, focus on an early memory. This is the starting point for your life-line.

With your paper horizontal, starting at the left hand margin, draw the line of your life, let it curve, wriggle or move up and down to indicate how different times of your life felt for you. Play games with your line! Mark different periods with symbols or pictures. Try to avoid words, but use a word or phrase if you are unable to think of another way of expressing what you want to say. Symbols often help to go deeper than verbal expression. If you like, use colours. Should you run out of paper turn over and continue on the other side. Take an hour or more.

When you come together as a group there are two other possible steps. (cf. Sharing, pp. 92 & 202).

(a) Share in pairs or threes, for twenty minutes or so, as much or as little as you wish. If stressful or painful insights have emerged in the course of the drawing, do not feel obliged to share them. Your privacy and that of others needs to be respected.

(b) Sit in a circle with your lifelines on the floor in front of you. For a quarter of an hour or so share how you felt about doing the exercise. How did it go for you? Should anyone wish to share something from their lifeline they are free to do so.

A way of ending off is to put all the lifeline pictures in a mosaic on the floor and quietly move round in a circle looking at them, and as you focus on a paper, pray for that person.

In describing this exercise I have drawn heavily on the work of Gordon and Soons.[7]

· **Life histories**

This is an even more informal sharing of past experience through individuals telling their life stories to each other. People need time to prepare on their own, or you may like to use Step 1 of the exercise on p. 259 to start you off. The way in which you listen to each other is crucial (cf. Sharing pp. 92 & 202). *Work and life resumé* on p. 187 is a more formal method which could be adapted to focus on your life stories rather than ministry.

xi. Using an article or book: various methods

An increasing number of thought-provoking articles and books are appearing on religious life: they could be a useful focus for a meeting. Various ways of doing this are suggested below.

– One member gives a resumé and raises questions for discussion.

– Everyone is given a copy of an article to study beforehand and asked to raise any questions, say what struck them or what they agreed or disagreed with.

– An article, chapter or book could be divided up between people and each asked to summarise their section and raise questions for discussion.

xii. Building a faith community

Working with religious communities and belonging to a lay community myself, I have come across and developed a number of exercises which encourage mutual faith sharing. I have chosen the ones which follow, either because I have found them especially powerful or because they are less well known. Further ideas can be found in *Wholetime: a handbook for workshops* by Gordon and Soons.[8] In all of them the suggestions for sharing together on pp. 92 & 202 are important.

· **Meditating on an object**

This may centre on a common object such as a rock, a candle or household object. Alternatively people may be invited to bring an object which means a great deal to them. Invite people to get to know their object, to relate to it, reflect on it and its purpose. Ask them to reflect on it theologically: what has it to say to you about God? What could you learn from it about God, yourself, and the relationship between you and God? After some quiet reflection, share in pairs or together.

· **Sharing a passage, poem or book**

Each person brings some passage, which may or may not be from the scriptures, or a poem and reads it aloud. This could be followed by saying why they have chosen it or by asking people to say if anything struck them. Alternatively, people could come with a book to recommend and say why it has been of use to them.

· Who am I?

Everyone draws a 5-segmented circle. Using words, colours or symbols, members fill in one of the segments in response to each question below:
>Who am I for God?
>Who am I for myself?
>Who am I for my Community?
>Who am I for my family/friends?
>Who am I for my colleagues/neighbours?

· A God experience[9]

Reflect on a time when you felt deeply touched by God.
What was it like for you?
Share this experience or part of it with the person next to you.

· What keeps me spiritually alive?

We are each responsible for trying to keep ourselves spiritually alive. It can be helpful to reflect on what helps you to do this. Give yourself some time (30 – 60 minutes) to reflect on this and then share as much as you wish. Listen to each person in turn until all have spoken, before any general discussion. A similar question is, "What sustains me in life?"

· Choices and consequences[10]

The first part of this exercise needs to be done in silence. Ask each member of the group to select a rose from a container. Invite each person to look at their rose. Admire its beauty. Then invite them to destroy their rose.

Allow people time to get in touch with their feelings about destroying the rose. (You may find several people felt unable to do so). Share together.

Reflect on and discuss what this has to do with justice.

· Discovering useful symbols

After helping people to centre themselves quietly, ask them to think of a symbol which is called forth by one of the following phrases (only use one).

>Who is God for me?
>How is life for me now?
>My religious vocation is like. . . .

Suggest they work with the first symbol they think of rather than search for a 'better' one. Invite them to mull it over gently and see what comes to mind. It may help to share in two's before sharing with everyone.

· **God, the church, and you and . . .**

Give everyone an A4 piece of paper and invite them to reflect on the relationship between four or five of the following: God, the church, the congregation, this community, myself, the world, work. Suggest they try to illustrate these relationships on their paper. Share in twos and in the wider group.

2. NURTURING YOUR RELIGIOUS VOCATION

The suggestions for sharing together on pp. 92 & 202 will be helpful in relation to all the exercises below.

i. Your founder/foundress

The suggestions below are different ways in which you could reflect on your founder or foundress. Clearly these could be adapted to a meeting with any significant person or group in your congregation. (cf. *Hints for leading a guided fantasy* on p. 206.)

· **A conversation with your Foundress**

This 30-45 minute exercise involves each of you having a personal conversation with your foundress and then sharing what you each wish to share about that conversation. The steps are based on those suggested by Progoff when having this sort of dialogue with someone.[11] One member could talk people slowly through the following steps.

Step 1: Ask people to reflect on their own life, beginning with the date and place of birth and then remembering eight or nine points in time when significant choices had to be made. Suggest they jot these down.

Step 2: Ask them to jot down, in a similar way, eight or nine significant occasions in the life of your foundress and the responses and decisions she made which shaped her future.

Step 3: Suggest they start an interior conversation with the foundress, discuss with her what is of concern to them, imagine her reactions and listen to her responses. What will she say about how you are living as a member of your congregation? How will she respond to what you are facing? Has she any advice? Suggest people jot down the conversation, letting their pen follow their thoughts. Give them time to do this until you judge they are nearing the end, then gently ask them to draw the conversation to a conclusion.

Step 4: When people have 'returned' to the group, suggest they share, possibly in pairs and then in the whole group, what this experience felt like and some of the insights reached in the conversation.

· A significant moment

Invite each person to pick a significant moment in the life of your founder and enter into his feelings.

Take 10-15 minutes over this. Then ask them "What is the moment saying to you now?" Pause for thought and then ask people to share their responses.

· A word in your ear

Invite people to sit comfortably, relax and close their eyes. Imagine your founder walks into the room and asks to address you. Read out some saying or passage from him or ask people by way of preparation, to bring one to read out. Suggest people listen and reflect on what they have heard in relation to the needs of the church and the world today, as though they had never heard the saying before. This is to help people to think in a new and fresh way about some significant inspiration of your congregation. Invite them to listen again and then take time to reflect, on their own, as to why your founder might be saying that to you now. In due course share in some way.

ii. Consider your charism

Living in a small community provides an opportunity to explore your initial charism and how it has been lived, used, developed and changed through the years, and identify its contemporary significance for you, the church and for society.

· An outline for personal and communal reflection

The charism of a congregation is not an object, it is a living and growing vision and inspiration which gives a congregation its characteristic style and focus of life and work. The facilitator describes the charism or the group clarify it together and then suggests the following steps.

Step 1: Personal reflection

(a) Give yourself time and space to reflect on your charism. You may find it helpful to pray through it quietly, to re-write it in your own words, to reflect on how it has affected your own life and work.

(b) How do you see yourself living out your charism in your small community? How is this different from when you lived in a large community? How do you intend to keep your congregation's charism alive in you rather than leave it between the pages of your constitution? What help, if any, do you need in doing this? Where and how you will get it?

Step 2: Community reflection

(a) Suggest people share as much as they wish from their personal reflection. It could be useful to see it re-written in people's own words or to do this together.

(b) Think creatively as to how your charism could manifest itself in your life and mission as a community. How will it affect those among whom you live, those with whom you work, your parish, and others? Your charism is a gift not just to your congregation but to the church, to the people of God, to humanity at large. How will you pass it on? How could you encourage others, especially lay people, to adopt and develop it in their own way and in secular society? You might work in pairs on different aspects of this.

(c) It may be appropriate to make a date in your community calendar for reviewing any decisions you have made.

· **Change and conservation**[12]

This exercise is based on the ideas about change and conservation discussed on pp. 25 & 73. Consider Figure 16.1 below.

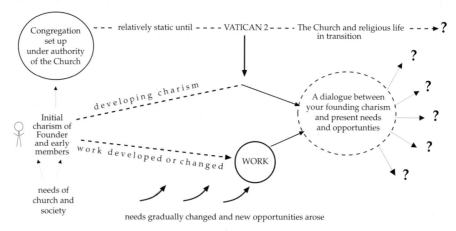

Figure 16.1
Development of your charism

For the original charism of your congregation to be fruitful in later times there have been changes, but through them all certain values, concepts or ideals have been conserved.

(a) What is it that you need to conserve from your religious heritage in order to be faithful to the charism which has been handed down to you?

(b) What is it that you need to change in order to conserve these things?

(c) What difficulties do you face in relation to making these changes?

(d) What *could* you do about them?

(e) What *will* you do about them? How can you set about it?

· **Personality choice**

Invite people to take half an hour on their own to think about one or more past or present members of the congregation whom they have known. Who have they found particularly significant or inspiring? Why? In what way were they living out the charism? After sharing with the group, suggest people reflect on what they can learn about themselves through their choice.

· **Sharing your charism with others**

The charism of a congregation was a gift at a time when it was needed. If it is a valid charism for all time it can be communicated to others, and developed in different ways according to the current situation and needs. It is a gift to the church – religious men and women, secular clergy, and lay people. Even if a congregation shrinks or dies, the charism could have been passed on into the life-blood of the church and flourish. That the charism flourishes is important.

Together list the lay people with whom you come into contact in your lives and work. Put them into categories such as colleagues, clients, benefactors, contacts, employees, employers, friends, relations etc.

Give each person or pair one category to focus on while discussing questions such as those below. Suggest they keep notes so they can share their findings with the rest of the group – or they may like to write something on a large sheet of paper.

(a) How do we feel about the lay people we are in touch with: what are our positive feelings? What are our negative feelings? Could we or should we involve lay people more? If so, how?

(b) In what ways are we or are we not on an equal footing with these lay people and they with us? Do we rely on them or do they rely on us? Is there a real 'give and take' between us? Could there be?

(c) How much do they know about our charism? Where does it touch them? To what extent are they influenced by it?

(d) How would we wish to see the charism deepening and developing in their lives? What could we do to help it to flourish in this way?

After 20-30 minutes call the groups together to share their findings. Discuss what people think as a result of all that has emerged. Is there anything of a practical nature which people want to work at immediately?

iii. Your vocational call

Invite people to reflect on their call to the congregation. You may do this by talking them slowly through the various life stages below: (cf. *Hints for leading a guided meditation* on p. 206.)

- when they first heard of or met members of the congregation. . . .
- when they first felt attracted. . . .
- their request to join. . . .
- preparing to enter – what it felt like for them, how family and friends reacted. . . .
- the day they entered. . . .
- their postulancy, first impressions, how they felt. . . .
- their novitiate, its ups and its downs. . . .
- key moments in their religious life, e.g. change of community, change of work, a retreat, etc. . . .
- the present moment: what is God saying to them through all this?

Or you may ask people to reflect not only on what drew them initially into the congregation but what it is that keeps them in it now. Invite people to share as much as they wish.

iv. Making your constitutions come alive[13]

One of the inherent dangers in having religious constitutions is that, because they set out the ideals by which people aim to live as members of a particular congregation, they can arouse all sorts of negative feelings. A group of religious were so concerned about this that they spent three days focusing on ways of making their constitutions come alive. We began by listing the feelings which made it difficult for them to live their constitutions. These included:

- guilt at not living up to them, "I lack the self discipline to take them seriously and work on making them meaningful in my life", "It is difficult to commit myself wholeheartedly when I know my enthusiasm waxes and wanes, I have so many pressures and demands already".

- fear of not being able to live up to the ideals caused reluctance to study them deeply: "not wanting to know", "quietly stifling them as too uncomfortable to live with", "impatience with myself", and a deeper fear "of not being sincere, and of what will be asked of me".

- negativity because "they are unrealistic and Utopian in practice though I accept the theory", "I am so familiar with them they feel stale", and "studying them is a waste of time, I don't know where to begin".

- feeling threatened because "the ideals set out are so contrary to my normal reactions".

We put together various ideas and exercises to help this group of sisters and their communities overcome the difficulties above and get help from their constitutions in the daily living of their religious life.

Small Communities in Religious Life

· Developing new attitudes

The developing of a positive attitude towards the constitutions is essential for making the most of them, and forms a necessary basis for personal reflection and community discussion. You might give people the material below and suggest they reflect on it privately before discussing it together.

The diagram below sets out the problem, so people recognise and acknowledge it. It states what is necessary for living the constitutions. This is related to what Fromm says about alienated and non-alienated activity (cf. p. 68).[14] The latter makes for authenticity. Realise that the constitutions set out ideals to be aspired to and striven for, a programme

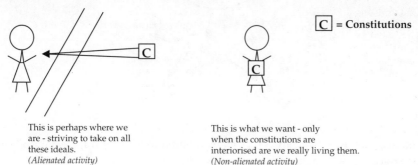

$\boxed{C}$ = Constitutions

This is perhaps where we
are - striving to take on all
these ideals.
(Alienated activity)

This is what we want - only
when the constitutions are
interiorised are we really living them.
(Non-alienated activity)

for life, rather than a set of precepts which people are expected to attain in the near future. They are meant to inspire and stimulate. To expect too much from ourselves or our communities is counter-productive and leads to discouragement and self-denigration.

Reflect on the thought, prayer, and effort which has gone into drawing up and revising the constitutions. Although rooted in the past they are intended to be a help towards living our particular charism today. It is a functional document which has to be appropriate for a wide variety of individuals, situations and communities.

· Personal exercises

The various suggestions below will appeal to different people. It is important to use an exercise you feel to be helpful.

Pray with the constitutions, for instance, meditate on a particular part, or use a sentence as a mantra, write out an article in the form of a prayer, or find a psalm connected with it.

Focus on the practice of a section for a limited time, such as a day or a week or for Lent, deciding how to remind yourself, and when to review how it is going.

Work on a trial web:[15] put down a phrase or word from the constitutions in the centre of a piece of paper and then jot down and connect up any ideas which it sparks off in you. The following example was centred on the idea of meetings.

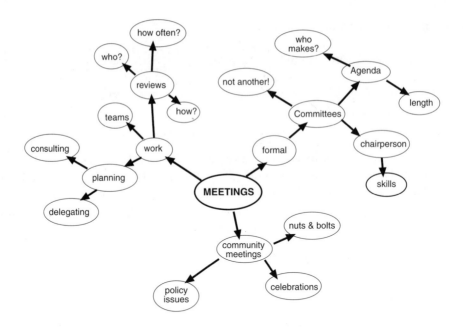

Learn key passages by heart. This can be a quiet meditative way of internalising particular articles which appeal to you.

Annotate or illustrate your constitutions by:

– interleaving blank pages for illustrations, personal comments or apt quotations;
– writing margin notes;
– underlining passages that particularly strike you as inspiring or challenging.

· Communal discussion

Go through a particular section of your constitutions:

Step 1: Underline the words/phrases which particularly apply to you as a community.

Step 2: Everyone asks themselves: What must I do inside myself, and what must I do or say in order to make these ideals affect me and my life and work?

Step 3: Share by listening to each other in turn before discussing together.

Step 4: Use one of the ideas below if you want to draw out practical conclusions.

Brainstorm the difficulties you face in making the constitutions a practical reality in your day to day living (cf. p. 203). Use the problem-tackling sequence on p. 168 to work through the common problems. When you are working towards solutions it is useful to differentiate between:

Small Communities in Religious Life

What will help you as an individual.
What will help you as a community.
How you can help each other.

Discuss in pairs how the constitution affects your everyday lives or fails to do so. As you listen to your partner, be accepting and supportive as well as challenging him to think more deeply about what he is saying. You might make a contract between you to focus on a particular section for a period of time and then review how things have gone.

As a community focus on particular sections for specified periods, using it in your prayers together. Think creatively of ways in which you will keep the chosen bit in mind.

3. REFLECTING ON RELIGIOUS POVERTY

In the face of the complex and daunting issues surrounding global injustice, poverty, starvation and oppression, there is a constant temptation to succumb to a feeling of utter powerlessness. The exercises in this chapter are offered in the belief that each person and each community **can** *make a difference at some level, and maybe at many levels. They have emerged from working with groups of religious who wanted to grasp this nettle, take a new look, and work out fresh ways in which their vow of poverty and their preferential option for the poor could take a deeper hold of their lives and lead to more practical action.*

i. Taking an option for the poor

Taking a preferential option for the poor can be seen as an attitudinal stance, a move, as it were, from being in the centre of the world among the comfortably off, to being on the edge, alongside those pushed to the margins, unwanted, unseen, rejected, ignored or oppressed. This is a move from looking at the marginalised as other, to trying to stand alongside them, be in solidarity with them and view things from their perspective. Clearly, this is no substitute for a direct experience of poverty or marginalisation, but nonetheless it can be thought-provoking and challenging and lead towards inner conversion. The ideas below are based on Figure 16.2 and could well be worked through over a period of time.

Step 1: Put up, or give people a copy of Figure 16.2. Suggest fifteen minutes or so of personal reflection or discussion in pairs or small groups. Alternatively you could build up, or give people, only the central features of the diagram and ask them individually or in groups to list those people on the margins, and then to list the practical effects of an inner orientation to standing alongside marginalised people. Pool and discuss your findings. (cf. Sharing pp. 92 & 202).

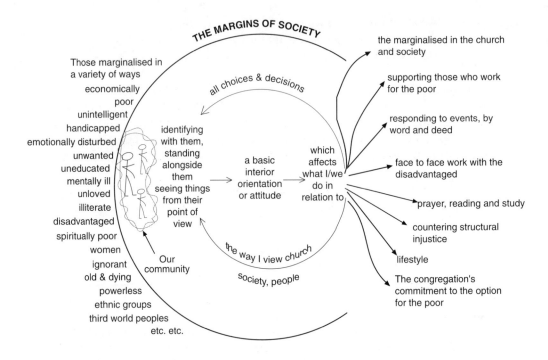

Figure 16.2
Orientation to those on the margins

Step 2: Take each of the topics listed on the right-hand side of the diagram and explore their possibilities without making any decisions at this point. They are not in any particular order. If this is done in pairs or sub-groups, get each group to start on a different aspect and move on from there, so all points get covered. Most of the sections which follow correspond to one of these aspects.

The following three questions are relevant to each of them:
    What could this entail individually and communally?
    What hinders me/us from taking action?
    What would encourage me/us to do so?

The marginalised in the church, congregation and religious community. Individuals and groups, with whose stance you may or may not agree, can be marginalised by the church both globally and locally in parish and diocese, by the congregation and by a community. Ask yourselves:
Who are marginalised in each of these areas and how is this manifest?
What are the dangers in congregational and community life for marginalising each other?
In what ways do we often justify ourselves in doing nothing about this? What stand might we take individually or communally?

Supporting those who work for the poor. What possibilities are open to *us*, within the congregation and outside it? How to make this more of a non-alienated than an alienated activity (cf. p. 68)? What particular justice and peace issues are any of us committed to or engaged in?

Responding to events by word or deed. Do any events, whether local or further afield, spring to mind to which we have responded or failed to respond?

Face-to-face work with the disadvantaged. Albert Nolan[16] identifies four stages of spiritual development through which we go, as Christians, in our relationship with and service of the poor. Compassion and relief work are his first step.

Earth your discussion by asking yourselves such questions as: Who are the marginalised people in our neighbourhood and in our town? What do we really understand by the term? What are the needs of marginalised people? Are we in touch with them, are they being cared for?

There are different approaches to this work: doing things *for* people which they are not in a position to do for themselves; doing things *with* people, thus working in partnership and making use of their insights, abilities and skills; and giving sufficient encouragement and support to enable people to do things for themselves. Ask yourselves: What sort of face-to-face work might we do with marginalised people, individually or as a community, or possibly with the parish or work colleagues? What approach would be the most appropriate? This may vary as the work develops. Would we envisage all being involved to the same degree or in the same way? How could we make it more likely that we learn from and are evangelised by those with whom we work? In the light of our primary purpose in living as a small community, would we see ourselves engaged in episodic, *ad hoc*, temporary face-to-face actions, or in long-term work with all the stress and struggle of seeing it through?

Prayer, reading and study. How can we ensure that through reading, listening to talks, and study we become better informed about and more committed to the poor, identifying more closely with them and increasingly seeing things from their point of view, rather than allowing these activities to let us off the hook of face-to-face work?

Countering structural injustice. For Nolan working for structural change of unjust systems is the second stage of spiritual development in relation to the service of the poor. It may well be undertaken alongside face-to-face work with the poor.

It can mean working with the well off or those in positions of power, in order to counter anyone or anything that keeps others in situations of disadvantage. Ask yourselves: In what ways are we or could we do this, individually and as a community? Structures in society embody the values of the majority and the powerful and do much to ensure that the division between rich and poor, oppressor and oppressed remain in place. How might we be colluding in keeping unjust structures in place? In what ways might we challenge these?

Life-style (cf. p. 73). Taking an option for the poor does not necessarily mean living as they do. How could our life-style and domestic arrangements witness to our option for the poor? In what ways could they be a counter witness? What do we or could we do about re-cycling and conservation? What personal habits witness to or are contrary to our option for the poor?

The congregation's commitment to the option for the poor (cf. p. 75). What has the congregation as a whole, or some communities or individuals done because of our option for the poor? If we as a community are taking some radical stance or action, how can we ensure that we share what we learn with others and possibly stimulate them to further commitment? How can we do this without being or appearing to be judgemental?

Is there any danger of us hiding behind the actions of others? How might we learn from and support them? As a congregation, are we too inward-looking, concentrating on our own poor, or should we recognise the poor among ourselves before going out to others?

Your attitude to yourself. How do we experience inner poverty and powerlessness? What could help us to come to terms with our own poverty, whether of health, age, abilities, etc.?

Step 3: Having explored various aspects of taking an option for the poor, decide as individuals and as a community what this option will mean in practice for you and your community. How will you keep yourselves up to your decisions? Will you set a time for reflecting on and learning from your actions?

ii. Solidarity with the poor[17]

Write the description of different categories of people on pairs of cut out paper footprints, e.g. 'homeless', 'AIDS victim', 'famine victim', 'refugee', 'lonely', 'abused', 'childless', 'person who had an abortion', 'person undergoing a nervous breakdown'.

Invite each person to take a pair of footprints and stand on them or sit with their feet resting on them. Give them time to reflect on and enter into the experience of the person whose footprints they are standing on. (cf. *Hints on leading a guided fantasy* on p. 206.)

In turn listen as each one shares the experience of 'being' that person. (cf. pp. 92 & 202).

De-brief yourselves and ask: What challenges us about the whole experience? Are there any implications for us in relation to what we might do personally or communally?

Small Communities in Religious Life

iii. The human face of need: encounters[18]

What follows is a suggestion to help communities to 'put a human face' on some pressing problems in society. It is often through a face-to-face encounter that we begin to understand the difficulties people are going through and realise that 'the poor' have similar hopes and fears to ourselves. This might sensitise us to the best ways in which we could help them, or work with them to enable them to help themselves. Nolan stresses that in the final analysis it is only the 'poor' who must and can save themselves.

One way of doing this, is for you as a community to identify some of the areas of need in today's society about which you are concerned e.g. unemployed people, alcoholics, homeless people (down-and-outs, young, women, one-parent families), drug addicts, families coping with handicapped members (young or old with senile dementia), prisoners, ex-prisoners and their families, AIDS victims or any other areas known to the community.

Choose one, or at most two, of these areas for deeper study. Try to gain first-hand experience of the need through personal contact with a victim of the need and/or someone who works with such people. This task may be carried out by one or two members. Before you meet anyone prepare yourselves by asking such questions as:

What do we hope to get from this meeting?

How can we put the person at ease?

What questions can we ask?

Have we any negative feelings, fears or judgemental attitudes we need to face in ourselves before we meet them?

How can we get them to 'tell us their story'?

How should we explain our interest? Are we in danger of seeming to be patronising, superior, curious, or inquisitive.

How can we help ourselves to begin to understand them, how they feel, what they think about life and other people who appear better off, their hopes and fears, and how they keep going?

After the encounter it could be very helpful to write down individually what has struck you, what you feel you have learnt, and any change in your own feelings or attitudes.

Share your experience with the community. It may be possible in some cases to invite a person along to meet the community.

iv. Money – how we use it: personal and communal reflection[19]

Aim: to help people become more aware of the roots of their personal attitude to money and increase their sensitivity towards others with different attitudes and ways of using it.

The questions below are a guide to personal reflection on the place of money in your life. It may help to jot things down for your personal use. Then share your reflections by listening to each person in turn without discussion until all have spoken (cf. pp. 92 & 202). The influence of an early experience on forming our attitudes to money is considered on p. 78.

(a) What does the word 'money' mean to you? How do you feel about money? What do you think about these feelings? Are you proud or ashamed of them?

(b) Think back to the formative years of your early childhood. How was money used at home? How important a factor was it? What still influences you from the way your parents and other significant adults spent or saved money?

(c) Think back to your school days. Did you have more or less than other children? What did you feel about this? Did others know or guess or comment? What effect did this have on you? Does it affect the way you see money and use it now?

(d) Think more generally around your childhood: relatives, friends and neighbours. Were people well-off, hard-up, or struggling? What influence did your social and cultural environment have on you? Was there an agreed or generally accepted hierarchy of values? Is some of this still affecting you?

(e) Your initial formation in religious life. How did attitudes towards money and community customs in its use strike you? What influences remain with you from those days? How strong or weak are these influences on you and your attitudes now? Have there been any significant events which have reinforced or changed your attitude to money?

(f) Now look again at your answer to the question, "What does money mean to you?". How would you explain to yourself, and possibly others, why you think and feel as you do about money and its use?

(g) Our attitudes towards money have probably been formed unconsciously over the years, but having alerted yourself to what your attitudes are and how they may have developed, you are now in a better position to exert some control over them. How happy or uneasy are you about your attitude to money and its use? What do you see as a better attitude? Why? Do you see this attitude reflected in the Gospels?

Changing one's attitude is a painstaking and slow business. It is encouraged by taking actions which are at variance with the attitude we are trying to change, for example, lending things we are possessive about. Reflection, journalling, examining whether your actions have been consistent with your old attitude or with the one you are trying to initiate, also help. You need to be patient with yourself. Pondering and praying about it will move you forward and help you to view others with more understanding.

After you have shared your reflections, pause while you ask yourself what has struck you from listening to everyone. Then share and discuss this.

4. TAKING A FRESH LOOK AT MISSION

Reflecting together on various aspects of your mission can renew your enthusiasm and motivation, stimulate new ideas, and provide encouragement and support. The ideas on sharing together on pp. 92 & 202 are relevant to all the exercises.

i. Reading the signs of the times

This meeting would be suitable both for a new community which is exploring what its particular ministry will be or by way of review for an established community.

Preparation. You might alert members to the subject a week or more before this meeting and ask them to let it go though their minds, or suggest people focus on different areas, for example, on the newspapers, radio or TV news, or listen to what subjects people in the work-place or neighbourhood are talking about. Alternatively, you may feel that people are more likely to raise key 'signs' if they are unprepared and spontaneous.

Introduction. Start by reading Matthew 16 v 2-3 in which Jesus challenged his followers to read, not the signs of the coming weather, but the signs of the time in which they were living. Give yourselves a few minutes to reflect on the message these two verses hold for you today.

Discerning the signs of our times. If people have prepared as suggested above, now is the time for them to share their thoughts (cf. pp. 92 & 202). This might be done in a straight-forward way by asking some of the following questions.

What do we see to be the needs and key issues of today: problems, trends, particular approaches or methods, new opportunities, and the general atmosphere?

What particularly strikes us as we look around us today (locally, nationally, or internationally)?

Another way would be to use the wall newspaper method.[20] Sit in silence with a large sheet of paper on the wall on which is written 'The signs of the times'. Suggest people write up any signs which strike them, using felt pens. Do this in silence for 10 or more minutes before you discuss.

If you decide to be unprepared and spontaneous, you could have a supply of recent newspapers and ask people to browse through them for ten minutes or so before asking:

What are your feelings as a result of your browsing?
What is this saying about society today?
What signs of the times do we discern from the papers?

Reading off the implications for ourselves. Jesus blamed those who questioned him, not because they did not see the signs, but because they failed to interpret them. Interpretation is a more difficult and demanding activity. It calls for reflection, honesty and an openness to committing oneself to action of some sort. Ask yourselves the questions below.

What are these 'signs of the times' saying to us about what needs to be done?

What facts about our situation do we need to take into account when discussing what to focus on? Clearly, there is such a complex web of needs, trends and issues that no one person or community could encompass more than a minuscule amount. Motivation makes for perseverance and creative action. Ask yourselves: Do we need more information? Information can lead to motivation. Should we take the next few months to explore the subject before deciding what we might or might not do? If so, how do we do this: books, talks, a course, reflection, discussion or in some other way?

What will we focus on? Will this be for an indefinite period or for a few months or a year?

How will this focus affect our mission and ministry? Would it be more feasible if it informs what we are already doing rather than for us to do something extra?

Do we need any training or particular skills, help or advice from persons or organisations with appropriate experience? Is this something we do on our own, or interest others in and seek co-operation for? If so, who: the parish, other churches, organisations or groups, or the congregation?

When do we review what we are doing? When do we take another look at the signs of the times to ensure we keep up with them? Make a note on your community calendar.

In thinking about the above, it could be worth reflecting on how elderly or infirm members of a community might be involved, not only through prayer but through such things as writing letters (e.g. for Amnesty International), telephoning, scanning newspapers, reading or gathering information. Taking action can be very gentle and quiet.

ii. Building up a picture of the local area

This exercise is particularly appropriate for a new community, one moving into a new area,or one wanting to review its ministry. Ask yourselves the following questions in order to gather information about your local area.

· **What do we mean by area?**

How wide will we cast our net when considering our ministry?

· **What do we already know?**

You may already have a more or less detailed picture of the locality through living in it or, for a new community, as you came to a decision about where to live (cf. pp. 48-4).

· What do we want to know?

Your list may include among other things: information about economic and social class groupings, the kind of employment people engage in, amenities and services, leisure activities and opportunities, educational facilities for all ages, parish life and the ecumenical scene.

· How will we go about getting information about the area?

You can and will learn about your area both by living in it and by seeking information, so the activity of building up a picture can be engaged in by every member, even if already busy in a job or elderly and house-bound. Some of these ways are:

working from home. Much may be learnt from local newspapers and, to some extent, from local radio, from callers and tradespeople, and from neighbours. You could hold a house-warming for various people or sectors of the community; or enter into correspondence in the local paper.

going on your ordinary round. As you travel through the area, shop, go to the launderette, library or church, take exercise, and visit a doctor or dentist, you will be able to pick up information from looking and listening. Read notice boards, chat to people you meet, ask questions, notice the condition of the houses, gardens, streets, bus shelters.

special visits. Go to see local people who work in the social services, in the caring or medical services, in teaching, youth or community work, and local journalists, clergy and church workers in the various denominations. Some you may already know. Get a list of local clubs from the library and visit some of them. Visit work places or factories. One way is to work at this systematically, dividing the geographical localities or areas of interest – church, social life, occupations, amenities and so on – between you. Another is to deliberately 'hang around' those places where people congregate and chat: the launderette, school gates, bus-stops, queuing in the post office, and listen or enter into conversation.

· How shall we explain ourselves?

It can build up your confidence if you prepare a few phrases to use, as appropriate, explaining what you are doing. If you are new to the area, you could say, "I'm just trying to get to know the area and get the feel of the place", "I like to familiarise myself so I can settle in better", "Doing this helps me to feel at home here". Those taking a fresh look at the place in which they have lived for some time, could use such phrases as, "We are trying to make an informal survey", or "We've been here for some time but so much has changed, we are trying to take a new look at what's going on", "We've been so focused on working at . . . that we feel we are a bit out of touch with the neighbourhood".

These questions may also be useful: "What strikes you about the parish?", "How does it feel to live here?", "What do you think I ought to know?", "How would you describe the area?" Most people enjoy being able to share their knowledge.

· **How will we take note of what we learn?**

Here again people work very differently. Some of the ideas below may start you thinking of a creative and interesting way which suits you.

> Have a personal notebook or pad in which you jot down such things as facts and figures, your feelings, things which strike you, conversations or anything else worthy of note. Spend a few minutes each evening or on returning home to ask yourself: 'What have I learnt?', 'What strikes me?', and make a few notes.

> Put up a large sheet of paper with key focal points, which again could be geographical or interest areas, on which you can note down what you have discovered, felt or seen. This could be done communally or individually.

> Have your own local notice board on which you display information, leaflets, cuttings or your own impressions – written or drawn.

· **How will we assimilate what we learn?**

Both personal and communal ways are suggested below.

Listen to yourselves. Pause long enough to get in touch with your own feelings about living in the area. Ask yourselves questions: How do I feel about the amenities, the shops and shopkeepers, people I meet in the estate or road, the parish, the way people respond, relate, look, and enter into conversation? Do I feel pleased, disappointed, angry, satisfied, compassionate or sad? What are my positive reactions to what I've seen and heard? What are my negative reactions to what I've seen and heard? What particularly strikes me? What is this saying to me at this stage of our exploration?

Reflect on what you have discovered. At some stage, or at intervals, you will need to spend time sharing and reflecting on your information, hard facts, feelings, hunches, and impressions.

How you do this is extremely important because different things strike different people. We perceive and interpret things differently. Our life experience, socialisation, training, prejudices, predilections, interests, and attitudes inform how we perceive. It can therefore be of immense value to share perceptions, listening to each other in turn and really hearing and understanding how each one sees and interprets the situation. In this way you are more likely to correct or adjust your perceptions, so they more nearly equate with reality.

Between you, your picture of the locality and its needs will become increasingly accurate. After listening to each other, and either coming closer together or drawing further apart in the way you perceive the area, the questions below may be useful.

Are we in danger of reinforcing each other in an inaccurate picture (whether positive or negative)? How can we check things out?

How have our common prejudices or past history affected the way we see things?

Are we being sufficiently objective? How would local people respond if they heard us talking now?

Are we in danger of seeing through rose coloured spectacles or being doom and gloom merchants?

iii. Discovering the real needs of local people

Having built up a picture of the area either from doing the exercise above or from living there for some time, jot down any self-evident needs you have noticed, and maybe some more hidden ones. The following suggestions may help you to penetrate beneath the surface and check your impressions with others, in order to discover the true or most critical needs of the area and avoid jumping to conclusions or being swept up in some activity, however worthwhile, before you have surveyed the field.

· **Test your findings**

Frame some of the conclusions you have come to in a tentative way or formulate questions about them which you can ask ordinary people or local workers: "One of the impressions I'm getting is . . . but I may be completely wrong. What do you think?"

· **Avoid committing yourselves before you are ready**

It may be wise not to allow yourselves to become involved definitively too soon in anything that is going on. Find a way of excusing yourself without offending people: "I am pleased to be asked but I really need time to think about all I am discovering . . .", "As a community we need to pool our ideas before we decide on anything.","I'm interested in what you are doing but I've decided not to take on anything until I and the community have surveyed the field". However, people may welcome your temporary help, in some activities where local needs are being met, such as a women's refuge, club, play group, centre for the homeless or drug addicts, or some church, youth or children's group. This would give you some first-hand experience without long-term commitment.

· **Do further research**

Follow up any area of unmet need by further research in any way you can think of:

Find out further facts and figures from the local authority or library;

Ask people who are suffering from this unmet need. Lovell[22] points out that only too often plans are made to meet the needs of others without actually consulting them. Ask yourself: "Is this a genuine need of theirs? If so, how can they themselves contribute to meeting it?";

Plan a short-term or one-off activity to test the water;

Organise an informal meeting, possibly over a buffet or shared meal, with key people in the area of your concern, in order to explore it together. Beware of causing offence to people, who may well be over-stretched, by highlighting areas of unmet need.

Use a simple questionnaire. Questionnaires are a useful device because they yield written first-hand information in a focused way. Experienced advice is needed when phrasing the questions: ambiguities, not suspected by those asking the questions, frequently confuse the recipients, and their answers can therefore be misleading. An even greater difficulty is the great reluctance of many people, especially the elderly, to 'fill in forms'. Often they are apprehensive that, in some way, officialdom is trying to interfere with their independence. Some schemes which have met real needs, have come into being because people visited friends and neighbours and, over a cup of tea, asked them about their needs and helped them to complete a very simple questionnaire. Sometimes it is better if no papers at all are in evidence. The enquirer asks some key questions and makes notes privately later. An example of such a questionnaire is given by Lovell in *The Parchmore Partnership*.[23] Multi-choice questionnaires can also be used in which respondents circle their answers.[24] It is important that the reasons for collecting information are explained, and assure people that all private information given will be treated confidentially. No one's name should ever be mentioned anywhere in connection with anything confidential without their expressed consent.

As before, when you have built up your picture of the needs, it could be useful to share your perceptions and reflect on what you now see as unmet needs. At this stage you are merely flagging them up, not deciding which ones you could or will deal with. Suggestions for coming to a decision are considered on p.107 and in *Chapter Thirteen: Decisions and Decion Making.*

iv. Our context: church and society[25]

The objective of this meeting. To help people become more aware and alert to what is going on around them in society and in the church.

By way of introduction. Explain that the clearer and more realistic people are about the world and church in which they live, the more likely they are to be able to operate effectively in it. They will be working in the light rather than twilight, gloom or darkness.

As can be seen from varying newspaper reports on the same occasion, any event is seen differently by those who participate in it or view it We each have a subjective perception of what is happening. We see reality differently and none of us sees it 100% objectively and as it really is. We live in a community, province, parish and neighbourhood in which there is a plurality of perceptions: we each have our own way of making sense of all we see and experience. Our perception of the world and church is likely to be a moving, changing and developing one as we read, relate to people, exchange ideas, experience things and reflect in the light of our beliefs about God and Jesus. We should not expect, therefore, to come to a common perception of what is happening 'out there' whether we are looking at the local scene, the country as a whole, or further afield. This meeting is not about trying to hammer out a common perception of church or society (an impossible task) but about opening ourselves to developing our own ways of seeing things and relating to people who see things differently It is an opportunity to clarify how both we and others see 'reality out there', to share some ideas and insights about our perceptions and, in that exchange, to alter, enlarge and develop our own perceptions and through viewing things from various perspectives, see them in the round and more realistically.

Personal preparation. Give people time to reflect on what strikes them about the church or society, and how they think and feel about it. This could be done for half an hour at the start of the meeting or people could be asked to think about it a week or so beforehand.

Focus of the meeting. Decide beforehand, preferably with the community, on the particular focus of the meeting. At one end of the scale you could focus on the local parish or neighbourhood and at the other you could focus on national or global issues. Clearly the local is affected by the global and therefore it is really a choice about which way you decide to enter the discussion.

Possible methods and questions. The three sets of alternative questions below are designed to penetrate increasingly beneath the surface of events and trends in order to be aware of their effect on you, your lives and your work. There is probably too much here for one meeting. You need to decide how deeply to work at this with your community. Some of it could be worked through together, and you might leave people with a question to mull over for themselves. In the questions below, substitute 'parish' for 'neighbourhood', 'diocese', 'the UK', 'the Church' or whatever you decide to focus on.

(a) Questions to do with getting at significant events or trends.

What are the key things which strike you as you reflect on what has been happening during the last X months in the neighbourhood?

What would you highlight if you had to describe your parish to a visitor from Australia (or to your superior general)?

If you had to give a talk on 'Current trends in our parish', what would you highlight?

Is there anything significant happening overtly or at a deeper level in your parish? What is it? What do you think and feel about it? What is its significance for you? What have you learnt from it? How has it affected you?

(b) Questions about the way significant events and trends affect and inform our actions and relationships.

What possible effects, good and bad, do the things you have highlighted and the ways you see and feel about them have upon:

- you as an individual?
- your work?
- your relationship with others?
- your relationships within your community or your province?

In what way, if any, do these things challenge you?

(c) Questions about using your perceptions.

In order to be most effective in your work and life:

- what could you do about how you perceive the parish?

- do you need to alter or develop your perceptions in any way? If so, in what way and how could you set about it? What or who could help you? What might hinder you?

- how can you handle other people's very different views about events and trends?

What is involved in responding critically and creatively to your own and other people's perceptions of what's going on 'out there' in church or society?

Conclusion: Ask yourselves some final questions.

What strikes you as a result of this meeting?

What, if anything, have you learnt from it?

Is there anything you want to do as a result, individually or as a community?

v. Women in the church and society

My own consciousness of the vital importance of struggling with the issue of feminism has been immeasurably heightened by listening to Joan Chittister, undoubtedly one of the prophets of today. I use the word 'struggle' because, as she says, we are still 'patriarchal women', socialised into a society and spiritually imbued with patriarchal values. She describes feminism as a new world view and a necessary one for both men and women if the destructive forces and oppressive systems are to be halted and reversed in time to save not only humanity but the very planet itself.[26]

Most of the following ideas emerged when a women's congregation wanted to suggest various ways in which a community or individual sisters could raise their awareness of the place of women in the church and to explore what they could – and possibly should – do about it. The list may stimulate you to think of others more suited to your community. Some of the items might well be linked together.

· A topical issue

Consider why the issue of women in the church has come to the fore. What do you think about it? Do you need to educate yourself about it? Ask yourself how it fits in with family relationships, society, the church, your congregation's traditions, and Mariology.

Joan Chittister argues that a feminist spirituality is necessary if people in the church and the world are to get a glimpse of the full face God: the spreading of the Good News requires it. "How is it possible to be a good Christian without being a good feminist?"[27] What are you doing as women in the church and what more might you be doing?

· Men and women

To have a truly feminist attitude is to believe in the basic equality and necessary complementarity of male and female characteristics. Study the particular gifts and approaches of both women and men though reading or inviting someone to talk about feminine and masculine qualities and values.[28] As a community you might gather together material on the subject to share in a meeting. Explore your personal thoughts and feelings. What contribution does or could your community make to the feminist debate?

· Clergy-women relationships

The questions below may stimulate discussion.

* Examine how you relate to clergy you meet. How would you describe these relationships? Discuss the sort of relationship you want to have and what action you could take towards developing it.

* Why have women been so 'voiceless' in the church? How do the women and ordained and lay men you know see this issue?

· How others see it

Identify different stances taken up by people on the continuum from militant feminists to entrenched chauvinists. Stand in the shoes of the various people and try to experience how they feel; try to understand why they feel so strongly about such things as the role of women in the church and society, sexist language, women priests and so on. Identify and explore your own prejudices and help each other to do so non-judgementally.

· The place of women

Collect newspaper cuttings which highlight the place of women in church and society: on abuse, battered wives, women priests, and on women who have made a name or have a prominent role. Use these to trigger off discussion. Is it worth focusing on one issue and exploring it more deeply? How could you better inform yourselves?

· Women in the bible

Members could choose one woman to reflect on and then ask themselves such questions as: Why did I choose her? What did she do? At what cost to herself? What has she to say to me or us *now* in relation to our mission and ministry. What opportunities might we be overlooking?

iv. Facing change and helping others do so

You are unlikely to help others face change unless you yourself are able to do so, both as individuals and as a community. The exercise below is aimed at helping you explore how you feel about innovations,and what helps and hinders you from considering them openly. I do not say 'accept' them because there are changes which may not be for the better and which you would do well to reject.

The facilitator of this session could introduce it by an objective statement about change, possibly followed by some discussion.

Change is and always has been endemic in church and society. The increasing speed of change can be frightening. In your ministry you are likely both to meet people who react, at times quite violently or in great distress, to the changes taking place in the church, and others who experience enormous frustration at the slowness of the institutional church to move forward. In your community, members may well veer towards one or other end of that continuum. Understanding more about change can help to prevent changes in an organisation, the parish, community, or neighbourhood becoming divisive. The need to make certain changes if we are to conserve what is of value to us, is considered on pp. 25 and 73.

Change is a natural and continual part of life. We have all changed enormously not only physically, but in our ideas and opinions, in the depth of our beliefs over the years. Change becomes more problematic if it is too fast; occurs in many areas of life at the same time; requires a complete reversal of direction; or upsets the inner model on which one bases one's life. Marris warns against "burdening ourselves with so many simultaneous changes that our emotional resilience becomes exhausted".[29] To be hesitant about accepting an innovation is a healthy reaction: to react against *considering* an innovation is not. People are likely to be at different stages: some may already have accepted innovations with which others are still struggling.

Step 1: Facing change in yourself[30]

Consider Figure 16.3 and then work through the questions on the next page.

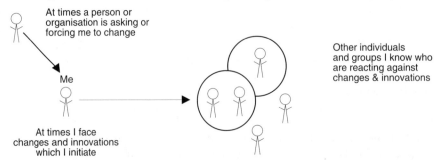

Figure 16.3
Facing change initiated by others

Small Communities in Religious Life

You can learn from your own experience of facing change. By and large do you welcome changes or are you on the cautious side? There may be things in the situation, in how the change is presented and by whom, or in you personally which affect your response. List what helps you consider change openly, even welcome it. List what hinders or prevents you from doing so, or causes you to react spontaneously against it.

Together collate your responses.

Step 2: Facing change as a community

Do a similar exercise in relation to interior and exterior things which affect the community response to change.

> What blocks or hinders you as a community from moving and changing; both within the community and outside it?

> What helps you as a community to move and change; both help from within the community and from outside?

After Steps 1 and 2 you may want to consider what practical steps you will take individually and/or communally in relation to change and innovation.

Step 3: Helping others to face change

Consider the lists of things which helped you face change, and things which caused you to react against it. Read off the individual or communal implications in relation to any individual or group in the parish, whom you want to come to terms with changes already in place or changes you wish them to consider. Decide whether and what you will do or say.

5. A COMMUNITY MISSION OR TIME OF RENEWAL

After a community has been in place for some time, it can settle down and even get in a rut, spiritually or in other ways. Ruts are neither challenging nor life-giving. One way of creating the right sort of disturbance of the comfortable *status quo* is to decide to set aside a particular period – a week, a month, or longer – which, while continuing your usual work, you will use as a time of spiritual renewal. This could be a time that you make special in some way both individually or corporately. It might be preceded by a day or days together, when you have more time to think and pray or focus on a theme. Different things suit different communities.

Possible themes. Below are various things you could focus on.

> *A previous chapter.* Study, mull over or reflect on what emerged and how you, as a community, are or are not living out the proposals.

> *A particular topic*, e.g. community, ecumenism, poverty, justice, prayer. . . .

Your constitutions and how you can make them come alive for you in a new way (cf. p. 222).

Your charism. Trace its origins and the way your predecessors have lived out, deepened and developed it over the years. How is it manifested in your lives today? How might *you* deepen and develop it? How could you share it more widely, remembering a charism is primarily a gift to the church? (cf. *Consider your charism* on p. 219).

Your religious heritage. Study the origin and early days of your congregation, possibly make a pilgrimage together to where it started, or ask your archivist to show you early documents or give you a talk.

The Scriptures. Take a particular part and decide how you can study it together by using commentaries, attending lectures, studying a book together, or in some other way.

Possible frameworks. There are various ways in which you could arrange to make this a special period of renewal or re-thinking:

by spending some extra time in corporate prayer together – silent or otherwise, a holy hour, a special Eucharist or agape.

by having a focus for a week or month, on a particular saying or quotation which, having reflected on, you put up where it can be a reminder.

by undertaking some regular corporate activity, for instance meeting to discuss, doing some faith-sharing exercise, going out together, or whatever it is that is likely to build you up as a real communion of people.

by members in turn suggesting how the following month could be a month with a difference.

by undertaking a review (cf. Chapter Fourteen).

by forming a partnership with another community or working in clusters of communities, occasionally meeting to see how things are going and to stimulate each other.

As well as celebrating the conclusion of your community mission you might consider whether there is any way of putting on a similar exercise for local people, in an appropriate way, in the neighbourhood or parish.

6. MOVING INTO RETIREMENT

The exercise below may be done some years before a person's retirement from a professional job. It is valuable to think ahead to this stage in one's life and ministry when a new freedom of choice and new opportunities will open up. This last stage of life is crucial for one's human and spiritual development.

Step 1: Picture the scenario: i.e. how you see retirement could be for you, so that you could live in a way which would be satisfying. The following questions may help.

What do I see my retirement to be for? Taking into account that God is not retiring me: what is God wanting of me? What inner changes is God hoping for in me?

What do I see my purpose (cf. p. 71) to be in my retirement, in relation to:

  – my own development and growth (human, spiritual, intellectual)?
  – other people?
  – my community, province, congregation?
  – people in the neighbourhood?
  – on wider front: region, nation, world?

How do I think and feel about retirement? What do I need at this stage? What are my positive and negative feelings about becoming older and retiring? Why do I feel this?

What needs have to be met in my retirement for me to feel and be settled and at peace:

  – physical needs: community base etc.?
  – spiritual needs: church, bible study, prayer groups etc.?
  – social needs: people, community, family, friends, groups, activities, hobbies, etc.?
  – intellectual needs: mental stimulation, reading, studying, discussion, etc.?

What am I going to do with my time (i) while I still have energy and can be active? (ii) when I slow down and become less active? For example, what will I do:

  – as a hobby?
  – in the house and garden?
  – outside the house?
  – connected with the church, parish, or diocese?
  – connected with the neighbourhood?
  – connected with others, organisations, community, or province?
  – elsewhere?

Are there any guiding principles or factors which stand out for me and which must be present?

Step 2: Moving into that scenario: this may be years ahead or it may be on the doorstep, or you may even be over the doorstep.

What do I have to do in relation to each of the above? What preparation can I make? What can be done at once? Are there skills I need to acquire or any form of training or study I could undertake formally or informally?

Try to schedule and date the various things so they are in some order.

Step 3: Reflection: Relax and reflect on what now strikes you about retirement. Meditate on all this with the Lord; how do you now see the opportunities of your retirement period and the responsibilities of it?

It could well be useful to talk this over with a friend or confidante as suggested on p. 167. It could also provide the basis for a community discussion.

Ad Multos Annos!

REFERENCES AND NOTES

1. Widdicombe, op. cit. (ref. 2, p. 59) pp 142-44. I have also included two or three ideas I found in *Sunday Plus*.
2. This meeting is based on original work by George Lovell.
3. Arbuckle, Gerald A: *Out of Chaos: Refounding Religious Congregations* (Geoffrey Chapman 1988 ISBN 0 225 66549 2). "To permit the entrepreneur to have the required freedom, the new venture should normally be established as separate from the existing operation. This will protect the entrepreneur against unnecessary on-site interference from members of the dominant organisational culture and from having to justify his or her actions." p.40 and p.125.
4. *Perfectae Caritatis 2. Decree on the Appropriate Renewal of Religious Life*, 1995. See also Resolution 5 of the Lambeth Conference 1968. "It calls upon communities to state their part in the present renewal of the church in particular by seeking to renew themselves according to the priorities of the Gospel and the original institution of their foundation." p.7.
5. Pope John Paul II: in *Forum*, Volume 23, July/August 1984, No. 109.
6. I am indebted to Jackie Rolo of the Grail community for this meeting.
7. Gordon and Soons, op.cit. (ref. 30, p. 94).
8. Ibid.
9. I am indebted to the Religious Sisters of Charity for this exercise which was worked out during their General Chapter in 1995.
10. Ibid.
11. Progoff, op. cit. (ref. 7, p. 159) p. 168.
12. Marris, op. cit. (ref. 4, p. 31).
13. This is based on work done in Central Ireland in 1984 with the superiors of an English Province of Sisters.
14. Fromm, op. cit. (ref. 2, p. 92) p. 21.
15. Widdicombe, op.cit. (ref. 2, p. 59) p51. This was developed by Gabrielle Lurser Rico in *Writing the Natural Way* (J. P Tarcher Inc, 1983) p. 28.
16. Nolan, Albert: *The Service of the Poor and Spiritual Growth* (Catholic Institute for International Relations, 1985. ISBN 0 946848 90 4, Justice Papers No. 6) identifies and describes four steps of spiritual development through which we, as Christians, progress in our relationship with and service of the poor:
   Stage 1. Compassion for the poor which can lead to relief work and almsgiving.
   Stage 2. Realising that poverty is a structural problem which can lead to social and political action.
   Stage 3. Discovering the strength of the poor and realising that they can and must, and indeed are the only people who can, save themselves. This can lead to being evangelised by the poor "God's chosen instruments in transforming the world".
   Stage 4. Moving from a certain romanticism, through disillusion and disappointment with them, to a real solidarity in which rich and poor work together from their different positions, with the advantages and disadvantages of both, to bring about material and spiritual liberation.

17. I am indebted to the Religious Sisters of Charity for this exercise which was worked out during their General Chapter in 1995.
18. Sr. Monica Breen and I worked on this for the English and Scottish Province of the Religious Sisters of Charity. Doing this exercise had a deep effect on several communities.
19. This section on finance draws heavily on work done with Sister Maureen Connor RA and is based on a paper used at the 1992 Chapter of the Assumption Sisters *'Questions destinées à amorcer une reflection collective sur l'argent'*, which, in turn, drew on the work of Henry Rougette (Centre Libre) France. Issues of an ethical and moral nature relevant to the whole congregation, such as investments are not considered here, but may well be relevant when considering how the option for the poor is lived corporately.
20. I am indebted to Gordon & Soons (ref. 7, above) for this wall newspaper method. It is described in *Wholetime*, p. 99
21. This is taken from an Avec Handout written by George Lovell and myself, 'Brief Notes on Discovering People's Real Needs'.
22. Grundy, Malcolm (Ed): *The Parchmore Partnership*, Chester House Publications (1995) pp. 36ff in which Lovell describes how a church group narrowly avoided falling into this trap when wanting to meet the needs of elderly people in a church neighbourhood.
23. Op. cit. (ref. 21 above) p.37.
24. Lovell and Widdicombe, op. cit. (Ref. 3 p.93). An illustrated questionnaire used with a congregation in church is described on p. 85.
25. This was also worked out with Sr. Monica Breen (ref. 18 above).
26. Chittister, Joan D: *Heart of Flesh: A Feminist Spirituality for Women and Men*, (William B. Eerdmans Publishing Company, 1998 ISBN 0 8028 4282 8).
27. Ibid. p. 41.
28. The shelves of most good book shops have several titles in this area. Joan Chittister's book in ref. 26 above is seminal, unique and thought-provoking.
29. Marris, op. cit. (ref. 12 above) p150.
30. This exercise is based on one worked out by George Lovell.

A Word in Conclusion

For several decades religious have been undergoing an exciting but demanding transition in their way of life, ministry and mission. The future into which the Spirit is impelling them is a journey of faith and hope. They are busily engaged in transforming ways of living and working which have served so well for so long, into ones which will better meet the new challenges and opportunities of a constantly changing world. A daunting task, served and supported by much scholarly research, prophetic writing, and radical thinking. Consequently religious are experiencing a welter of new and enriching ideas and insights, and are faced with difficult choices and decisions. They are having to think for themselves, separately and together, as never before. They must assess the value and relevance of old and new thinking about religious life and mission for them and their situation, if they are to avoid the ever-present danger of adopting things in vogue which simply do not fit them and their circumstances.

This book was born out of the felt need of religious at grass roots for help in doing their own thinking as they moved from known and familiar concepts and habits to explore ways of embodying new insights into their religious way of life. It sets out as clearly as I can what I am learning about doing that. It is not a survey of work I have done with religious, nor a summary of contemporary thought and research into religious life, nor yet a profile of the shape and form of present-day communities. It is a collection of thinking tools for those in or concerned with small communities to help them grapple with new ideas about *their* vocation, *their* apostolic work, *their* circumstances, and *their* context. It is about processes that help people think in depth, and, therefore, a necessary companion to the plethora of materials that expound religious life today.

When people use the approaches, methods, and tools described in this book, it is a constant adventure into new awareness and understanding. For me, it has been a demanding and exciting journey. I have met situations, opportunities, and difficulties I had not previously encountered and seen better ways of doing things. All this is to be expected, in fact it is a validation of the processes being used.

I offer this book because I am convinced of the enormous contribution religious have to make to the church and society world-wide. I yearn to see this potential released as fully as possible. This is why I have dedicated so much time and energy over the years to working with religious. My hope and prayer is that this book will be a means of consolidating and extending the work I have done.

It has been a great privilege to be invited into the lives of so many religious, their communities and congregations. As a non-religious, albeit a longstanding member of a lay community, the Grail, I have been inspiried and challenged by so many close and stimulating relationships and encounters from which I have learnt so much – and continue to do so.

Bibliography

Alvarez, Jean 'Focussing a Congregation's Future' in *Human Development*. (The Jesuit Educational Centre for Human Development, Cambridge USA)

Arbuckle, Gerald: *Strategies for Growth in Religious Life* (St Pauls 1986) vol. 5 no 4 1994
Out of Chaos (Paulist Press NY; Geoffrey Chapman UK)
The Seed Must Die . . . (Veritas)
'Chaos – The Preface to Creativity: Anthropological Insights' in *Signum Documentation Service for Religious* vol. 16 no 5 1988
'General Government, Its Leadership Role Today' in *Review for Religious* Nov/Dec 1984
'Out of Chaos, Religious Life, Mythology and Refounding' in *Signum* vol. 16 no 6 1988
'Innovations in Religious Life' in *Human Development* vol. 6 no 3 1985
'Mythology, Revitalization and the Refounding of Religious Life' (*Review for Religious* vol. 46 no.1 1987)
'Provincials as Cultural Revolutionaries, The Role of Provincial Superiors Today' in *Review for Religious* March/April 1983
'Refounding Persons and Administrative Leadership, Practical Planning' in *Signum* vol. 16 no 7 1988
'Selling the Refounding Model to Provincials and Congregations' in *Signum* vol. 16 no 8
'Suffocating Religious Life, A New Type Emerges' in *The Way* no 65 Summer 1989

Arbuckle, Gerald A and Fleming, D L 'Understanding Refounding and the Role of Conversion' in *Religious Life: Rebirth Through Conversion* Alba House NY 1990

Alvarez, Jean 'Focussing a Congregation's Future' in *Human Development* V, Winter 1984

Augur, George G 'Religious Life Revisited' in *Human Development* vol. 19 no 4 1997

Barry, William A 'Sage Advice for Times of Great Change' in *Human Development* vol. 20 no 4 1999

Batten, T R and M *The Human Factor in Community Work* (Oxford University Press 1965)
The Human Factor in Youth Work (OUP 1970)
The Non-Directive Approach (Avec Publications 1988)

Beesing, Maria Nogosek, Robert J and O'Leary, Patrick *The Enneagram, A Journey in Self-discovery* (Dimension Books 1984)

Briggs-Myers, Isabel *The Manual for Myers-Briggs Type Indicator* (Consulting Psychological Press 1962)

Bishops' Conference of England & Wales in *Reflections* 24 September 1993

Brown, Rob and Brown, Margaret *Empowering Leadership* (Nicholas Brealey 1994)

Brueggermann *Shaping the Coming Age of Religious Life* (Seabury Press NY 1979)
The Prophetic Imagination (Fortress Press Philadelphia 1978)

Bunker, S. et al (editors) *Diggers and Dreamers: The Guide to Communal Living* (Digger & Dreamers Publications 1997)

Burns, J. MacGregor *Leadership* (Harper and Row NY 1978)

Buhlmann, Walter *The Coming of the Third Church*
'Prophet and Servant, The Role of the Apostolic Religious in the Church' in *Mission Today* nos 23-27 March 1984

Cada, Lawrence et al *Shaping the Coming Age of Religious Life* (Seabury Press 1979)

Casals, Pablo *Joys and Sorrows* (New York 1970)

Chamberlain, David *Babies Remember Birth* (Jeremy Tarcher 1988)

Chittister, Joan D *Heart of Flesh: A Feminist Spirituality for Women and Men* (William B. Eerdmans Publishing Company 1998)
    Women, Ministry and the Church (Paulist Press 1983)
    'Climbing the Eight Mountains of Religious Life' in *Signum* vol. 6 no 9
    'Religious Life: Questions for a New Beginning' in *Signum* May 1996
Clark, David *Basic Communities: Towards an Alternative Society* (SPCK 1977)
Clarke, Katherine M Leadership 'When It's Time for Adaptation' in *Human Development* vol. 19 no 3 1997
Coghlan, David *Reviewing Apostolic Religious Life* (Columbia Press 1996)
    'Change Processes in Catholic Religious Orders' *Advances in Organization Development* vol. 3 Ablex NJ 1995
    'Change as Re-Education, Lewin Revisited' *Organization Development Journal* vol. 12 no 4 1994
    'Collaborative Leadership in Apostolic Ministry: Behaviour and Assumptions' in *Review for Religious* Jan/Feb 1988
    'Levels of Participation in Apostolic Religious Life' in *Human Development* vol. 9 no 4 1988
    'Religious Orders and Consultants: Questions and Answers' in *Religious Life Review* vol. 26 no 128
Coghlan, D and Ottoway, R. N 'Change Agents in Religious Life' *Human Development* vol. 11 no 4 1990
Coghlan, D and McIduff, E 'Structuring and Nondirectiveness in Group Facilitation' in *Person-Centred Review* vol. 5 no1 1990
Conway, Nancy and Alvarez, Jean 'Decision Making by Consensus' in *Human Development* vol. 9 no 2 1988)
Cooper Marcus, Claire *Easter Hill Village: Some Social Implications of Design* (University of California)
De Bono, Edward *The Five Day Course in Thinking* (Penguin 1967)
de Hueck Doherty, Catherine *Poustinia: Christian Spirituality of the East for Western Man* (Avec Maria Press 1975)
de Mello, Anthony *Sadhana, A Way to God* (Image Books, Doubleday 1984)
de Waal, Esther *The Rule of St Benedict: A Life Giving Way* (Geoffrey Chapman 1995)
Dillistone, F W *The Power of Symbols* (SCM Press 1986)
Door, Donal *Option for the Poor: A Hundred Years of Vatican Social Teaching* (Orbis Books NY 1983)
Dorit, F and Warm, P *Collaborative Communities* (1996)
Egan, Gerard *You and Me: The Skills of Communicating and Relating to Others* (Brooks Cole USA 1977)
Farley, Margaret *Personal Commitments, Beginning, Keeping, Changing* (Harper & Row 1986)
Fiand, Barbara *Wrestling with God* (The Crossroad Publishing Company NY)
Fellowship of Intentional Communities *Communities Directory* and *Communities: Journal of Cooperative Living* (FIC. Rutledge, MO 63563 USA)
Fox, Matthew *Original Blessing* (Bear and Company 1983)
Fromm, Erich *To Have or To Be* (Jonathan Cape 1978)
Futrell John Carroll 'Evaluating Apostolate Communities' in *Human Development* vol. 7 no 2 1986
Gill, James 'Indispensable Self-Esteem' in *Human Development* vol. 1 no 3 1980
Gordon, Esther and Soons, Hubert: *Whole Time A Handbook for Workshops* (Grail Publications 1996)
Gottemoeller, Doris 'Community Living: Beginning the Conversation' in *Signum* Feb 2000
Grundy, Malcolm Ed. *The Parchmore Partnership: George Lovell, Garth Rogers, and Peter Sharrocks* (Chester House Publications 1995)
Guggenbuhl Craig, Alolph *Marriage, Dead or Alive?* (Spring Publications Geneva 1977)

Harmer, Catherine 'Community: Intentional or . . .?' In *Signum* January 2000-07-15

Harnan, Nicholas 'What About the New Life? A Prophetic Challenge for the New Millennium' in *Signum* January 2000

Huddlestone, Mary Anne 'The Quest for Intimacy' in *Human Development* vol. 20 no 3 1999

Jackson, Hildur (Editor) *Creating Harmony: Conflict Resolution in Community* (Gaia Trust, Denmark in association with Permanent Publications, UK 1999)

Jarvis, Irving and Mann, Leo *Group Think* (Collier MacMillan 1977)

Kabat-Zinn, Jon *Mindfulness Meditation for Everyday Life* (Judy Piatkins Publications 1994)

Khan, Hasrat Inayat *The Sufi Message* vol. 10 (Barrie and Radcliffe 1964)

Kubler Ross, Elizabeth *On Death and Dying* (Tavistock 1970)

Leddy, Mary Jo *Reweaving Religious Life: Beyond the Liberal Model* (Twenty-Third Publications USA 1990)

'Beyond the Liberal Model' in *The Way* Supplement 65 (Summer 1989)

Lee, Bernard J 'A Socio-Historical Theology of Charism' in *Review for Religious* vol. 48 no 1 (January/February 1989)

Lewin, G Ed. *Conduct, Knowledge and the Acceptance of New Values in Resolving Social Conflict: Selected Papers on Group Dynamics* (Souvenir Press London 1973)

Lippet, Ronald *Phases of Organisational Change*

Lonsdale, David *Dance to the Music of the Spirit* (Darton, Longman and Todd 1992)

Lovell, George: *Analysis & Design: A Handbook for Practitioners and Consultants in Church and Community Work* (Burns & Oates 1994)

Avec: Agency & Approach (Avec Publications 1996)

Consultancy, Ministry and Mission: A Handbook for Practitioners and Work Consultants in Christian Organizations (Burns & Oates 2000)

Human and Religious Factors in Church and Community Work (A Grail Publication 1982)

The *Church and Community Development: An Introduction* (3rd edition (Avec Publications 1988)

Lovell, George, Middleton, Jane and Smith, Hilary *A Process Model for the Development of Individual and Collective Vocations* (Methodist Diaconal Order Occasional Paper no 1 1996 Methodist Publishing House)

Lovell, George and Widdicombe, Catherine *Churches and Communities: An Approach to Development in the Local Church* (2nd edition 1986)

Lurser Rico, Gabrielle *Writing the Natural Way* (J. P Tarcher Incorporated 1983)

McCollum, Maureen Ed. *Of Clogs and Stocking Feet* (CRC 324 Laurier Avenue East, Ottawa K1N 6P6 Canada 1992)

McLeod, Frederick 'Trends in Spirituality' in *Review for Religious* March/April 1988

Malone, Janet *The Dance of Leadership*

Marris, Peter *Loss and Change* (Routledge and Kegan Paul 1974)

Merkle, Judith A *Committed by Choice: Religious Life Today* (The Liturgical Press 1992)

Metcalfe, Bill *From Utopian Dreaming to Communal Reality: Co-operative Lifestyles in Australia* (University of New South Wales Press 1995)

Shared Visions, Shared lives: Communal Living Around the Globe (The Findhorn Press, Scotland, 1996)

Moran, Mary Jo 'Leadership in this Age of Change' in *Human Development* vol. 20 no 3 1999

Morgan, Elizabeth, Weigel, Van B and Debaufre, Eric *Global Poverty and Personal Responsibility, Integrity Through Commitment* (Paulist Press NY 1989)

Morgan, Marlo *The Mutant Message Down Under* (Thorsons 1994 Harper Collins USA. 1991)

Morris, Desmond *Manwatching: A Field Guide to Human Behaviour* (Jonathon Cape 1977)

Neal, Ernest *Hope for the Wretched* (Agency for International Development 1972)

Neal, Marie Augusta *Catholic Sisters in Transition: From the 1960's to the 1980's* (Michael Glazier USA 1984)

Near, H *The Kibbutz Movement: A History* (Oxford University Press 1992)

Newman, John Henry *Meditations and Devotions* (Sheed and Ward 1930 arranged by Enid Przywara)
    Essay on Development of Doctrine

Nhat Hanh, Thich *Be Still and Know: Meditation for Peacemakers* (Pax Christi & The Fellowship of Reconciliation 1987)

Nolan, Albert *The Service of the Poor and Spiritual Growth* (Catholic Institute for International Relations 1985)

Nouwen, Henri J.M *Reaching Out* (Collins Fount Paperback 1980)

Nygren, D and Ukeritis, M 'Religious-Leadership Competencies' *Review for Religious* 52 (May/ June 1993)

O'Connor, David F 'Dysfunctional Clergy & Religious' in *Human Development* vol. 2 no 4 1990

O'Murchu, Diamuid *Poverty, Celibacy and Obedience: A Radical Option for Life* (The Crossroad Publishing Company NY 1999)
    Quantum Theology, Spiritual Implications of the New Physics (The Crossroad Publishing Company NY)
    Reclaiming Spirituality (The Crossroad Publishing Company NY)
    'What Are Religious Talking About These Days?' in *Signum* February 1998
    'Religious Decline and Revival' in *Signum* vol. 16 no 5 1988
    'Religious Sisters: Eclipsed by HIS-STORY' in *Signum vol.* 26 no 9

O'Donoghue, Helena 'Religious Community as Apostolic Resource' in *Religious Life Review* no 114

Petrie, Pat C*ommunicating the Kingdom, Communication Skills for Christians* (Grail Publications 1992)

Plaskow, Judith and Christ, Carol P *Weaving the Visions, Patterns in Feminist Spirituality* (Harper & Row 1989)

Potucek, Carolyn *A Community-Based Approach to the Re-entry Process* (Columbia Biblical Seminary & Graduate School of Missions Columbia South Carolina May 1991)

Progoff, Ira *At a Journal Workshop* (Dialogue House Library NY 1975)
    Process Meditation (Dialogue House Library NY 1975)

Rahtjen, Bruce with Kramer, Bryce and Mitchell, Ken *A Work Book in Experiential Theology* (A Publication of Association in Experiential Theology Incorporated 1977)

Rashford, N S & Coghlan, D in *Human Development* 1988

Renfro, Jean Marie 'Religious Charism: Definition, Rediscovery and Implications' *Review for Religious* vol. 45 no 4 (July/August 1986)

Rogers, Carl *On Becoming a Person: A Therapist's View of Psychotherapy* (Constable 1967 3rd reprint 1972)

Schillebeeckx, Edward *Meditations and Devotions: Jesus in our Western Culture,* (SCM 1986)

Schneiders, Sandra M *New Wineskins: Re-Imagining Religious Life Today* (Paulist Press 1986)
    'Congregational Leadership and Spirituality in the Postmodern Era' in *Review for Religious 1998*

Schwartzburd, Leonard 'The Risky Confrontation of Friends', *Human Development,* vol. 9 no 2 1988

Seifat, Harvey and Clinebell, Howard *Personal Growth and Social Change: A Guide for Ministers and Laymen as Change Agents* (Westminster Press 1969)

Shaffer, C and Anundsen, K *Creating Community Anywhere: Finding Support and Connection in a Fragmented World* (Tarcher/Putnam 1994)

Sperry, Len 'Neurotic Personalities in Religious Settings' in *Human Development* vol. 12 no 3 1991
    'Passive Aggression in Organisations *Human Development* vol. 11 no 2 1990

Stamp, Gillian 'The Tripod of Work' February 1987 *A Brunel Institute of Organisation and Social Studies Occasional Paper (BIOSS)* The University of West London
    'Well-Being and Stress at Work' *BIOSS Occasional Paper* September 1988
    'The Enhancement of Ministry in Uncertainty' *BIOSS Occasional Paper*

Svoboda, Melanie 'Community Living: A Question of Balance' in *Signum* January 2000

Tenny, Anna Maria 'Re-Designing the Vows – A Model of Religious Life for Mature Christians' in *Signum* December 1999

Timmerman, Joan H in 'Sexuality and Spirituality' in *Human Development* vol. 20 no 3 1999

Whitmeyer, C et al (editors) *In the Company of Others: Making Community in the Modern World* (Tarcher/Putnam 1983)

Widdicombe, Catherine: *Meetings That Work, A Practical Guide to Team Work,* (St Paul's, 1994; 2nd edition The Lutterworth Press, 2000)

The Roman Catholic Church and Vatican II, Action Research into Means of Implementation (Unpublished thesis for Degree of Master of Philosophy, Institute of Education, London University 1984)

Wilson, George B 'Applying Your Criteria in Making Choices About Ministry' in *Human Development* vol. 15 no 2 1994

'Of Mission Statements and Missions' in *Human Development* vol. 17 no 2, Summer 1996, p. 11

Wittberg, Patricia: *Creating a Future for Religious Life, A Sociological Perspective* (Paulist Press NY 1991)

'Transformations in Religious Commitment' *Review for Religious* (vol. 44 no. 2. 1985)

'Dyads and Triads, The Sociological Implications of Small Group Living Arrangements' (*Review for Religious* vol. 49 no.1 1990)

Working Party on Collaborative Ministry set up by the Bishops' Conference of England and Wales, *The Sign We Give* 1995 (Matthew James Publishing 1995)

Index of Names

Index

Terms may make sense only after reading particular sections of the book. The
emboldened numbers refer to the main treatment of a topic.

Small Communities in Religious Life

Facilitators 29-30
Failure 144, **169-70**
Faith community 90, 216
Faith sharing 84
Fantasy journey, see Guided meditation

Feedback 124-6
  negative 53
Feelings dealing with 140-1, 149-51
  negative 141, 150
Finance **64**, 78, **230**
Flow model 186
Founder/Foundress 218-9
Free day 213
Freedom 80
  to be oneself 80
  to pursue one's vocation 80
Friendship 81, 156
Future, looking towards 154

Good Neighbours Scheme 92-3
Grail community 17, 22
Ground rules 202
Group Think 41, 174.179
Guided meditation 150, **206**
Guideposts 155

Hardiness 156
Health 46
Home base 48

Inadequacy 149-50
Indicators of change 124
Individual needs 79
Information, getting 175, 232-6
Informing the congregation 50-4, 177
  others 50, 65, 177
Injustice 227
Involving people 43, 109

Job-sharing 153
Joining in existing work 108
Journalling 145, 167

Koinonia 81, 83

Laissez-faire 28
Large communities 52
Leadership 95-6
  approaches 99
  check list 102
  forms of 95
  functions 96-9, 100
  levels 128

Leadership team, see Provincial team
Learning 108, 234
  from experience 143
  from meetings 204-6
  organisation 121
Letting go 146
Lifecycle 37, 145
Life style 73, 228
Lifeline 146, 215
Listening 200, 201, 210
Living singly 88, 163
Location 48
Losing a member 163
Loss 149

Meditation of a newcomer 57
Meetings 197-205
  facilitation 199
  participation 199
  preparing 200
  timing 198
  types of 198
  unpopularity of 197
Members, selection of 45-7
  losing 163
  new 161-2
  of new community 51
Ministry 48, 71, **76**, **105**
  deciding on 107-8
Mindfulness 139, 159
Mission 19, 48, **76**, **105**, 231
  statement 68, 71-3
Missioning – see Commissioning
Models **34**, 48
Money – see Finance
Moving house 142
  in 55-8
Myers-Briggs 60, 76, 93

Needs 112, 211, 212
  balance 84
  community 83
  human face of 229
  individual 79, 212
  local neighbourhood 106, 112, **235**
Neighbourhood, involvement 43, 109
  perspective 54
  shape 55
New members 161-2
Non-alienated activity 68
Non-Directive **29-30**, **101**, 118
Noxiants 71, 112